The Essential
Paul Elmer More

The Essential
Paul Elmer More

A Selection of His Writings

EDITED WITH AN INTRODUCTION
AND NOTES

BY

BYRON C. LAMBERT

FOREWORD BY RUSSELL KIRK

ARLINGTON HOUSE   NEW ROCHELLE, N.Y.

"The Demon of the Absolute" is from Paul Elmer More, *The Demon of the Absolute* (copyright 1928 © 1956 by Princeton University Press), pp. 7 through 29. Reprinted by permission of Princeton University Press.

"The Doctrine of the Logos" is from "The Doctrine of the Logos," pp. 277-296, "The Logos" (continued), pp. 297-329 in *Christ the Word* (copyright 1927 © 1955 by Princeton University Press). Reprinted by permission of Princeton University Press. Some footnotes are More's original footnotes, others are the notations of the editor. See the notes at the end of this chapter for clarification.

To Phyllis

Library of Congress Catalog Card Number 79-189372

ISBN 0-87000-162-0

MANUFACTURED IN THE UNITED STATES OF AMERICA

Contents

POLITICS AND SOCIETY

Foreword

The greatest of American critics, Paul Elmer More, was no professor, but an editor. For some years he gave to *The Nation* an elevation and a dignity since unequalled in American periodical literature. For mastery of humane letters and critical insight, too, More has no peer in this country.

Someone called him "the American Sainte-Beuve," but More is better than a trans-Atlantic copy of a French critic: he stands with Coleridge, Sainte-Beuve, Samuel Johnson, and three or four others in the first rank of the critical art. I think it probable that his books—though for years many of them were out of print—will be read when few other American writers of his time are remembered.

Out of More's deliberate solitude in New Hampshire, during 1897 and 1898, there grew the eleven volumes of the *Shelburne Essays* and the three volumes of the *New Shelburne Essays*. For range of subject and originality of observation, nothing in the bulk of American literary criticism can bear comparison with these essays. From those years until 1937, More was deeply involved in the philosophical and literary and even political controversies of the day.

Commanding in presence, fearless and witty in argument, immensely learned, More never gave ground before the fierce opposition to that Humanism which he and Irving Babbitt reinvigorated in American thought. In the course of his life, he travelled from Calvinism to Skepticism to Platonism to Anglicanism; and yet a high consistency runs through his mature works.

The Humanism of More and Babbitt and their friends was the Roman *humanitas*, those disciplinary arts that bring harmony to a man's soul and teach him right reason, dignity, and honor. Dr. Lynn Harold Hough, in his *Great Humanists*, describes the work of five men: Aristotle, Cicero, Erasmus, More, and Babbitt. To be one of so select a company is remarkable distinction; but More deserves it.

With Pico della Mirandola and the Humanists of the Renaissance, More was convinced that the dignity of man depends upon the existence of a power greater than man, and upon insights transcending ordinary experience. John Dewey and his associates, in 1933, somewhat alarmed at growing interest in the American Humanists, made a disingenuous attempt to capture the word "humanism" by issuing what they called "The Religious Humanist Manifesto." Now Dewey's friends, with few exceptions, were not religious men; and when Dewey himself was asked why he employed certain religious overtones in his writing, inconsonant with his naturalistic theories, he replied that to cut away rudely the last vestiges of religious sentiment must wound some persons unnecessarily; they should be accustomed more gradually to the divorce of reason and religion.

Doubtless this was kindly, but it scarcely was candid. The "humanism" that the Deweyites endeavored to promulgate survives today as a kind of league of militant atheists, devoted to such undertakings as "sex education"; and the Deweyites have let the word "religious" go by the board. More and Babbitt have won that battle, after all, and most men nowadays who respect the humane disciplines would not question the validity of their claim to the humanistic succession.

Seneca, Sir Thomas Elyot, Edmund Burke, and Benjamin Disraeli were among More's preceptors in public concerns; the great Anglican divines informed his theology. I think that probably his most important book is *Aristocracy and Justice* (1915). By the time that book was in print, our Time of Troubles had commenced, and throughout the world the god-terms Progress and Efficiency and New Morality and Democracy began to shake upon their feet of clay. The process of disintegration of the old liberal order, with its unchastened optimism, since then had hastened on from disaster to disaster. So it is that *Aristocracy and Justice*, and many of More's essays, might have been written last year, if relevance is in question.

As Santayana wrote in 1926, "That comfortable liberal world was like a great tree with the trunk already sawed quite through, but still standing with all its leaves quietly rustling, and with us dozing under its shade. We were inexpressibly surprised when it fell and half crushed us; some of us are talking of setting it up again safely on its severed roots." Perceiving that modern thought had gone wrong on first principles, More applied to this bent world the ethical convictions of the humane tradition.

More declared forthrightly that to react against folly and crime is the part of a wise man, and that no young man of intellectual power and sensibility ought to dread being called a reactionary. More's voice was lonely enough in 1915, say; but since then most of us have become reactionaries of one sort or another, reacting against the ferocious clutch of ideology and an amorphous humanitarianism. Radical notions of social perfectibility, and humanitarian notions of man's natural goodness, will bring us not to a domination of sweetness and light, More suggested in his essay, "The Philosophy of War," but to terrors beside which the Thirty Years' War might seem pallid; and war after war, since he wrote, has provided proof for his argument.

Like Dr. Johnson, More detested cant; and so he outraged the sentimentalist. He hated and dreaded the triumph of technology, the age of the engineer, the mechanization of life, and the destruction of true leisure. Many understand now the reasons for his vaticinations.

Today we are swept along by the terrible currents that, as More knew, broke through the dikes of the traditions of civility more than half a century ago. If some of us are to fight our way to shore, we need More's chart. This collection of More's writings, carefully selected by Dr. Lambert, should make More's insights easily available to a generation confusedly longing for normative knowledge.

Russell Kirk
Mecosta, Michigan

Introduction

In 1967 the Phaeton Press republished the eleven volumes of Paul Elmer More's *Shelburne Essays*, almost a half century after their completion—and neglect.[1] Such a venture gives renewed hope to those who have wept in Babylon that there might be a rebirth of aesthetic standards in the high places of culture. One remembers that just about the time the sophists had all of Attica to themselves, Socrates and Plato appeared; and it was in the ruins of the Temple that Josiah rediscovered the lost Book of the Law. May it ever be thus; and may all such finders be the keepers!

At the height of his powers, panoplied in encyclopedic learning, elevated by such historical vision as is given to few men, and fully convinced of the eventual triumph of the truth of the Ideal world, More could yet say with a measure of bitterness that he supposed he was "at once the least read and the worst hated author in the country."[2] It was no time, in those brassy years following the First War, for a classicist and conservative to walk in the Grove. More would have had to possess godlike vision to imagine that he would ever be read again.

But that was "a time, and times, and a half time" ago. After another war, interest in More began to reawaken, slowly. Russell Kirk's *The Conservative Mind* (1953) was an undoubted freshet, in which More is introduced as a modern heritor of Burke's politics of imagination and consecration.[3] Then Austin Warren wrote "The 'New Humanism' Twenty Years After" for *Modern Age*, in 1958.[4] The spring was beginning to flow. That same year Robert M. Davies wrote *The Humanism of Paul Elmer More.*[5] In 1960, A.H. Dakin brought out what is now the definitive biography of More, *Paul Elmer More.*[6] Thereafter Daniel Aaron published *Paul Elmer More's Shelburne Essays on American Literature* (1963),[7] and Francis X. Duggan presented his analysis of More's criticism, *Paul Elmer More* (1966).[8] One may say that this is not much about a major American critic; and it is not. Still it is a cloud, a little bigger than a man's hand.[9]

For whose bones could jump to life again—ever—who had once written that the rights of property were dearer than the right to life? Or had dared declare that social humanitarianism was the broad road to political collectivism? Or had announced that education and culture could be saved only by the creation of a "natural aristocracy"? Or had said that ethical and esthetic principles could never be divorced, when everybody knew that art had come of age in its separate world of limitless self-expression? Or had advocated a return to the Classics just when the study of the ancient languages had been pronounced officially dead and adjustment-to-what-is made the only logical pursuit for the living? In the words of one hostile reviewer, it was men like More who had given the hemlock to Socrates.[10] No accusation against the man seemed too absurd.

Judging from a distance of fifty years, More's warnings about the perils before his world now seem demonstrably pertinent, and his enemies graphically myopic. As early as 1900 he was arguing that unrestrained subjectivism in the arts would result in their collapse into a million little cells of unintelligible pain and bravado. While all around him were applauding President Eliot's elective system at Harvard and demanding the lowering of collegiate admissions standards in the name of service to their communities, More predicted that such a course would end up with politics on top and learning on the bottom of the collegiate totem and with the utter debasement of the college degree. Now it seems that More's only failure was overmodesty in his protestations; even he could not envision students seizing a president's office and demanding the right to design their own curricula on the flawless assumption that, after all, who could know better what they wanted? Most Americans think that the evils of moral and legal permissiveness had to wait until the Sixties to become manifest. More, before the First World War, was using New York City as a demonstration lesson in the growth of crime because of an unwillingness of the American courts to convict criminals.

George Roy Elliott, of Amherst, said of More that he was an "extraordinarily severe thinker" who had come at a time when severity of thought was "extraordinarily out of fashion."[11] Seward Collins, replying to the charge that More was "impertinent to his age" (the word today is "irrelevant"), said no man is in "more vital contact with his age than when he is attacking it in every detail."[12]

Like his fellow St. Louisan, T.S. Eliot, whose spiritual odyssey he shared in more ways than one, More journeyed eastward, "reversing the frontier." If we follow Davies, More's life can be seen in three stages: the first, beginning with his birth in St. Louis in 1864 and closing with his emergence as a man with a mission from his two-year hermitage at Shelburne, New Hampshire, in 1900; the second, from 1900 to 1915, devoted to literary criticism and editorship, the years of the *Shelburne Essays*; and the third, from 1915 to 1937, the period of ripe maturity, absorbed with philosophical, historical, and religious studies.[13]

More's adolescence and early years of intellectual turmoil were like those of anyone else, if the usual pattern is rebellion, bewilderment, and restless experimentation. Giving up Christianity at sixteen, he took up reading voraciously in the German Romantics and writing lyrics and tragedies in the authentic *Weltschmerz* manner; thereafter he reacted into a hard rationalism, under the discipline of which he made plans for a "new philosophical system" based on Democritus; then he drifted into impressionism and the study of literature as a creation of the *élan vital*. These first years saw him as a published poet, novelist, translator of Sanskrit and Greek, editor of Plato and Aeschylus, biographer of Franklin, historian of ideas, classical scholar, and literary critic. More would have us forget that he tried teaching Latin, Greek, and Sanskrit to young gentlemen and ladies for a few (a very few) distressful years; would not think it important to dwell on his degrees from Washington University and Harvard, except that at Harvard he met the man who changed him from a romantic to a classicist, Irving Babbitt; would ask that an affair of the heart remain suitably buried; would have us mention that his retirement to the mountain hut in New Hampshire enabled him to settle upon literary criticism as a career and gave him a name for eventually fourteen volumes of essays; and would have us note that finding himself, he found Henrietta Beck as a wife (1900) and a literary editorship on the New York *Independent* (1901).

The second or middle period of his life is the one for which he is best known, for these are the years in which he achieved his critical reputation. After a two-year editorship at the *Independent*, he went on to become literary editor of the New York *Evening Post* (1903–1909), then literary editor and editor-in-chief of *The Nation* (1909–1914). During these laborious years he wrote over six hundred articles, editorials, and reviews, carried on a heavy correspondence, met the deadlines of the presses unfailingly, and published the first nine volumes of the *Shelburne Essays*. The subsequent two volumes of the *Essays*, published in 1919 and 1924 respectively, either date substantially from or are based on work done in the years up to 1915. His "quest of the spirit" was as active as ever in this noonday of his life, but ordered and deepened; and his writings reveal an increasing stress on the ideals of classical humanism and a growing concern for educational, economic, and political matters. His opposition to philosophical monism (absolutism), romanticism, socialism, science, and humanitarianism became more pronounced. He believed, as Collins has said, that the Western world had "gone wrong on first principles," and he traced the roots of these evils as far back as Alexandria and gnosticism, noting the tributaries farther up the line, like Baconian empiricism, Deism, Rousseau, Romanticism, Hegel, Marx, Darwin—all contributing manifestly to the modern vogue of naturalism and to the collisions and madnesses of the twentieth century. His own response to these evils was the advocacy of a thoroughgoing dualism, based on Plato, which stressed the need for individual resistance to the centrifugal pull of things outside the human will and a bracing-up of human character at its center by a strengthening of the "inner check," that daemon which says *"No"* to impulse and so develops the will to refrain. The climactic expression of More's dualism can be found in "Definitions of Dualism," the concluding section of *The Drift of Romanticism (Shelburne Essays*, Eight Series, 1913). More's political and educational beliefs reach their highest expression two years later in the very next, the Ninth Series of the *Essays*, called *Aristocracy and Justice*, in which More calls for a reestablishment of classical educational standards and a return to distinctions in cultural life.

It was not really until the last period of his life that he was dubbed a "New Humanist" and became known as a co-leader with Irving Babbitt of a band of writers seeking to restore classical and human values to literature. Ironically he had already begun to part company with some of his closest comrades, even as they rallied together between 1928 and 1930, under the banner of the *Bookman*, the *Forum*, and the *American Review*, to turn back the anti-Humanist assaults of the *New Republic*, the *American Mercury*, and the disciples of the New Criticism. More was reluctant to contribute an essay to Norman Foerster's *Humanism and America* (1930), which was supposed to be the *vade mecum* of Neo-Humanism and a tribute to More and Babbitt, but when he did he settled on "the relation of humanism to religion," a theme he knew he would have to handle delicately so as "to avoid cross-purposes with the other contributors."[14] More had been reconverted to Christianity between the publication of the first edition of *Platonism* (1917) and the writing of *The Christ of the New Testament* (1924), and it had put a certain distance between More and Babbitt, who could not quite accept More's having new views.

In a letter to T.S. Eliot, dated July 9, 1930, More lamented,

"After all theology is the only really interesting subject, and I
get so little of it in conversation or letters."[15] Intimations of
More's growing absorption with religious questions would not
have been hard to find, had anyone cared to look. In the essay,
"The Paradox of Oxford," included in the Ninth Series, More
had spoken of a possible reconciliation of the Classical and
medieval traditions in a synthesis which would embrace "the
higher and . . . the less dogmatic elements of each."[16] And in
the preface to *Platonism,* More wrote, "I can foresee no restoration of humane studies to their lost position of leadership
until they are felt once more to radiate from some spiritual
truth."[17] More had felt a religious hunger for years, he confessed later in *Pages from an Oxford Diary,* but it was not until
taking up the serious study of Plato in *Platonism* and *The
Religion of Plato* (1921) that he saw humanism to be helpless
without the alliance of religious faith. Thus was born the idea
of *The Greek Tradition,* the writing of which was to take him
twenty years. *Platonism* became a corollary and introductory
volume to the study, while *The Religion of Plato* was made the
first book in the project.

There followed *Hellenistic Philosophies* (1923), *The Christ
of The New Testament* (1924), *Christ The Word* (1927), and
The Catholic Faith (1931), in the course of which books More
moves from a theistic humanism to a full acceptance of the
doctrine of the Incarnation. A concise summary of the "Tradition" can be found in More's subsequent *The Sceptical Approach to Religion* (1934). More also published two volumes of
polemical theology and criticism in those late years, *The Demon of the Absolute* (1928) and *On Being Human* (1936),
which along with *The Sceptical Approach to Religion* he made
into a three volume "New Shelburne Essays" series. Then with
F.L. Cross he co-edited *Anglicanism* (1935), an anthology of
seventeenth-century religious literature, and with Samuel P.
Cowardin, Jr., collaborated in *The Study of English Literature*
(1936), a text for beginning students of literature. The autobio-
graphical *Pages from an Oxford Diary,* published posthumously in 1937, was his last book and a delicately personal

summation of his philosophical and religious postions.

The last lesson of life, he said in the *Pages*, was just this: "We are intellectually incompetent and morally responsible."[18] Born knowing nothing, we strive through many errors to learn little that is final. Not certain what we are supposed to do, we curse ourselves both when we act and when we do nothing at all. Yet the intuitive sense of right and wrong is there; we know we are free to choose. Despairing of finding any rationalistic account of this world that is satisfactory, we ask if our intuitions and experience do not point to a realm beyond, whose truths can be apprehended only by the imagination, or by symbol. We consent finally to the beckoning finger of faith, and following, sense the ever-deepening certainty of being in the right way, find our hope more and more confirmed by our experience, discover our feeling of responsibiliity converted into religious obedience, and come "at last to a reality that is beckoning out of the unknown and to a waiting land of the spirit."[19] This far Plato had journeyed; hence, his heaven of divine Ideas, standing unshaken above the world of change and illusion and finding embodiment below only in poetry, religion, and the voice of conscience. But Plato could go no further; "something still was wanted, a voice that should have the authority of revelation from above rather than the plausibility of persuasion from below."[20]

This confirming revelation More found in the Christian doctrine of the Incarnation. More's thesis was "that Greek literature, philosophic and religious, pagan and Christian, from Plato to St. Chrystostom and beyond that to the Council of Chalcedon in 451 A.D., is essentially a unit and follows at the centre a straight line."[21] Plato had demonstrated the terrible duality in things, how above the material universe stood the everlasting realm of Ideas, how God from his vantage point in the Ideal world worked to impose order upon the ever-resisting chaos of the lower world, and how in the heart of man could be seen the same struggle between the spirit and the flesh, between reason and emotion, will and impulse. The Incarnation had overcome this duality. Christ had perfectly har-

monized the upper and lower natures in himself; he had
united the divine and the human; he had bridged the distance
between the One and the Many. He was the world of impersonal Ideas made palpable in the flesh and God's long-suffering
purpose to perfect nature made visible in a person. The Greeks
had held that there was a rational principle, a *logos*, holding
the cosmos together, and that men were fashioned with a logos
in themselves which could recognize the divine Logos, wherever it appeared. Christ demonstrated that the divine principle was *personal* and purposeful. Christ's descent to death was
the expression of God's willingness to take the responsibility
for the pain and brokenness of the world upon himself, while
his resurrection manifested his actual power over nature and
the processes of death. The Incarnation was God's bid for the
comradeship of men in the work of bringing· order to the
universe, and Christ's Ascension, God's proof not only of the
immortality of the soul, but of the sanctification of the flesh.

For More, the Incarnation was the resolution of the problem
of evil. "If there be any meaning in the tragic end of the
Incarnation, if the Cross have any cosmic significance, it must
be simply this, that God as the Author of an imperfect world,
so through his suffering made himself voluntarily its re-
deemer."[22] And again: " . . . The Incarnation . . . reveals God
as a personality somehow involved in the failure of His own
handiwork and somehow redeeming the evil of the world by
participating in the penalties of imperfection." Except by this
divine condescension men could not know how the consequences of their deeds "reach out . . . into the eternal world
. . . to the very heart of God." The Incarnation, therefore,
revealed sin to be finally this: disloyalty "to One who has
counted upon us for aid in the bitter war with Necessity,"
ingratitude to the One "who has honored us with the call to
partake in the glorious work of creating order and beauty and
joy." "God became man in order that man might become
God."[23]

At the very end of his life what More longed for was a "gift
of persuasion" to bring the world to the truth he had found for

himself.[24] He was convinced that by losing touch with the Judaeo-Christian tradition, the modern world was "in peril of sinking back into barbarism."[25] As a first corrective step, he wanted to recover the insight of the early Christian fathers that the logos in man can participate in the divine purpose of the universe, and that all the wisdom of the sages and all true literature has been (and is) the response in the heart of man to the manifestation of the Logos in the world. The high function of art and letters, therefore, is "to build here and now a home for the soul in the world of Ideas," and the purpose of the critic and the scholar is "to trace the operations of the logos, to distinguish its genuine expression in literature from shams, to know the truth, and so to dwell in the calm but active leisure *(scholé)* of contemplation." The true scholar is a *logios,* a Logos-seeker, who recovers the avenues of communion between man and God and keeps them "in fee for generations to come";[26] and the goal of his effort is the harmonious synchronization of spirit and form.[27]

More wanted to bring about the reintegration of ethics and esthetics, which had been gradually separated since the time of the Renaissance, and so bring order into modern culture. More called himself a "humanist" in the sense that he insisted on strengthening that feature in man which distinguishes him from the animals. For More what made man a *human* combination of mind and matter was not only his reason, but his imagination. While the reason in man reached out for the eternal Ideas, it was only through man's imagination that he could lay hold on them. Therefore, the task of art was to clothe the eternal truths of the Ideal world in such illusions of form as would open the imagination of men to their influence. Following Eliot, More says although one can determine whether a piece of writing is literature or not simply by applying literary standards to it, one cannot judge the greatness of literature solely by literary standards; its greatness can only be determined by its faithfulness to the truths of Heaven.[28] Only as man becomes more Godlike, does he become more geniunely human, and only as he knows more divine truth does he find more adequate means of expressing it. The rift between man and nature, between reason and passion, between the good and the beautiful can be healed only by the ethical imagination.

It was the dominance of the ethical imagination that More wanted to see reestablished in the laws, literature, and institutions of men. In literature it meant adherence to the Great Tradition; in science, the perception of "something other and different lurking beneath natural law and peering out at the observer with strange enticements";[29] in law, the awareness of the ancestral cost of bringing us to where we are, the willingness to listen to voices from over the distances of human experience, and distrust of easy solutions for longstanding wrongs; in education, the revival of classical studies at the core of the curricula, meaning their use as discipline for the mind and character. More said once that by imagination he meant the habitual grasp "in a single firm vision of . . . the long course of human history and of distinguishing what is essential therein from what is ephemeral."[30] The ethical imagination was both catholic and selective; it was "the presence of the past in the present," stored knowledge, stored sensitivities, Burke's "unbought grace," passed on from generation to generation, always capable of enrichment by added experience, yet always in danger of impoverishment by neglect or rejection.

"Humility and commonsense," More would say, these were the qualities too often lacking in the long history of human thought. His quarrel with rationalistic thinking was that it tended to get lost in "its own unreal abstractions," "reducing all existence to one order," either mechanical or spiritual.[31] Whether it be a Marx, a Plotinus, a Hegel, or a Dewey, the great "reasoner" always beheld the cosmos as a completely systemized reflection of his own presuppositions; the more logical and complete the theory, the more absurd and fatuous the results. The *absolute* was the immemorial demon in the house of intellect.

More's quarrel with the romantics and humanitarians was not that of the hardened cynic. What he protested against was their surrender of judgment to sentiment. He traced modern societal disorganization to Rousseau, who externalized the true dualism of man's moral struggle within himself into the false dualism of the struggle between man and society. Almost overnight, men, conceiving themselves liberated from "sin," had to put the blame for their failures elsewhere and so transferred the causes of evil to society at large. Was there poverty? The king and the constitution were to blame. Were there superstition and ignorance? The Church was to blame. Were there cruelty and immorality? Christian marriage and the monogamous home were to blame. And so the assertion went that the whole trouble was men had forgotten how to live according to "nature"; therefore, what they needed was to throw over artificial "rules" and form a new conscience by doing as they pleased! As for society, sympathy was the only cement needed to restore it to a state of fraternal peace. More points out that the fallacy in such a theory is that sympathy is a highly ambiguous emotion; one can "weep with those that weep" and simultaneously rejoice in one's own contrasting good fortune. In a sentimental society when interests clash, he said, sympathy will finally unmask as selfishness.[32]

More's quarrel with science was that it had given rise to the widespread popular notion that the universe was a closed system of natural causes. While More recognized that the popular world-view was not a representation of what scientists of his day were actually thinking, nevertheless the false world-view was there, continuing to spawn all sorts of religious, social, and political evils. So all-pervasive was this notion of a self-generating system of nature that it constituted a dangerous new monism for the public mind, grandiosely fastening itself on every aspect of thought and life in modern civilization. Philosophy itself was no longer free. The dominant "schools" of thought were only naturalism working itself out under different guises, whether as pragmatism, vitalism, neo-realism, phenomenology, behaviorism, or analytical philosophy.

Essentially More's quarrels with contemporary education, art, and theology were for the same reason: they were all tools of monistic naturalism. Artists of the expressionist sort and philosophers of the pragmatic sort, imagining themselves to be "in tune" with what was happening, were more and more out of touch with reality. Modernists had rejected the Logos and so were actually creating a subhuman culture. Identifying themselves with the beasts, they would inevitably come to accept bestiality as a manner of life. By contrast, More would say, consider the frankness of Homer. The *Iliad* and the *Odyssey* show human lust and ambition caught in a tangle of blind war and tumbling gods, yet presented in such a way that individuality of character and the fatefulness of individual choice are never lost in the wide vistas of battle or the interpositions of Olympus. Homer sees his whole panorama from above, from an elevation which could have been won only from strife with himself and the sure knowledge of what endures in human experience. The vision is objective; we scarcely think of the poetry as the work of a man at all; yet we know it was shaped by a human imagination fully aware of the paradoxes in human behavior and the unaccountable meddlings of fate. Homer avoids the biases too often found in the development of literature. He treats of sex and violence, but not lasciviously as do the naturalists. He is moral, but not moralistic like the Neo-Classicists. He is instructive, but not didactic. He is concerned more with what engenders awe than with what produces wonder, the beau ideal of the Romantics. His ideas are truly living things, woven into the action, not schemata or commentary.

More's conservatism was, therefore, not that of the philistines. He was both too proudly reactionary and too humbly self-critical to be a Bourbon. No capitalist could have gotten away with saying what More did about the sanctity or property; and just as equally, no saint could have declared the insubstantiality of earthly rewards so convincingly.

Call him a "reactionary," and he would not only accept the term, but heroically reconsecrate it:

> . . . The saying has gone abroad that strength means joy in change and that he who would question change is reactionary

and effeminate; and so in the name of progress and virility we drift supinely with the current. . . . But reaction . . . is essentially to answer action with action, to oppose to the welter of circumstance the force of discrimination and selection, to direct the aimless tide of change by reference to the coexisting law of the immutable fact, *to carry the experience of the past into the diverse impulses of the present*, and so to move forward in an orderly progression. If any young man, feeling now within himself the power of accomplishment, hesitates to be called a reactionary, in this better use of the term, because of the charge of effeminacy, let him take courage. The world is not contradicted with impunity, and he who sets himself against the world's belief will have need of all a man's endurance and all a man's strength. The adventurous soul who today against the reigning scientific and pragmatic dogma would maintain no vague and equally one-sided idealism . . . will find himself subjected to an intellectual isolation and contempt almost as terrible as the penalties of the inquisition, and quite as effective in producing a silent conformity. If a man doubts this, let him try, and learn. Submission to the philosophy of change is the real effeminacy; it is the virile part to react.[33]

More added nothing to his credibility by such ethical and political sacrifices. But—he was a severe thinker when severity of thought was out of fashion. G.R. Elliott once said of More that he was "devoid of even the most innocent flatteries."[34]

More's conservatism was in the line of Burke's. It was prescriptive, venerative of the long past, indwelt with "the sense of mysterious presence out of the invisible world"; in other words, imaginative in the high sense of that term.[35]

. . . The instinctive distrust of uncontrolled human nature and the instinctive reliance on the imagination are the very roots of the conservative temper, as their contraries are the roots of the liberal and radical temper, the lack of imagination, if any distinction is to be made, being the chief factor of liberalism and confidence in human nature being the main impulse of radicalism.[36]

How could this man be American? Yet he was American, and his earliest aim was to establish an American criticism.

Duggan has pointed out how it was More who discovered that
virtually the whole of German romanticism is contained in the
writing of Thoreau. More's work on the New England region-
alists anticipates Carl Van Doren's; his analysis of Poe and
Hawthorne was ahead of Harry Levin's by fifty years; his thesis
that "the most significant strain in American letters is the
strain of darkness, morbidity, and preoccupation with evil" has
been echoed by Robert Spiller and Randall Stewart.[37]

His opponents have accused him of being humorless, olympian, and stodgy. His pupil, Stuart Sherman, after breaking
with More, caricatured him as pompously aloof and unwilling
to meet his fellow-countrymen half way, the veritable
"bishop" of American criticism who required that human nature be base and that America be governed by a half-dozen
great families![38] Yet those who disagreed with him most vio-
lently admitted he spoke from a breadth of learning which few
could match. Mencken confessed that More was the "nearest
approach to a genuine scholar" America had. Those who said
he had no sense of humor somehow missed reading "Oxford,
Women, and God" in the Eleventh Series, "Byron's 'Don
Juan' " in the Third Series, and the preface to the Tenth Series.

Now a word about this anthology. I call this collection *The
Essential Paul Elmer More* because it presents the "essence"
of his thought in all of those fields in which he worked. It is an
attempt to provide a digest of his working ideas, not just in
literary criticism, for which he is best known, but in philosophy, politics, religion, and education. Those essays have been
chosen which best reveal not only his fundamental conceptions about such questions as the nature of existence and the
function of criticism, but those which also illustrate the way in
which he related the different disciplines in which he worked.

More was a *true* cosmopolitan and a reproach to the pseudo-
cosmopolites of contemporary bias, since he regarded sophisti-
cation as more than a matter of knowing what was going on
everywhere in the present ("keeping relevant"); he insisted
always upon the witness of *all* history to any issue that was

raised, and he could quote Plato in the Greek, the *Bhagavad Gita* in the Sanskirt, Lucretius in the Latin, and early Christian rhetoricians with as much ease as he could Matthew Arnold, Sainte-Beuve, or Goethe in their respective languages. He was an astonishing American—at least for our times. He was independent of his age as no "relevant" critic or thinker could ever hope to be. It was because of this that he gave the impression of being academic, whereas he spent only a small portion of his life in the academy, the better being involved with writing newspaper articles, reviewing current fiction, and being an editor of a national journal. No recluse, More was hugely involved in that blistering controversy with the anti-Humanists in the late Twenties. He was at home with modern writers as diverse as Donald Mitchell, Lafcadio Hearn, and Baron von Hügel.

The criteria governing the selection of the essays for this volume are therefore easily explained. I wished first to avoid duplicating the work of Daniel Aaron, whose *Shelburne Essays on American Literature* amply introduce More's contribution to American criticism; therefore, none of More's work on American writers is included in this anthology. I do not consider such an omission damaging, not only for the reason that the public has access to it now in both Aaron's anthology and the republished *Shelburne Essays,* but because More did the better part of his labors in English, continental, and classical literature, fields which he regarded as of far greater importance than the American to his task of restoring enduring standards of taste.

Most important, I wanted to include selections which would illustrate the themes which absorbed More most, namely those on dualism, tradition, imagination, faith, moral law, common sense, humility, illusion, the teleology of history, and standards of taste. I wanted those which would demonstrate both his scholarship and his originality of insight; those which would have warm, public appeal, and yet show the chaste strength of his style; those which both he and his contemporaries, friend and enemy alike, regarded highly; those for which he is remembered by a later generation; and those undeservedly forgotten. The collection had to show More's catholicity of interest, his range of learning, and his development, although the limitations on space and the arrangement of the essays do not permit emphasis on the last.

The one feature of this collection of More which sets it apart from all other anthologies of his work, including his own for the Oxford Press, is the inclusion of certain shorter pieces done by him for journals now defunct, which show the master at his offhand best and therefore sharpen the focus of the ideas being treated in each section. "Marginalia," from the *American Review*, is More's last word, literally, on what he meant by "dualism"; it stands first in Section I. The four brief pieces, beginning with "The Scholarship of Ideas," closing out the Third Section, are drawn from *The Nation* and the *New York Independent*. "Wealth and Culture" and "Progress," in Section IV, are lifted from the pages of *The Villager*. There are many other pieces, not included here, deserving rescue.

The other, and weightier, titles are, of course, taken from the various volumes of the *Shelburne Essays*. But there is one exception. "The Doctrine of the Logos" is an essay consisting of the culminating two chapters of *Christ the Word*. While More never intended that these chapters should be published as a unified article, together they constitute such a consummate piece of condensation and climax that they can almost stand alone. It is hoped that by reprinting them in this way they will create in the reader a curiosity to look at the original work; and if this happens, it will more than warrant my separating them for awhile from their native habitation.

The arrangement of the essays under the four headings of "Philosophy and Religion," "Literature," "Education and History," and "Politics and Society" is an attempt to provide a logical order for the reader, who would otherwise amble desultorily through an unarranged collection; here the different headings represented an attempt to couple certain areas More tended to view as naturally linked together. The grouping of the essays is arbitrary; some could fall easily under two or more heads, because of the way in which More integrated morality and esthetics, for example, or history and religion. "Victorian Literature" could be carried under the heading, "Philosophy and Religion," for instance; but it gave better depth to the section on literary criticism to be placed there, especially since More's criticism was molded by his classical learning. "Criticism" and "Rousseau" are rich studies in cultural history, and "Natural Aristocracy" could be viewed as social criticism; yet they are not placed under these categories, because "Criticism" is an important study in a certain body of *literature*, "Rousseau" demonstrates the futility of humanitarian socialism, and "Natural Aristocracy" pleads for the education of aristocrats by reforming the curricula of the schools and colleges. In all, I tried to get balance and proportion in the arrangement of the essays, so that they properly reflect the order and emphasis of his thought. The second section on literary criticism is, thus, a little longer than the others, since the professional judgment of literary works took up the better part of his life; but the section on "Philosophy and Religion" is placed first, since the essays there grouped state the first and last principles by which More made his judgments about literature, education, and society. It is for this reason, too, that "Criticism," "Natural Aristocracy," and "Justice" are placed at the head of their respective sections, for they provide an introduction to and summary of the principles developed by the other pieces in that section. Readers behaving the way they do, I have tried to place those essays which state More's principles most succinctly at the beginning of each division of the book.

It is regrettable that limits on space made it necessary to exclude an essay like the wonderfully warm and appealing "My Debt to Trollope," from *The Demon of the Absolute;* or the sinewy outline of his dualistic philosophy in "Definitions of Dualism," from the Sixth Series; or a work like *Pages from an Oxford Diary*, that delicately brief and beautiful autobiography of More, which is like nothing else More ever wrote, more a poem than an essay, more a confession and credo and "last lingering look" than a book, more

Like pious incense from a censor old,
. . . taking flight for heaven without a death.

Perhaps these compositions deserve solitary editing and republication anyway.

The translations of the foreign passages are mine, except where I could find a standard translation in a dictionary of foreign phrases or an edition of the author in question. Where the meaning of the foreign phrase or quotation is obvious from the context, I leave it untranslated. More could expect his reading public to be familiar with Latin, since it was a requirement for both a high school diploma and a college degree at the turn of the century. More could expect the college graduate of his day to know one or more modern foreign tongues, as well. Alas, the same cannot be expected of the "life-adjustment" generation. I risk insulting the learned, I fear, by translating the obvious into the swinging parlance of today, while I alienate the popular reader by leaving even one foreign word untranslated. I can only hope that there will be enough readers, like myself, whose knowledge of Latin, Greek, French, and German has gone rusty, that they will secretly bless the editor for taking their embarrassment into account.

I have taken the liberty of omitting those of More's footnotes which would have had only contemporary interest and added information of my own which would help identify a name or clarify an allusion otherwise obscure to even the well-read of today. Again I probably err on the side of doing too little; but I was not trying to edit a text for the use of entering freshmen. I have also rendered More's notes consistent in arrangement, where they varied over the years from one manner of treatment, like carrying translations in a parenthesis following the foreign passage quoted, to another, like carrying references from scripture or the classics in the margins; and the footnotes are not only newly numbered but numbered consecutively within each essay. At the request of Mrs. Harry B. Fine, More's daughter and the owner of the copyright for a large number of the essays, I have left More's spelling untouched. This will explain the slight inconsistency between the spelling of the pieces from More's books, based on the Oxford English standard, and that in those pieces which appeared only in American journals, whose editors followed Webster's International.

I should like to thank the Phaeton Press, Mrs. Harry B. Fine, and Mrs. Edmund G. Dymond for permission to reprint from the *Shelburne Essays,* volumes I, IV, V, VI, VII, IX, and X; and Princeton University Press, for the permission to reprint "The Doctrine of the Logos" from *Christ the Word.*

My abundant thanks are due Mrs. Annette Bruhwiler, Director of the Rutherford Campus Library, and her staff, especially Mr. Robert Stanbury and Miss Joyce Crenshaw, for all their assistance in locating many needed books and references demanded in my study of More; the Newark Public Library for granting me special privileges photocopying hundreds of pages of Morean articles and reviews, long out of print; Dr. Rene Silva, Chairman of the Department of Foreign Languages at the Rutherford Campus, and members of his faculty like Mrs. Ingrid Lotze, Mrs. Lucy La Porta, and Mr. Irwin Radezky, who checked my translations from the German, Italian, and French respectively; and Mrs. George Bleyle, of Passaic Collegiate School, Passaic, New Jersey, who assisted me with the Latin; Father Dean Timothy Andrews, of the Hellenic University, Brookline, Massachusetts, who helped me with More's references to certain early twentieth-century Orthodox theologians; to the New York University Library, the Rutgers University Library of New Brunswick, New Jersey, the Newberry Library of Chicago, and the Trenton State College Library, Trenton, New Jersey, for photocopying out-of-print articles of More from their files of magazines and newspapers; and above all to Fairleigh Dickinson University and its Provost, Dr. Richard M. Drake, for making a grant available without which the study of the Morean materials and the typing of the manuscript could not have been done.

I wish to thank Dr. Charles Angoff, editor of the Fairleigh Dickinson University Press, for his generous advice about printing this collection of essays; and to acknowledge the help of the late Professor Gorham Munson, one of the original New Humanist group, who encouraged me to continue in these studies; Dr. Russell Kirk, who kindly consented to add the foreword to the book and so bring the lustre of a widely respected name to my editorial labors; Mrs. Evelyn Prince, my secretary, and the members of her staff, for managing the uncounted thankless errands and telephone calls which interrupted the already over-expanded annoyances of a dean's office; and my wife, who kept believing that the work could be done.

Let me add a couple of last words. First, this has been a labor of love, pursued in such snatches of time as a modern college administratorship would allow, a few minutes after lunch, a sentence upon arising, a paragraph after a night of committee work, some Saturday mornings in the libraries, a few more precious Sunday evenings, permitting concentration enough to revise, correct, and connect one effort with another, sometimes separated by weeks, even months of administrative duty or crisis. In a word there has been no time, no proper leisure for even this limited scholarly effort, such being the result of our labor-saving devices, shortened· work hours and much vaunted progress! Those who have leisure do not know what to do with it, and those who need it cannot find it or afford it.

Secondly, there is no question in my mind that someone else should have undertaken this work. More deserved better than an editor of such modest attainments as my own. But there was no one else, so far as I could see, who had determined to do anything to preserve some of the work of this unusual critic. My one hope is that this book will provoke enough interest to stimulate the great to look at More again seriously. If I have helped call attention to a vital link between our cultural past and the hungry generations yet unborn—and More is one of our few links—perhaps I have done all that I have been called to do. In this present darkness, I have had the privilege of locating an unspent candle and relighting it.

Byron C. Lambert
Fairleigh Dickinson University
Rutherford, New Jersey

1   Paul Elmer More, *Shelburne Essays*, First Series through Eleventh Series (eleven volumes in all). New York: Phaeton Press, 1967. Hereafter, "SE I", "SE II", etc.

2   From a letter to Prosser Hall Frye, December 29, 1922, quoted in Francis X. Duggan, *Paul Elmer More*, No. 106 in *Twayne's United States Author Series*. New York: Twayne Publishers, Inc., 1966 (p.i). Hereafter, "Duggan."

3   Russell Kirk, *The Conservative Mind from Burke to Santayana*. Chicago: Henry Regnery Co., 1953.

4   Austin Warren, "The 'New Humanism' Twenty Years After," *Modern Age: A Quarterly Review*, Vol. III, No. 1 (Winter, 1958–59), pp. 81–7.

5   Robert M. Davies, *The Humanism of Paul Elmer More*. New York: Bookman Associates, 1958. Hereafter, "Davies."

6   Arthur Hazard Dakin, *Paul Elmer More*. Princeton, New Jersey: Princeton University Press, 1960. Hereafter, "Dakin."

7   *Paul Elmer More's Shelburne Essays on American Literature*, Selected and Edited by Daniel Aaron. New York: Harcourt, Brace, and World, Inc., 1963.

8   See footnote 2 above.

9   I have not listed unpublished studies and dissertations concerned directly with More, but the interested reader may refer to a list of titles in my article, "More Redivivus," *The University Bookman*, Vol. VII, No. 4 (Summer, 1967), p. 92.

10 Francis Hackett, "Mr. More Moralizes," *The New Republic*, Vol. XXVI, No. 331 (April 6, 1921), pp. 163–4.

11 George Roy Elliott, "Mr. More and the Gentle Reader," *The Bookman*, Vol. LXIX, No. 2 (April, 1929), p. 143.

12 Seward Collins, "Criticism in America: I. The Origin of a Myth," *The Bookman*, Vol. LXXI, No. 3 (June, 1930), p. 357.

13 Davies, p. 62.

14 In a letter to Robert Shafer, July 17, 1928, quoted in Dakin, p. 271.

15 In a letter to Eliot, July 9, 1930, quoted in Dakin, p. 292.

16 See SE IX, pp. 80, 88, 100.

17 Paul Elmer More, *Platonism*, Second Edition, Revised. Princeton: Princeton University Press, 1926, p. ix.

18 Paul Elmer More, *Pages from an Oxford Diary*. Princeton: Princeton University Press, 1937, Section XXXII. Hereafter, "POD."

19 Paul Elmer More, *The Sceptical Approach to Religion, New Shelburne Essays*, Volume II. Princeton: Princeton University Press, 1934, p. 193.

20 Paul Elmer More, *Christ the Word*. Princeton: Princeton University Press, 1927, p. 29. Hereafter, "CW."

21 Paul Elmer More, *The Religion of Plato*. Princeton: Princeton University Press, 1921, p. vi. Hereafter, "RP."

22 POD, Section XXIII.

23 *Ibid.*, Section XXIV.

24 *Ibid.*, Section XXXIII.

25 RP, p. vii.

26 CW, pp. 300–1.

27 Paul Elmer More, *The Catholic Faith*. Princeton: Princeton University Press, 1931, p. 72.

28 Paul Elmer More, *On Being Human, New Shelburne Essays*, Volume III. Princeton: Princeton University Press, 1936, pp. 194–5.

29 SE VI, p. 172.

30 SE IX, p. 36.

31 Paul Elmer More, *The Demon of the Absolute, New Shelburne Essays*, Volume I. Princeton: Princeton University Press, 1928, p. xii. Hereafter, "DA."

32 SE VI, p. 238.

33 SE VII, pp. 267–9. Italics are editor's.

34 George Roy Elliott, "Mr. More and the Gentle Reader," *The Bookman*, Vol. LXIX, No. 2 (April, 1929), p. 143.

[35] DA, p. 122.
[36] SE IX. p. 168.
[37] Duggan, pp. 147–8.
[38] Stuart P. Sherman, *Americans*. New York: Charles Scribner's Sons, 1923, pp. 321, 326, 333.

PART I

Philosophy and Religion

Marginalia[1]

Two foreign students recently, one from Switzerland, the other from Sweden, have consulted me about my philosophical theories, which they are studying for the doctor's degree in their respective universities. To both of them the dualistic thesis stood out as the binding thread running through all my work. This is an obvious view, which has been accepted by every critic, so far as I know, who has written on the subject. But it is as true as it is obvious that dualism may vary widely in its connotation, and my own use of the term has perhaps a certain peculiarity which needs to be noted. Emphatically I have not meant by it to set up an ironclad rival to the various metaphysics of the One. My intention has been much less ambitious than that, and implies no more than this, that in every field of experience, if I push my analysis to the end of my resources, I find myself brought up against a pair of irreconcilable, yet interrelated and interacting, contraries, such as "good" and "bad," "mind" and "body," the "One" and the "Many," "rest" and "motion." The dualist is one who modestly submits to this bifurcation as the ultimate point where clarity of definition obtains. Beyond this he refuses to follow reason in its frantic endeavor to reconcile these opposites by any logical legerdemain in which one of the controlling factors of consciousness is brought out as an Absolute while the other disappears in the conjuror's hat. The dualist, in other words, though he may do homage to the reasoning faculty as the governor of practical conduct, yet balks at its pretension to discover in its

own mechanism the ultimate source and nature of Being. He
remains half-brother to the sceptic, whereas the monist is a
metaphysical dogmatist.

I have said that it is the function of reason to deal with the
contraries of experience in the field of "practical conduct." But
this, it may be said, is only the superficial aspect of dualism; for
the root of the matter, it should seem that we must look not
to the logical faculty at all, but must penetrate to some deep
substratum of the temperament or the emotions, to some obscure region of the soul itself, out of which spring the conflicting impulses to the religious and the worldly life. There, in that
darkness where definitions fail us, lies the origin of the apparent and definable bifurcations. It is a division of what finally
interests, and the nature of the dividing force, in so far at least
as it touches religion, can be studied better in Newman perhaps than in any other English writer.

More than once Newman has said that from an early age
the two things which seemed of importance to him were
God and his own soul. One can understand why he put the
matter in this form; yet I think an attentive reading of his
works will show that what stood out for him against his own
soul was not so much God as the whole Otherworld of
which God may be the sovereign King but which can never
be absorbed into his being. God indeed is present to Newman's mind; and at times, as in the great passage of the *Apologia*, comes magnificently to the front. But in general I
do not find that sense of a personal Lord and Lover dominating his imagination as it does, for example, a St.
Theresa.[2] Rather, his imagination is haunted by that invisible realm beyond or outside of the range of the senses,
which was called Ideal by Plato as constructed of Forms, or
Ideas, seen by the eye of the soul, or Noetic by the later
Platonists as grasped by the *nous,* or Spiritual by St. Paul.
This to Newman, as I take it, even more than the being of
a personal God, was the one thing important, the one thing
he must make real to his soul against all the distractions of

the world. For the mystery of this sense of the Otherworld is that, though never an illusion, it is strangely elusive. To this paradox Newman returns more than once in his books, the most elaborate passage being that in *The Idea of a University*, which I have quoted in an appendix to *The Religion of Plato*.[3] It is never an illusion, I say; never a power that deceives or allures into evil and error; but it is elusive, impalpable, slipping from our grasp when we think we have it most firmly fixed, and hard to make concrete to the imagination and to impose on the will; lying like the shadowed reflections of the sky on the surface of a quiet pool but vanishing away when a breeze ruffles the mirror. The glory of Newman's genius as a master of language lay in his power of conveying to the reader some derivative notion of the reality of that noetic sphere of which he himself was, apparently by birthright, a citizen. In this gift, and not in philosophic argument, where in truth Newman was not strong, resided his royal prerogative over the souls of others; there we get the force of his chosen notto, *cor as cor loquitur;*[4] there by feebler wings he can be followed at a distance,

> *Sailing with supreme dominion*
> *Thro' the azure deep of air.*

But beside this realm of the Spirit lies another kingdom, that of nature, as we call it, which is not at all retiring or evasive. Rather it is visible, palpable, insistent, ever clamorous of attention. It is not elusive, but by a strange paradox illusory, the very heart and fountain of illusion. That is to say its real substance is less than its apparent substance, and its promises end in deception, disappointment, sometimes even in despair. But of the noetic world the truth and substance become more real by testing, and its promises are more than fulfilled if you grasp it tightly, cling to it, and obey its laws. And it follows too that just as the noetic world grows more real and solid, this phenomenal world loses in reality and substance. This is a law of experience to which Newman was keenly awake, and there is no more characteristic passage in his works than this in the first volume of his *Parochial Sermons*:

> And should it so happen that misfortunes come upon us (as they often do), then still more are we led to understand the nothingness of this world; then still more are we led to distrust it, and are weaned from the love of it, till at length it floats before our eyes merely as some idle veil, which, notwithstanding its many tints, cannot hide the view of what is beyond it;—and we begin, by degrees, to perceive that there are but two beings in the whole universe, our own soul, and the God who made it.

That, I take it, if we think of "God" as a synonym for the noetic world where He abides, points to the centre of Newman's religious life and is the core of his message. Certainly, at least, it is that in him which enchained so many of my younger years.[5]

*   *   *   *

A lovelier ode to spring was never indited than Horace's *Solvitur acris hiems,* in which we can almost hear the breaking of the fetters of winter and catch the chanties of busy men as that draw their boats down to the sea, and can see the Graces once more dancing their rounds on the flowered meadows. All the earth is filled with the joy of the great resurrection. And then the moral: O little men, be not deceived. Think not that your winter is to be followed by any spring. From such long hope the brevity of life cuts you off. Already the night is closing upon you, and you are on the way to that dull home of death where no joy is and from whence there is no return. This is not the only ode in which Horace bids us forgo the long hope— *spem longam reseces;* such a deprivation is the very root of his philosophy, *carpe diem,* snatch the day and be not credulous of any morrow.

Nor was the idea peculiar to Horace among the pagan poets.

Catullus gives it a new pathos by expressing it in his tripping hendecasyllables: The sun may trick his beams and flame once more in the forehead of the morning sky (to borrow Milton's adaptation in "Lycidas"), and the wasted moon may round out her orb, but for us when once our little light has set—

Ours is nothing but one long night of slumber.

And then I turn to the most fragrant of the Christian poets:

> *How fresh, O Lord, how sweet and clean*
> *Are thy returns! Ev'n as the flowers in spring. . . .*
> *　　Grief melts away*
> *　　Like snow in May,*
> *As if there were no such cold thing.*

No one can read Horace and George Herbert together without feeling that a whole world of emotion has slipped in between them; for the very gist of Herbert's song, in the lines that follow, is hope, the long hope, that the returning spring bade the ancient poets cut away. We do not often, I think, pause to consider the change that came into the world with the advent of this new hope. Christianity may seem to have failed in so many ways; it has done so little for the morals and intelligence of civilization, so little to mitigate the evils of social and international injustice, so little to impose restraint on the insurgent passions of mankind; but this one thing it has effected, the offering of hope, the long hope, to the souls of individual men. You cannot forget it, cannot hide away the fact:

> *Une immense espérance a traversé la terre.* [6]

Goethe, in one of those strange glimpses into the secret of Christianity that occasionally pierced his pagan armor, has used this for what is perhaps the most dramatic moment in *Faust*. His hero has gone through all the learning of the age, and found nothing but emptiness and disappointment. In his distress he has called for help upon the Earth-Spirit, with whom he claims kinship, and he has been contemptuously rebuffed. There is nothing left for him but escape from the fret of living into the deep slumber of oblivion. The cup of poison is at his lips, when from the cathedral nearby there floats through his window the refrain of the Easter song, for it is the dawn of that day when the new hope was born:

Christ is arisen!

The contrast would have been even more startlingly effective if the Easter chant had been preceded by the great speech in which Faust strips off the various decorous illusions of life, ending with the curse upon patience and hope. But with all his dramatic sense Goethe lacked the faculty of dramatic construction, as could be shown by other scenes in *Faust*. For instance, Gretchen's heartbroken prayer to Mary should have been made in the cathedral and followed closely by the terrible answer of the monkish chant: *Dies irae, dies illa,* instead of being separated by so much irrelevant matter. But we must not be hypercritical. As it stands, that juxtaposition of Faust's despair with the pledge of the world's hope is a stroke of pure genius.

I like to think historically of the advent of this hope as indicated by three quotations from the Greek. The first is from the great chorus of the *Agamemnon* of Aeschylus: "Sing woe! sing woe! but let the good overcome." It is, as it were, a desire, not a hope, but a desire prophetic of fulfillment.

The second is from the *Phaedo* of Plato, giving Socrates' intimations of immortality to his circle of timid friends on that last day of seeming defeat: "Fair is the prize [of immortality], and the hope great."

And the third was the utterance of another, also on the day of seeming defeat: "In the world ye shall have tribulation; but be of good cheer, I have overcome the world."[7]

1   The "Marginalia" were short sketches on a wide range of subjects which More left unfinished at his death. The first twelve, destined to be his last effort at publishing, were carried in the *American Review* for November, 1936, and covered the topics: a parody of Goldsmith's "Hermit" in an old copy of *Don Quixote;* some new thoughts on Shorthouse's *John Inglesant;* Whittier's "Pennsylvania Pilgrim"; a mysterious vocal summons to the next life; Woodhouselee's memoirs of Henry Home Lord Kames; how he induced the Bodleian Library to install paper-cutters; on the liabilities of writing about contemporary authors; on Mrs. Meynell's "Christ in the Universe"; dualism (Section IX, here reprinted); how he forsook Calvinism; his odyssey through Brahmanic theosophy; and Horace's *Solvitur acris hiems* (Section XII, the second of the two sections here reprinted). See the *American Review*, Vol. VIII, No. 1, pp. 1–30. I have chosen to put these selections first since they provide a short, clear introduction to what More meant by dualism and faith.

2   St. Theresa (1515–1582). Spanish nun and mystic

3   See Appendix C, *The Religion of Plato.* Princeton: Princeton University Press, 1921, pp. 350–1.

4   "Heart to heart conversation."

5   Section IX ends here; section XII follows.

6   "An immense hope has passed over the earth."

7   John xvi: 33.

The Doctrine of the Logos[1]

Our hasty survey of the literature from the fourth Gospel to the Council of Chalcedon has been directed to bring out this one fact, that the Greek Fathers of the age were concerned with the dogma of the Incarnation as the all-important basis of Christianity, so important that beside it every other question sinks into comparative insignificance. It might seem that religion was narrowed and impoverished by this focusing of attention upon a single point, but I think such a view will not be advocated by anyone who considers all that is involved in this article of faith, or who knows how thoroughly this same problem has again absorbed the minds of theologians during the past century. It is not a little thing to believe that Jesus of Nazareth was the Son of God as well as the Son of man. And when this myth, in itself the amazing consummation of Hebrew prophecy, comes to us interpreted through the Hellenic philosophy of the logos, surely anyone may be satisfied with the richness of its content. And so I propose, in these remaining pages, to show what this dogma meant to the ancient Church and, incidentally, what it may mean to us.

At the outset we are met by a difficulty. How shall we translate the term *logos* and its derivative *logikos?* For the first we have grown accustomed to "word," following the Latin usage of *verbum* (though the Tertullian *sermo* was perhaps a nearer translation); and this would be fairly adequate if we could always remember that the original for which it stands meant, as its Latin and English substitutes in themselves do not mean, both an unexpressed thought within the mind and a thought expressed in words. It denotes, that is, in the most general way what is mental or spiritual as distinguished from what is physical or material, and so is often synonymous with "wisdom" or the Platonic "Idea" or, as we shall see, "purpose"; it signifies both the "large discourse of reason, looking before and after," and the means by which mind or spirit declares itself in operation or communicates with other minds and spirits. On the whole it will be better, and will cause no embarrassment, to employ the term *logos* itself as if it were Anglicized, as indeed it almost is. But for the derivative *logikos* we have no such ease. Neither "verbal" nor "spiritual" is a tolerable translation, while "logical" has become so restricted in meaning as to have lost all its religious value. In this dilemma the lesser of two evils is to fall back on the literal transcript, despite its awkwardness and its liability to misunderstanding. I must ask the reader to forget the connexion of "logical" with formal logic as a technique of syllogistic reasoning, and to take the adjective as signifying simply "that which is related to logos" or, more specifically, "that which consciously possesses logos." Such indeed was the common usage among theologians.

Now to these ancient theologians, trained in the tradition of Hebrew prophecy and in the language of the Academy and the Porch, the whole extent of the universe was permeated with logos. Looking upon the populous tribes of plants and animals, impressed, as Aristotle had been in an earlier age, by the curious adjustment of part to part in their structure and by the mutual adaptation between them and their environment, moved above all by the mystery of their beauty which seems to transcend any conscious or unconscious need in their own existence, the Fathers could explain such phenomena only as the work of a shaping and governing intelligence. To this creative logos they attributed the miraculous growth of a plant from the seed; from this they derived the cunning provision of nature by which the hare and other defenceless animals were prolific, whereas the lioness, as they thought, bore only one cub at long intervals. Only so could they understand the wisdom of the birds, which brought these aerial passengers to and fro over the wide expanses of sea and land, the providence that teaches the ants to lay up their winter store, and many another activity of the lesser creatures for which science could offer no satisfactory account. Christ, they believed, was alluding to the mystery of the logos when he bade his disciples to consider the lilies of the field, which of themselves could take no thought yet were arrayed in beauty beyond even the glory of Solomon. Above all, these theologians, like the philosophers before them and, we may add, like many a poet since, were filled with awe by the greater spectacle of inanimate nature,—the majestic revolution of the stars, the recurrent swell of the tides beneath the moon, and the restraining of the vexed waters of the sea within their bounds. These things, they argued, do not happen by chance or by some blind law of corporeal matter. All this that we see, exclaims an unknown writer, is a manifestation of the "holy and incomprehensible logos."[2]

But if the phenomenal world, including plants and animals, is a manifestation of some controlling logos, it is still not logical in the sense that it consciously possesses logos; for that gift we must look elsewhere. "What a piece of work is man! how noble in reason!" Hamlet exclaims; "how infinite in faculty!" Now that *noble in reason* is precisely what the Greek theologians meant by distinguishing man from other creatures as alone logical. By virtue of that faculty he, and he only, enters into the life of animals and comprehends the actions which they perform under the impulse of a reason not consciously their own. He weighs the stars and measures their orbits; to him the light of the setting sun and the birth of morning become instinct with the joys of beauty; so that the heavens are unrolled before his eyes like a celestial book. While the body sleeps, something of his mind goes forth to wander in distant places and creates for him marvellous adventures. And what else is all this but the work of a "logical soul," which enables him to behold the invisible reasons that lie behind the forms and motions of things visible?

And man is logical not only by possession of the faculty of

thought and comprehension and by the gift of silent discourse within his own mind, but he is endowed also with the faculty of language, by which he embodies his ideas in symbolic sounds and signs and sends them forth to live a kind of life of their own.[3] Thus it is that logos communes with logos, and a man knows himself to be not solitary in a friendless world, but member of a great society of kindred souls.

So far the philosophy of the Church is scarcely distinguishable from that of the Porch. The divergence begins, and grows as wide as the removal of the heavens from the earth, when this doctrine is made the basis of religion. It was inevitable that the Stoic, from his conception of a conscious logos in the highest division of nature, should think of the power which governs the whole of nature as possessing the same consciousness; and what is such a power but God? There are in fact passages, and many of them, in Cleanthes and Epictetus and the Roman Stoics wherein the cosmic logos is endowed with all the characteristics of a deity worthy of homage and love; but if the disciples of Zeno sometimes worshipped, it was yet at the price of sacrificing their principles. So far as the logos could be regarded by them consistently as God, it was a divinity within and of the world, the "spirit within" and the "inexorable fate" of Virgil, and their religious emotion properly assumed that pantheistic tinge which has coloured so much of the naturalism of later ages:

> A presence that disturbs me with the joy
> Of elevated thoughts; a sense sublime
> Of something far more deeply interfused,
> Whose dwelling is the light of setting suns,
> And the round ocean and the living air,
> And the blue sky, and in the mind of man.[4]

I would not deny the exquisite charm of such a feeling towards nature; nevertheless, even at its best and purest, pantheism is a kind of halfway house, and no abiding place for the spirit of man. He who stops there will find himself after a while turned out upon the common highway, obliged to journey forwards to belief in a frankly personal deity, or backwards to an avowed atheism.[5] And so we meet with a curious lack of equilibrium in these ancient pantheists of the Porch. At times they beheld God and worshipped; but the backward direction was ever the easier and more consistent course for them. The legitimate goal of Stoicism, as indeed its real starting point, was the scientific conception of the universe as a product of unconscious, unpurposing, mechanistic energy, for which the feeling of reverence is a meaningless sentimentality; its native mood, as we see it in Marcus Aurelius, is rather resignation towards things as they are than adoration of a Being beyond these tides of mortal change.

Now to the Christian, for all he borrowed from the Stoic philosophy, the ultimate merging together of spirit and matter seemed to savour of the Arian blasphemies which had lowered the logos to be an integral part of creation.[6] Save in his most unguarded hours he was never a pantheist; God for him was always a Creator living outside of that which He created, immanent by His power, but essentially transcendent; the logos in the world was merely the image, or effluence, of a higher Logos identical with the wisdom and will of a supermundane Person.

To us of today, perhaps, with our larger knowledge of the complex construction of the universe and our theory of evolution, the chief interest in the logos will be its connexion with the idea of purpose, or teleology. Now the teleological view of existence was not unknown to the pagan philosophers, and in particular it plays a dominant rôle in the system of Aristotle. But the Peripatetic conception of *telos,* though in ethics it made purpose the guiding principle of conduct, quite definitely excluded the notion of cosmic purpose, and that in two ways. In the first place Aristotle looked upon the universe as without beginning or conclusion, as uncreated and eternally the same. In this scheme there is no progress from grade to grade in time, from species to species, but a coexistent scale of species showing a kind of geometric pattern. Each species is a finished unit, having its own end, while within the species each individual has a *telos* in itself, a potential perfection of its own nature, to which it may or may not actually attain. And in the second place, though Aristotle might seem to have raised teleology to its highest point by his conception of God as the absolute final cause, as the object, that is, of all desire and thus the source of all motion in the moving worlds, yet in reality he rendered the idea jejune by depriving this first cause of any reciprocal participation in the transactions of time. His God, so far from being personal, is not even an efficient cause, but a pure abstraction lifted out of all contact with things as they are. Aristotle perceived design in the world, but did not infer from this an interested designer; in other words his cosmic *telos* is in no proper sense a purpose, an end proposed by an agent who adopts means to its fulfillment, though without such an implication it is hard to see just what force is left to the term. A static impersonal teleology must be set down as one of the grandiose confusions of human thought.

Beat about as we will, there are only two conclusions in which the philosophic mind can abide. Either, as the Hindu in his more courageous moods taught, the whole thing, this globe and this life, are utterly without design, a phantasmagoria in which we can detect no meaning and to which we have no right to apply any interpretation, not even that of chance, a huge illusion of ignorance which simply vanishes into nothing at the touch of knowledge; or else, if we see design in the world, then there is no holding back from the inference of the theist. The agnostic will say that this is to fall into anthropomorphism. It is. But design itself is already an anthropomorphic term; and to admit the existence of design while refusing to see that it implies purpose, and to admit the existence of purpose while refusing to acknowledge a purposing mind, is the folly of halfheartedness. On the other hand the agnostic who, denying plan and purpose, thinks he can stop short of the philosophy of pure illusion, resembles a man who boasts that he can walk on water.

It is here that Christianity brought consistency to the

teleology of the schools by going behind the logos of the Stoic and behind the Aristotelian *telos* to Plato's intuition of a divine Providence, which is further vitalized and enriched by grafting it upon the lore of the Hebrew prophets and the faith of the gospel. For the logos of theology was not only the manifestation of design in the world, but the wisdom of foresight *(pronoia)*, a divine *purpose* realizing itself through the ages in the economy of creation and salvation, "the manifold wisdom of God, according to the eternal purpose *(prothesis)* which He purposed in Christ Jesus."[7] It is true, of course, that the Fathers had no more notion than did their pagan contemporaries of development in the scientific sense of the word; but it is true also that the *logos-pronoia-prothesis* of Christianity can be adapted perfectly to our modern views, is in fact a very natural complement of any tenable theory of evolution.

The comely order of the world, that which we mean by calling it a cosmos, was, then, to the Christian a reflection of the logos as creative purpose; while in the soul of man the logos answers to logos not as an inert reflection, but as a conscious participation. Thus to Basil, looking upon nature under the glorifying rays of the sun, it seemed as though he could hear the ancient word of commendation, "God saw the light that it was good"; and to Clement it seemed that he could behold the Lord "resting in joy upon the work of His hands."

But there was another side to the picture. This cosmos, stamped and sealed as it is with the divine signature, is yet subject to strange imperfections and marks of error,—calamities of the heavens, floods and disasters upon the earth, among living creatures the cruelty of life that depends on the death of other lives. And consider the state of man. We appear to be made for knowledge and admiration; yet how often our heritage of happiness is exchanged for cloying pleasures, and our aspiring desires into ugly lusts with their uglier consequences —sickness, envy, madness, and all their train. Read the pages of history, and it will appear almost that the divine logos has been not so much thwarted by man as turned into a diabolical ingenuity of evil. Hence the question that has troubled the

minds of all philosphers and all theologians, the insistent dis-
tracting query: *Unde malum?*

By the Greek philosophers generally evil was defined as a
form of ignorance, with the Socratic corollary that knowledge
and virtue are identical. That is to say: taking evil to be by
definition that which results in discomfiture and misery, they
held that no man will knowingly choose his own perdition.
Theoretically such a view would seem to be sound, but in
practice, as Aristotle showed, it fails to explain our conduct.
How shall we reconcile it with the common fact of experience,
which Ovid has expressed in the familiar epigram: "I see and
approve the better, I follow the worse"?

Christian theologians, on the other hand, however they
wrangled in other matters, agreed almost without exception in
stressing the human (or the Satanic) will as the prime factor in
evil. With their theory of creation they were bound to regard
existence in itself as essentially good, and to define evil as a
negation of existence, or, so far as it could be called positive,
as an uncaused revolt of the created will against God's will.
"Man," says Methodius, speaking for the orthodox Church,
"was created with free will, not as if anything already evil
pre-existed which it lay in the power of man to choose if he
wished, . . . but the act of obedience or of disobedience to God
is the only cause. That is the very meaning of free will."[8] Now
this association of evil with the will certainly touches a profound psychological truth; and it has this great advantage, that
it accords with our sense of responsibility for wrongdoing
which is one of the ultimate facts of human consciousness, and
which the Greeks, including Plato, fully recognized but found
difficult to reconcile with their equation of vice with ignorance. We consider the inanimate world, and the interruptions
of order may perhaps have the appearance of inevitable law,
as though they were necessary parts of a larger design; or we
regard the miseries of human life about us, and again we may
seem to discern the operation of an ineluctable fatality, as
though men were the puppets of inheritance and circumstance. But we look then into ourselves, and the more honest

and penetrating our gaze, the more deeply are we convinced, despite all the apologetic devices of reason, that to our own undoing we have deliberately chosen the perverse ways of wrong, that the disease is inherent in our very heart and will. The responsibility for evil, the Christian says, as Plato had said before him, lies with man, not with God. All this is well and plausible, yet something still is omitted. The innate sense of responsibility may point to the will as the errant faculty, but the question persists: how can we hold a man, how can we hold ourselves, accountable unless, when the will makes its decision, it does so with full knowledge of the consequences of our acts? In some way both the will and the intelligence must be concerned together in our definition of right and wrong.

So judged, I am inclined to admire the Athanasian theory of evil as that which, of all theories before or after, draws most deeply from the wells of human experience, and as the most thoroughly Christian.[9]

According to this theory the world, as the evocation of the divine logos, was originally without blemish, fashioned to be the fit and perfect home of creatures composed of soul and body. And the souls of men, for whom this dwelling was prepared, were created in the likeness of God, and as such possessed the special faculty of seeing and knowing their Maker; they were designed to be members of the great society of holy beings, angels and archangels, whose life consists in the joyous contemplation of spiritual things.[10] All this is implied by calling man "logical." But the principle of mutability is inherent in the very nature of all created things alike, only with this difference that to man was given the capacity of free will and self-determination which was withheld from inanimate objects and illogical animals. In this union of free will and mutability lies the honour of man, but also his peculiar peril of responsibility. His true motion, that for which he was designed, should be ever upwards to his Creator and towards a clearer vision of the fair realities of the spirit *(ta onta kai kala);* there is his goal, and in that direction he acquires the unity and uniformity and happiness and safety which he craves.[11] But this motion of the soul towards what is akin to its nature but ever beyond its perfect comprehension, requires a continuity of attention and energy not easy for a creature of whose very essence mutability is a constituent; there is needed a constant effort of the will, while this effort of the will is conditioned by a clear intuition of the object to be attained. Hence arise the hesitation and reluctance of the soul, its fitful purpose, and its turning away to the less exacting contemplation of itself and its own activities in the body. The beginning of evil for Athanasius was thus a kind of *rhathymia*, that slackness of attention or failure of energy, at once the cause and the effect of ignorance, which hinders the soul, as St. Paul lamented, from pressing on to "the mark for the prize of the high calling of God."[12]

This was the Fall, when, caught by the delusion of forbidden power that appeared to lie within their grasp, men fell into desire to themselves, humouring their own way above the contemplation of things divine. It was as if man, by shutting the eyes of the spirit, created about himself an artificial darkness, wherein these bodies and the dull objects of our touch seem alone to be visible *(blepomena)*, while the realities of the spiritual life fade into invisibility. That which was intended to be an instrument is converted into an end, and all the orders of being are thrown into disarray. The whole scale of values is inverted; pleasure assumes an importance not properly belonging to it; new desires spring up with new objects of desire, which in their fulfilment produce greed, injustice, theft, adultery, murder, and all the train of criminal aberrations. By the defalcation of man the world is altered into something which had no place in the original design of the Creator. In the widest sense of the word this state of mind is idolatry, which, taking its start from sluggishness of will, ends in worship of mere idols of the imagination instead of the eternal realities.[13] "He (the Logos) was in the world, and the world was made by him, and the world knew him not";[14] in the self-engendered night of evil man has ceased to be logical.

Such is the Athanasian account of evil. And on the whole I doubt if philosophy, or psychology if you prefer the word, has ever shown a profounder insight into the actual working of the human soul. For, when stripped of its mythological trappings, it is just this infirmity of *rhathymia* that drags us down from spiritual peace and unity to the tragical conflict of the pleasures of the senses; it is this compound of sloth and ignorance that creates the slough of sin into which the life of man has fallen. So far analysis of the actual experience of life may carry us into the *what* of evil. But the theory of Athanasius, it will be observed, is not metaphysical: it does not explain *why* this defection of will should trouble the energy of a creature endowed with free power of choice and having his natural good displayed before him; it leaves the ultimate *whence* of evil a mystery involved in the very act of creation, still unreconciled with any conception of an absolute cause. And in this it agrees, better perhaps than its expounder knew, with the dualism of Plato's *Timaeus,* which simply posits evil as a final inexplicable Necessity in the nature of things.[15]

The Athanasian theory of the fall of man, whether it be taken as history or allegory, accords well with the actual condition of the world: on the one side a God whose logos has gone out in a vast work of creation, on the other side the most highly endowed creature, the conscious percipient of the divine purpose, falling away to worship of idols of his own imagination. As Athanasius says, "man, the logical, created in the image of deity, was disappearing, and the handiwork of God was in process of dissolution."[16] Certainly He who wrought the design would not suffer it to perish, nor permit His purpose to be utterly frustrated, though it might be temporarily marred and hindered. And certainly "it will appear not inconsonant that the Father should effect salvation of the world by means of that through which He created it."[17] The logos was the instrument of creation, it should be the instrument of restoration: that is the sum of the Christian scheme of Soteriology. Now the mere notion that the salvation of man comes through the logos is not new; it animates the Idealism of Plato, though the word com-

monly employed by him is *nous,* reason, and it gives force to
the dogma of the Stoics. But by association with the Messianic
belief of Israel something is added to the philosophy of the
logos which Greece had never known.

In the synoptic Gospels Jesus is regarded as the Son of God,
and this belief is carried on and deepened in the body of the
fourth Gospel. But also in the prologue to the fourth Gospel the
idea is thrown out that the Saviour of the world is the creative
logos of God. Implicitly then, though the statement is not
made explicitly, the Son of God and the Logos of God are one
and the same: the Son as the Logos is identified with the creative wisdom and purpose of diety, the Logos as the Son is
hypostatized into a person beside the person of the Father. At
one bound the philosophy of the logos has become a religion.
And there is a striking corollary to this thesis: the Logos hypostatized as the only begotten Son bears a different relation to
God the Father from that borne to God the Creator by the
logos within man. We too as possessors of the word may be
called after a fashion children of the Most High and sons of the
Father, but as creatures of His will we are not of His substance
and nature, however we may be like Him; and on this difference depends the possibility of our present state of disgrace.
The distinction was made in Origen metaphysically by calling
the Logos the eternally begotten Son, whereas the birth of
man is an event in time. Athanasius expresses the same idea
scripturally by a quaint interpretation of the words of Genesis:
"Let us make man in our image, after our likeness." The Father, he says, is here speaking to the Son (hence the "us"); the
Logos-Son is the image, whereas man is created in the likeness
of the image, to possess as it were "certain shadows of the
Logos and so to be not the Logos but logical."[18] It follows also
that when we speak of the human logos we do not think of this
as an hypostasis distinct from the hypostasis of the man himself,
but as the characteristic quality of man as man.

The drama of redemption then will be the interaction between the Logos-Son of God and the logical nature of man,
whereby the effects of sin will be cancelled and man shall be

restored to the likeness of the image in which he was fashioned. In that drama the great event, the *peripeteia* so to
speak, is to the Christian the Incarnation; but this is by no
means an isolated incident or unrelated to the general course
of history. Rather, as Justin declared in the passage quoted at
the beginning of our study,[19] all the wisdom of the philosophers, all the precepts of the lawgivers and the example of the
sages, had been a response in the heart of man to the manifestation of the logos in the world. Justin might have added that
literature and art, so long as they remain true to their high
function and do not sink into mere flattery of man's baser
instincts, are an effort to interpret life and the phenomena of
nature in the light of the logos, and to build here and now a
home for the soul in the world of Ideas. And for the scholar the
finest and most comprehensive name ever yet devised is the
old Greek term *logios*, signifying one who is skilled to trace the
operations of the logos, to distinguish its genuine expression in
literature from shams, to know the truth, and so to dwell in the
calm yet active leisure *(scholê)* of contemplation. The scholar,
the *logios*, in that noble sense of the word, is he who by study
and reflection has recovered the birthright of humanity and
holds it in fee for the generations to come.

But in our darkened state the drag of the flesh is heavy, the
seductions of the world are insidious, the weight of sin, as the
Christian would say, overwhelming, so that, left to itself, the
spirit of man might seem bound to sit for ever in a closed
prison with only narrow and fleeting glimpses of the larger
light. Hence there was needed a more direct illumination than
is afforded by the logical order of nature and life, and to the
Christian the special work of redemption began with the self-
revelation of God to Israel through the inspired lawgivers and
prophets. I fancy that to the reader of today—though it would
not have been so a few years since—the most surprising feature of patristic literature is the constant and systematic conversion of the Old Testament into an allegory of the Logos.
This reinterpretation of Scripture was begun for the Jews
themselves—so far as the records are extant—by Philo; it was

turned to the service of the new faith by the earliest Christian writers and developed with all the extravagance of an uncritical imagination, particularly by Origen who raised the allegorical method of exegesis into an erudite bibliolatry. Whenever the voice of God is heard or the angel of the Lord appears, it was taken to be a direct revelation, not of the Father, but of the Logos-Son; types of Christ were discovered in the most unexpected places, all prophecy centred upon the coming event of the Incarnation, and every word, each syllable, was probed for hidden treasure. It need not be said that much of this interpretation is from one point of view without critical or historical basis; yet one may well doubt whether our present habit of rejecting the whole method and of minimizing the prophetic element of the Old Testament is not equally erroneous in the other direction. Many of the passages supposed by ancient theology to refer to the coming Messiah may have had quite a different and more literal meaning to the contemporary Jews; but to read Scripture without perceiving that an undefined Messianic hope was an inheritance of the Hebrew race throughout the ages, that in their subsconscious mind, as we might say, the notion of a divine deliverer lay always dormant, ready at any moment to flash out into clear expression, that the whole course of Israelitic history unrolls as a kind of mystical progress towards one grand event, to overlook the fact that the New Testament is a close continuation of the Old and a consummation of what had been long preparing, not to see that the Johannine Logos is the secular realization of the unquenchable Messianic hopes and can be read back legitimately into the ancient theology of Israel as, so to speak, its implicit *telos*,—this, I say, is the greater failure in scholarship and a more unpardonable dereliction of intelligence. Bibliolatry has slain its thousands, but bibliophoby may slay its tens of thousands; for it is still true that the letter killeth.

Thus from one point of view the Incarnation may be regarded as the closing event, in the fulness of time, of a long series of transactions, while from another point of view it is unique in character. Hitherto the Logos might be known as a creative and providential and admonitive force, manifesting itself indeed to those who could read the signs, but always as a director behind the scenes; now, at the climax of the drama, it comes forth upon the stage and takes its part openly among the actors, a veritable *deus ex machina.* The meaning and purpose of this theophany were concentrated by Irenaeus into a brief formula, which the Church never forgot, and about which Athanasius in particular wove the fabric of his *De Incarnatione* as a tremendous fugue upon a single theme: "God became man in order that man might become God."[20] The divine Logos, that is to say, condescended to the conditions of human life, in order that the logos of man might be raised to its prerogative as conscious bearer of the likeness of God. In that act of re-creation the Greek theologians by analysis discovered four leading moments: (1) revelation, (2) imitation, (3) grace, (4) vicarious atonement.

I. Obviously the epiphany of the Logos is first of all and through all an act of revelation. The consequence of the Fall, as a declension of the soul from allegiance to the Creator to concern with the creature was, in a word, idolatry. To the early converts this idolatry appeared primarily as the worship of images and of the innumerable gods who were themselves creatures fallen from grace, if not mere phantoms of human conceit; but the most stubborn foe of the Christian, as it had been of the Platonic, faith was that homage to the idols of the reason which wears the mask of philosophy. Call it Stoicism or call it Epicureanism, call it science or deism or realism or mere indifference or what you will, the most insidious and obstinate enemy of religion was, and is, the subservience of the mind content to see in the world only a huge fatalistic mechanism or a heterogeneous product of chance or, as the modern Darwinians would have it, a monstrous combination of both. Whatever form the error may take, it is a denial of the Logos as the creative wisdom and purpose of God, a magnification of the creature, a refined, but none the less devastating species of idolatry. Against this defection to idols, whether of the imagination or of the reason, God had protested by the majesty of

His works and more directly through the mouth of inspired sage and prophet appealing to the silent witness within the breast of every man. There was needed a more definite and immediate manifestation of the truth, and this to the Christian was given when the Word became flesh.

The Word became flesh: it is a portentous saying, not easy for men of our day to accept in its simplicity, nor did it make its way in the ancient world without contradiction and ridicule; to the Greek it appeared at first as foolishness and to the Jew a stumbling block. I would not slur over these difficulties, but there are certain considerations, not unknown to the Greek apologists, that may mitigate the objections of reason. In the first place if there be a God, is it not reasonable that He should reveal Himself? Is it not the case that, so far as we are concerned, an unrevealed God is the same as no God? that an unrevealed God might as well not exist, properly speaking does not exist, for us? The Great Unknowable does not offer a subject very fruitful for contemplation or very serviceable for the wants of mankind. And, secondly, if God was to reveal Himself, how could this be done effectively save through some such act as the Incarnation? How should the poison of idolatry be counteracted save by some miraculous intervention manifesting the existence of a divine purpose in the world yet not of the world? How can we conceive purpose save as the will and intelligence of a person directed to the accomplishment of some end? How could man be made to grasp the reality of a person except under such conditions as surround and limit his own being? How otherwise could such conditions be assumed than through the visible embodiment of the Logos as an historical event in time and place?

All this is conveyed in the saying: The Word became flesh. But it is important to add that the Greek theologians, though they held the appearance of the Logos in human form to be a *true* revelation of God, were emphatic in declaring it to be not a *complete* revelation of God. Over and over again they are careful to assert that the expression Father and Son applied to two persons of the Godhead, while true so far as it goes, is only the translation into human language of a mystery which transcends the human understanding, and that the exhibition of the divine attributes in the life and death of the incarnate Logos did not exhaust the fulness of the divine essence. This reverent reservation was the excuse, if any there be, for their employment of such terms as infinite and omnipotent and omnipresent and the like abstractions in their definition of that which might better have been left undefined; it was a not wholly fortunate way of avowing that what we know of God by revelation is the truth but only a little of the truth.

II. The purpose of the special manifestation of divine purpose, if the play on words be permitted, was that man, made in the image of God and logical, but fallen into illogical idolatry, might be restored to his high estate, and that so the frustrated plan of creation might be fulfilled; or as some would say, preferring the language of Aristotle to that of mythology, that man in the course of time might attain in actuality to the potential perfection of his nature. So God, at the opportune moment, revealed Himself in order that man might recover, or reach, the divine likeness by imitating what he beheld.

Now this doctrine of imitation, as I have said elsewhere,[21] was not discovered or invented by those of the new faith. It lies at the very core of Plato's theology and so of the Greek tradition; and it has never been expressed more clearly than in the great passage of the *Theaetetus*, of which echoes can be heard in endless variations through the literature, pagan and Christian, of the following ages:

> "But it is not possible that evils should cease to be—since by reason of necessity there exists always something contrary to the good—neither can they have their seat among the gods, but of necessity they haunt mortal nature and this region of ours. Wherefore our aim should be to escape hence to that other world with all speed. And the way of escape is by becoming like to God in so far as we may. And the becoming like is in becoming just and holy by taking thought. . . . God is never in any wise unjust, but most perfectly just, and there is nothing more like to Him than one of us who should make himself just to the limit of man's power."

At first thought on reading these words, one may ask what Christianity has to offer that is not here; but second thought makes one aware of a subtle difference. And then if, with this passage in mind, one turns to the sermons of Gregory Nyssen on the Lord's Prayer and the Beatitudes,[22] in which the Platonic doctrine of *homoiôsis*, or imitation, is developed into a marvellous treatise on the Christian life, one sees how profoundly the sentiment has been transformed by its reference to the Incarnation. The change might be expressed, though inadequately of course, in epigrammatic form by saying that in Platonism man imitates God by becoming just and holy, whereas in Christianity man becomes just and holy by imitating God. With Plato, even when his philosophy slants most strongly towards religion, the ethical Ideas are the outstanding reality, the fixed point of belief, while God, for all that we hear of creation and providence, remains still a somewhat shadowy figure, now appearing and now fading into the background. It is precisely otherwise with the Christian. To him the ethical Ideas owe their cogency to the fact that they are personified in the Logos, and we are able to make them our own by imitating the Logos as revealed in a life passed under human conditions. "No one but His own Word," says Irenaeus, "could tell us the things of the Father. . . . And we could not apprehend them otherwise than by seeing our Master and hearing his voice, in order that by imitating his actions and fulfilling his words we might be brought into communion with him."[23]

It is properly the human aspect of the Master's life that draws us first as we read the gospel narrative, his unblemished purity and strong humility and his love for God and man.[24] The clear beauty of his character acts as an almost irresistible incentive to imitation, or at least to the desire of imitation; while his perfect humanity is like a voice saying in our ears: Thou too canst live today as he once lived, and so win for thyself such purity and humility and love. And then, perhaps, something in the story, those surprising sentences that had no place on merely mortal lips, the signals of a miraculous power and authority held in check,—something warns us that here is man yet also more than man. We remember the prologue to his life in the fourth Gospel: "In the beginning was the Word, and the Word was with God, and the Word was God. . . . And the Word was made flesh, and dwelt among us."[25] And so remembering, if we are capable of rising to the high theology of the Logos, we discover a new meaning in these virtues set before us as models, a meaning so sublime that, as Gregory says, the very thought thereof affects us with a dizziness like that which comes upon one who from the edge of a lofty promontory looks down upon the remote floor of the sea. He who, imitating the purity of Jesus, purges himself of the clinging passions of the world, will discern in his own heart, as in a burnished mirror, a living image of the transcendent holiness of the Father. If he imitates the humility of Jesus, he will then know that he has set himself to follow after one who, though he thought it not robbery to be the equal of God, yet humbled himself to the endurance of human infirmities and to the Cross. And beyond this purity and this humility lies the sublime charity moving within the circle of the divine nature and reaching therefrom out towards creation, of which mystery we get a glimpse in the saying: "God so loved the world that he gave his only begotten Son."[26] Does the Great Commandment imply that here, in the highest reach of imitation, we should be included in this love not by passive reception only but by active participation?

That and something more than that. In the fifth of his sermons on the Lord's Prayer, when he comes to the clause on the forgiveness of trespasses, Gregory, trembling for his own audacity, ventures to hint at a strange inversion of what might seem to be the natural order of things. Our duty and our hope of happiness, as he has shown, depend on making ourselves like to God; but here on the contrary we are bidden to ask that God should become like to us, that He should forgive *as and if we forgive.* In pointing to this reciprocity in the law of imitation, Gregory touches on an amazing enigma of the economy, which yet, as we see if we stop to reflect, is based on necessity. For any true similarity must be mutual, and A cannot resemble B unless at the same time B resembles A. And so, with a slight change in the language of the famous maxim, we may say indeed that God imitated (*i.e.* became) man in order that man might imitate God; but we may add in our thoughts that without the second clause the first would be void and meaningless. We may even go further and assert that the moral response of human nature is the cause and inevitable condition of the divine condescension, as though God could not have loved Himself and the world were there not potentially in the heart of man a similar love of his fellows and of God.

By such steps as these we are brought to comprehend how the Platonic doctrine of *homoiôsis,* being interpreted through the words of Christ, "he that hath seen me hath seen the Father,"[27] acquired a precision and a power which rendered it capable of converting the world.

III. Imitation is the effort of the human will, stirred from its lethargy by the spectacle of our celestial exemplar, to shake itself free of the idolatrous desires of the flesh and to recover its pristine, or native, energy. But the will of man, whatever the cause, is desperately enfeebled, and the heart of man deceitful above all things, and there is no health in us. How shall we, unaided and of our own volition, regain what we have deliberately cast away? It is from thoughts such as these, confirmed seemingly by direct experience, that the Christian has developed the doctrine of grace. The Logos, he believes, did not simply in the Incarnation reveal itself to the logos of man as an inert object to be imitated, but came with power and purpose, with that effluence of the spoken word which passes from person to person and draws them together as it were by invisible bands. We touch here a mystery of psychology as well as of religion which our fumbling science has not yet sounded. We feel the mystic force upon us in our intercourse with men, when familiarity ripens into friendship or beyond friendship into love; we know it as something that goes out of the beloved or admired person, and gradually subdues our spirit to his. And this was what drew the disciples to Jesus when they lived with him in Palestine, drew them with a compulsion of love and homage which seemed to surpass the measure of human influence, and which came to a climax in the ejaculation wrung from the doubting Thomas: "My Lord and my God!"[28]

Nor is this attraction limited to the means of sight and hearing. In the last discourse, recorded by the author of the fourth Gospel, Jesus, wishing to console his disciples, assured them that his going away was even expedient for them, since only so, in the severance of physical ties, should they enjoy fully the purer communion of the spirit:

> "And I will pray the Father, and he shall give you another Comforter, that he may abide with you for ever,
> "Even the Spirit of truth, whom the world cannot receive, because it seeth him not, neither knoweth him: but ye know him, for he dwelleth with you, and shall be in you."[29]

Jesus was not thinking of a third person in an imaginary Trinity, as his words might at first seem to imply and as they came later to be interpreted (or recast) under the mythopoeic influence of the age. Certainly he was but expressing in vivid metaphorical language the fact that, though he was departing in the body, his spirit should still be with them and in them, as indeed he says explicitly in the very next verse: "I will not leave you comfortless, *I will come to you.*" The thought is exactly the same as that with which the first Gospel concludes: "Lo, I am with you alway, even unto the end of the world." The Holy Ghost, then, is just another name for the Grace of God, whether it be said to proceed from the Father or from the Father and the Son; it is the inner compulsion of spirit upon spirit, of deep calling to deep, by a law of personality of which the outer manifestation is seen in the working of revelation and imitation. And prayer, defined by Plato and the Fathers as the soul's discourse with God, would be the voluntary disposition of the human logos to receive the gracious influence of the divine Logos.

> Sure they do meet, enjoy each other there,
>   And mix, I know not How nor Where.
>   Their friendly Lights together twine,
>   Though we perceive 't not to be so,
>   Like loving Stars which oft combine,
> Yet not themselves their own Conjunctions know.[30]

IV. So far we have considered the economy as a revelation of the living Logos, with its extension in imitation and grace, but our definition of this last term as the meeting and merging together of twin activities, divine and human, points to a deeper thought drawn rather from the death and resurrection than from the life of Christ,—the thought of redemption as a vicarious atonement. Here confessedly the light is dim, and the Catholic Church has wisely left the matter in the region of pious conjecture without formulating its theories into a creed or fixed dogma. In the West these theories, following the rabbinical temper of St. Paul, have tended to assume the colour of a legalistic or forensic procedure. Sin, from this point of view, is defined as a transgression of the law of God or as an offence against His divine majesty, in either case as a crime punishable by death. And since, for one reason or another, man is incapable of satisfying the requirements of infinite justice, God Himself pays to Himself the penalty by the surrender of His only begotten Son to the ignominy of the Cross, and so redeems the culprit by an act of vicarious atonement. In the East also the view of Christ's death as the purchase price for sin comes up here and there, but commonly with this curious difference. To the Oriental mind it was the devil who must be placated; man by his disobedience has sold himself to the adversary, and Calvary is regarded rather as a ransom paid by God to man's now rightful lord than as a satisfaction to Himself as judge. Occasionally this transaction takes an odd and really immoral slant from what must be deplored as an almost instinctive admiration among the Greeks for successful trickery, even swindling. The Son of God by appearing on earth masked

in human form deceives the devil into supposing, and acknowledging, that in the death of this perfect and representative
man he shall have received full value for his claims, only to find
that he has brought into hell one who is able not merely to
release himself but by his resurrection to deliver the world.
Satan, as we should say, has played his trump card, and lost the
game, though, in view of his further machinations, it cannot be
said that he takes his defeat like a gentleman.

But these were aberrations of fancy that filtered into the
faith from the surrounding mass of superstition. Behind them
lies the feeling that in the Incarnation we see the middle act
of a long drama in which divinity and humanity are enacting
their appropriate parts. In this view the human nature of
Christ would be not *a* man (as indeed it was never so considered in the orthodox belief), but mankind; and thus, as symbol
or representative or epitome of the race, or as all three at once
(since to the mystical intelligence these three things have a
way of losing their distinction), would be paying the penalty
for the sins of all men once for all. The beginning of our evil
was a turning away from the light to that darkness wherein
were engendered the manifold brood of ruinous illusions. And
for us this course, if followed without check, leads on and on
to the extinction of the logos within us, has in fact already
brought us to the verge thereof. The voluntary death of the
divine Logos in its assumed humanity would then be a kind of
anticipation and prophetic fulfilment of man's destiny, while
the resurrection of humanity by the power of the Logos would
be a guarantee of the victory of man's spiritual nature over the
grave.

Thus, though from one point of view, the crucifixion may be
regarded as only a vivid consummation of the life of our great
exemplar ("And I, if I be lifted up from the earth, will draw all
men unto me"),[31] to the more mystical eye, and contemplated
under the law of sympathy or solidarity which governs the
universe we know not how or why, it would be an act of
vicarious atonement, whereby the incarnate Logos, taking
upon himself the sins of the world, opens to all fallen souls a

door of escape from the hell of idolatry. To the mind of theologians trained in the subtle ambiguity of Greek thought, these two views, imitation and redemption, the reaching of the logos from below upwards and its reaching from above downwards, merge together almost indistinguishably in the drama of the divine economy; they are both, in fact, embraced in the Irenaean theory of recapitulation.

So far the records are plain reading. But here and there we come upon suggestions of a play within the play, which the Christians borrowed unwittingly from their gnostic rivals, and never quite forgot, nor yet ever fully admitted. It will be remembered that in the Valentinian mythology the fall and restoration of man had been anticipated by a similar drama among the Aeons of the Pleroma, or, otherwise expressed, were a continuation of the agony of the celestial Sophia. And some relic of that belief, simplified and purified, I seem to detect in such a saying as that of Valentine's critic, Irenaeus: *unum genus humanum, in quo perficiuntur mysteria Dei.*[32] What are these mysteries which can only be carried out in the human race, which the angels desire to behold and cannot, to which the doubting frightened eyes of the early believers were directed by the spectacle of a suffering God?

Some notion of what this portent might mean is given by the age-long dispute of theology over the question whether the Incarnation was, as it might be called, an afterthought for the sake of repairing a miscarriage in the original plan of creation, or was purposed from the beginning and so was only incidentally related to the fall of man. This difference of interpretation, discoverable in the writers of the New Testament and carried on through generations of scholars, came to a head among the schoolmen in the contention between the Thomists who supported the former view by such texts as I John iii, 5 and II Peter i, 4, and the Scotists who derived the latter view from the more imaginative language of St. Paul in Ephesians i, 9–12 and Colossians i, 19. In the Occident, so far as I know, the echoes of this ancient battle have long since died away;[33] but in the eastern Church they may still be heard in the debate between such doughty champions of orthodoxy as Androut-sos[34] and Rhôssês.[35] "The perfection of man," says Rhôssês, who holds the more mystical view, "is bound up with the perfecting of religion, and the necessity of perfecting religion involves necessarily the Incarnation of the Word of God in that Person in which there would be not only a perfect imparting of divine truth, power, and life, but also a perfect human vehicle to receive this imparted (divine truth, power, and life). . . . Hence the Incarnation of the Word would have been necessary for the perfection of man even without (man's) sin. Still more did it become necessary because of the fact of sin, since man did slip into sin by the wrong use of his reason and free will."[36]

It might be well to stop at this point, nor search with profane and futile curiosity into things beyond our utmost comprehension; and here, in any manner of explicit theorizing, the orthodox theologians did draw the line. Yet there is a bare hint now and then, a mere fluttering of the veil of silence, indicative of strange and unacknowledged guesses at the meaning of the *mysteria Dei*. Such, for instance, are the halting speculations of Gregory Nyssen and others, even Athanasius, about the inevitability of imperfection in the world, owing to the fact that the very process of creation, as a passage from what was not to what is, involves change, and so introduces an element of mutability and fallibility into the sum of existence. Is this a cautious way of admitting Plato's *Anankê*, Necessity, into the universe as a second cause conditioning the efficiency of the divine cause? And if the result of creation is from the beginning faulty, what then of the Creator? Is He without fault? And if the Incarnation with its tragic climax is no adventitious event imposed on the creative benevolence by the arbitrary sinfulness of man, but an integral part of the eternal plan, how then? What becomes of the notion of omnipotence when the will of the omnipotent can be executed only through such a concession to the need of adversity, and victory is only possible through defeat? *Pathei mathos,* "by suffering comes wisdom," was said by Aeschylus, having in mind the fatality that besets all mortal schemes; must that principle be extended upward to the deity? We shudder, perhaps, at such a thought; yet, after all, how can we think of purpose save in connexion with obstacles and limitations to the will of him who purposes? And then, if the dogma of vicarious atonement leads us to find in the Incarnation an act of gracious pardon for man's miserable failure to stand beside his Master as a servant who has been called to help in the slow and toilsome task of shaping a cosmos out of chaos, who perhaps was created to that end, is it also an appeal to man's pardon—I will not say for sin, God forbid, but yet for some limitation there where we should look for perfect strength? Can there be the least shadow of truth in the audacious words of the poet,

> For all the Sin wherewith the Face of Man
> Is blacken'd—Man's Forgiveness give—and take?

Long before such an inference the Fathers of the Church would have drawn back in pious alarm, and properly, since it springs from a presumption of knowledge where we are professedly ignorant. Yet, on the other hand, the doctrine of the Logos as the divine purpose fulfilling itself only through sacrifice and suffering must shake our confidence in the smug commonplaces of theology; the *mysteria Dei* are not to be clarified by the enumeration of empty absolutes. We shall believe that in some way the brief enactment in Palestine, with its tragic climax on Calvary, is an epitome or symbolic rehearsal of a secular drama at once of creation and redemption wherein the protagonist is God Himself. By the dogma of vicarious atonement the pains and losses and failures of our mortal state become part of a cosmic agony, and any feeling of resentment at the real or seeming injustices of life fades away into awe before the spectacle of the Cross.

In the end we come back to the word "purpose" as decisive of our philosophy and our religion.

Now there are those, and always have been, who fail to perceive in their own consciousness anything more than a vortex of sensations cohering together for a few years about some shadowy centre of gravitation, why no one can guess, and then losing themselves forever in the stream of phenomena that flows on and on to no conceivable goal. To talk of purpose in a world so constituted is mockery. For such men, if they have the courage of their conviction, I do not see what reasonable creed is left but that of the Epicurean: "Let us eat and drink, for tomorrow we die."

Again there are those for whom this visible universe is no more than an ocean of ephemeral illusions, but who nevertheless have no doubt of a spiritual law holding irresistible and relentless sway in its own separate sphere. The call within to exercise the ethical will is clear and peremptory, yet all the desires and activities connected with this transitory life are frustrate from their inception and end at last in nothing, meaningless all as is the very principle of individual consciousness. For these men I do not see what resting place remains short of the absolute mysticism of India. Purpose, if they are consistent, must be identified by them with a determination to escape utterly from a purposeless existence into some Nirvâna of impersonal timeless bliss, to the nature of which no clue is given by the hopes and fears of the conscious soul in its earthly pilgrimage. Such was the creed put into the mouth of Buddha when he attained to supreme enlightenment under the Bô tree:

> Through many births, a ceaseless round,
> I ran in vain, nor ever found
> The Builder, though the house I saw,—
> For death is born again, and hard the law.

> O Builder, thou art seen! not so
> Again thy building shall arise;
> Broken are all its rafters, low
> The turret of the mansion lies:
> The mind in all-dissolving peace
> Hath sunk, and out of craving found release.

And, lastly, there are those who admit no such limitation to the law of purpose, but from all they learn, within and without, infer the being of a divine Builder, whose voice they think they hear calling them to labour with Him in the execution of a great and difficult design. For them this transient life is replete with lessons of infinite purport, and the outspread glories of this world, through the impediments of imperfection, bear to the discerning eye "authentic tidings of invisible things." These men, whatever their professed creed, belong to the Greek tradition, as followers of Plato and as believers in the incarnate logos; and if they hesitate to associate that belief with the ecclesiastical dogma of Christ the Word, they have at least the *anima naturaliter christiana.*

Certainly Jesus himself taught the doctrine of purpose conceived in the heart of a heavenly Father. The indications of purpose he beheld everywhere, in the beauty of the lily, in the fall of a sparrow, in the destiny of populous cities; and his summoning of men to repentance was to the end that, through a life of purity and humility and love, they might bring their wills into harmony with the will of God, and so be prepared for participation in that kingdom on earth and in heaven of which he, Jesus, presumed to call himself the Lord.

---

1   This selection is made up of the climactic tenth and eleventh chapters of *Christ The Word*, the fourth volume of the *Greek Tradition*, published in 1927. Both chapters in the original book were carried under the same title as is used here. The two chapters not only sum up the book, but essentially state More's personal credo, his Platono-Christian insights here rising into an eloquent poetic and theological unity. He wrote a complementary volume, *The Catholic Faith* (1931), which develops in more detail several of the themes suggested by these chapters. No portion of *Christ The Word* has ever been anthologized before.

2   *Ep. ad Diogn.*, vii.—The preceding sentences and many that follow in this and the next chapter are a cento from Athanasius and other Greek theologians. To give the references for all such passages would clutter up these pages intolerably. [More's note]

3   The λόγος προφορικός. [More's note]

4   Wordsworth, *Lines Composed Above Tintern Abbey*, ll. 94–99.

5   The former, for example, was the path taken by Wordsworth, as may be seen by comparing the *Tintern Abbey* from which I have quoted with the religious

note of his later poems. Lucretius virtually went the other way. [More's note]

6   So Athanasius, *Contra Ar.*, ii, 11. [More's note]

7   Eph. iii: 10, 11.

8   *De Libero Arbitrio*, 265 (Migne). [More's note]

9   The following exposition of the Athanasian theory of evil is based on the opening section of the *Contra Gentes*. [More's note]

10   Συνδιαιτᾶθθαι τοῖς ἁγίοις ἐν τῇ τῶν νοητῶν θεωρία –these "spiritual things," *noêta*, are the Platonic Ideas. It is noteworthy that Athanasius does not merge them into the being of God. [More's note]

11   Compare the importance of the single word θκοπός in *Laws*, xii. [More's note]

12   For *rhathymia* as a cause of evil implicit also in Greek intellectualism, see [More's] *Religion of Plato*, chap. ix. Cf. *Sophist* 254a τὰ γὰρ τῆς τῶν πολλῶν ομματα καρτειρέὶν πρὸς τὸ θέιον ἀφορῶντα ἀδόνατα.

This also, removed from the sphere of theology, is Aristotle's notion of δύναμις and ἐνέργια reaching their ἐντελέχεια in pure θεωρία. And Plotinus, among his other views, held evil begins for the soul when it turns from the contemplation of Being to consideration of its own state of Becoming (I, viii, 4). [More's note] The scripture quoted is Phil. iii:14.

13   It is not fantastic to compare this reduction of all evil to a form of idolatry with the ἐίδολορμα which Plato, in the *Sophist*, held to be the characteristic activity and the initial error of those who sought for reality in the shadows of appearance instead of in the eternal Ideas. When he declares that sophistry is the "primary falsehood" in the heart, he is merely saying in other language what Christ means by calling Satan "a liar and the father of lies." [More's note]

14   Jn. i:10.

15   Ch. X, "The Doctrine of the Logos," closes. The paragraph which follows is the opening statement of Ch. XI, "The Logos (continued)." Op. Cit., pp. 296–7.

16   *De Incarnatione*, vi. 1. [More's note]

17   *Ibid.*, i:4. [More's note]

18   *Ibid.*, iii, 3. The logos of man differs from the πρωτότυπον in being τρεπτός, subject to mutation. This is not to say that the divine Logos, as ἄτρεπτος, is fixed in stark immutability, but that through all its changes its essential nature remains unaffected. In man change is of the radical sort designated by the Stoics as "passion," πάθος. See *De Inc.*, iii, 4; Gregory Nyssen, *De Hominis Op.*, 184c (Migne), and *In Verba Faciamus Hominem*, 264a, c (Migne). [More's note]

19   A quotation from Justin's *Apology*, II, x, in which Justin states that the wisdom of the philosophers before Christ was merely a laying hold of "the fragments of the logos."

20   So it is the fashion to translate the formula as given, e.g. *De Inc.*, liv, 3: αὐτὸς γὰρ ἐνηνθρώπηθεν ἱνα ἡμέῖς θεοποιηθῶρεν. A more exact version would be: "For he himself put on human nature (or, came to live among men) in order that we might be made like to God." The *theos* of the compound is a word characteristically Greek in its fluidity, and may mean "god," or "a god," or a "godlike being." Here the third sense is evidently intended, and there is nothing in the orthodox use of the formula to warrant the sort of mysticism implied in the meaning "god." [More's note]

21   See the *Religion of Plato*, 37 ff. [More's note]

22   I should reckon these sermons *De Oratione Dominica* and *De Beatitudinibus* together about the finest treatise on Christian ethics known to me. They ought to be made available in separate publication, properly edited with text, translation, and notes. [More's note] Gregory of Nyssa (c. 332–398) was a Greek theologian and bishop of Nyssa in Cappadocia.

23   *Contra Haer.*, V, i, 1. [More's note]

24   The place of these three virtues in the teaching of the Gospels I have discussed in *The Christ of the New Testament*, chaps. v and vi. [More's note]

25   Jn. i:1, 14.

26   Jn. iii:16.

27   Jn. xiv:9.
28   Jn. xx:28.
29   Jn. xiv:16, 17.
30   Cowley, *Friendship in Absence*. It should be noted that by virtue of a certain ambiguity inherent in the Greek mode of speech the doctrine of grace in the eastern Church never raised the problem which so much troubled the West. *Charis* means both a benefit conferred and the gratitude for such a benefit. It is both active and passive, or, more precisely, like so many similar words in Greek signifies a certain relation or kind of activity between two agents without defining the direction of that activity; as Sophocles says (*Ajax*, 522), χάρις χάρινγόρ ἐϭτιν ἡ τίκτουϭ' ἀεί. *Charis* thus implies a mutual activity between God and man, and there is no place for an antinomy between grace and faith. [More's note]
31   Jn. xii:32.
32   *Contra Haer.*, V, xxxvi. [More's note] The Latin phrase reads, "One human being in whom is perfected the mystery of God."
33   It was, however, still active in the seventeenth century. See Brémond, *Le Sentiment religieux*, IV, 398 ff. [More's note]
34   Chrestos Androutsos (1869–1935).
35   Zekos Rhôsses (1838–1917).
36   Rhôssês, Σύετημα Δογματικῆς 465, quoted by Frank Gavin, *Some Aspects of Contemporary Greek Orthodox Thought*, 173. For the contrary view of Androutsos, see his Δογματική, 168. [More's note]

PART II

Literature

Criticism[1]

Of all Matthew Arnold's books I sometimes think that not the least precious is the slender posthumous volume published by his daughter in 1902. It was long his habit to carry in his pocket a narrow diary in which he jotted down engagements for the day, mingled with short quotations from the books he was reading to serve as amulets, so to speak, against the importunities of business. The quotations for a selection of years printed by Mrs. Wodehouse from these *Notebooks* form what might be called the critic's breviary.[2] Here, if anywhere, we seem to feel the very beating of the critic's heart, and to catch the inner voice of recollection and duty, corresponding to the poet's "gleam," which he followed so devoutly in his life. I do not know to what work in English to liken it unless it be the notebooks containing quotations from Marcus Aurelius and Epictetus written down by the author of the *Characteristics* with his comments, which Dr. Rand edited in 1900 as the *Philosophical Regimen of Anthony, Earl of Shaftesbury.*

Nor is it mere chance that Matthew Arnold and Shaftesbury should have left for posthumous publication these private memoranda, which with all their differences of form and substance are in their final impression upon the mind so curiously alike; for the two men themselves, in their outlook on life and in their relation to their respective ages, had much in common, and there is perhaps no better way to reach a dispassionate understanding of the virtue and limitations of criticism than by comparing Arnold with his great forerunner of the early eighteenth century. Both men were essentially critical in their mental habit, and both magnified the critic's office. "I take upon me," said Shaftesbury, "absolutely to condemn the fashionable and prevailing custom of inveighing against critics as the common enemies, the pests and incendiaries of the commonwealth of Wit and Letters. I assert, on the contrary, that they are the props and pillars of this building; and that without the encouragement and propagation of such a race, we should remain as Gothic architects as ever." And the purpose of Shaftesbury in upholding the function of criticism was much the same as Arnold's; he too was offended by the Gothic and barbarous self-complacency of his contemporaries—the Philistines, as he might have called them. As Arnold protested that the work of the English romantic revival was doomed "to prove hardly more lasting than the productions of far less splendid epochs"; that Byron was "empty of matter," Shelley "incoherent," and Wordsworth "wanting in completeness and variety," just because they lacked critical background; so his predecessor censured the literature of his day. "An English author would be all genius," says Shaftesbury. "He would reap the fruits of art, but without study, pains, or application. He thinks it necessary, indeed (lest his learning should be called in question), to show the world that he errs knowingly against the rules of art."

Against this presumption of genius on the one hand and the self-complacency of Philistinism on the other, both critics took up the same weapons—the barbs of ridicule and irony. With Shaftesbury this method was an avowed creed. His essays are no more than sermons on two texts: that of Horace, "*Ridiculum acri Fortius et melius magnas plerumque secat res*—a jest often decides weighty matters better and more forcibly than can asperity"; and the saying of Gorgias Leontinus,[3] which he misinterprets and expands for his own purpose, "That humour was the only test of gravity; and gravity of humour. For a subject which would not bear raillery was suspicious; and a jest which would not bear a serious examination was certainly false wit." With this touchstone of truth he proceeds to test the one-sided enthusiasms of his day, the smirking conceits, the pedantic pretensions, and the narrow dogmatisms whether of science or religion. "There is a great difference," he says, "between seeking how to raise a laugh from everything, and seeking in everything what justly may be laughed at. For nothing is ridiculous except what is deformed; nor is anything proof against raillery except what is handsome and just." The comic spirit is thus a kind of purgation of taste, and a way of return to nature. How deliberately Matthew Arnold used this weapon of ridicule in the service of sweet reasonableness, which is only his modern phrase, a little sentimentalised, for eighteenth-century nature; how magisterially he raised the laugh against his enemies, the bishops and the great austere toilers of the press and the mighty men of political Philistia, no one needs be told who has enjoyed the elaborate irony of *Culture and Anarchy* or of *Friendship's Garland.*

Sweet reasonableness, or "sweetness and light," to use the phrase as Arnold took it from Swift's *Battle of the Books,* is, I have suggested, little more than the modern turn for the deist's nature and reason; how nearly the two ideals approach each other you may see by comparing the "good-breeding," which is the aim of Shaftesbury's philosophy, with the "culture" which is the end of Arnold's criticism. "To philosophise," said the former, "in a just signification, is but to carry good-breeding a step higher. For the accomplishment of breeding is, to learn whatever is decent in company or beautiful in arts, and the sum of philosophy is, to learn what is just in society and beautiful in Nature and the order of the world." I have wondered sometimes whether Matthew Arnold had these words in mind when he formulated his definition of culture; whether his famous command is really but another echo from the ancient quarrel of the deists. The whole scope of the essay on *Sweetness and Light* is, he avows, "to recommend culture as the great help out of our present difficulties; culture being a pursuit of our total perfection by means of getting to know, on all the matters which most concern us, the best which has been thought and said in the world [Shaftesbury, too, like Arnold, is insistent on the *exemplaria Græca*]; and through this knowledge, turning a stream of fresh and free thought upon our stock notions and habits."

There is, I trust, something more than a pedantic curiosity in such a parallel, which might yet be much prolonged, between the author of *Culture and Anarchy* and the author of the *Characteristics*. It proves, if proof is necessary, more clearly than would any amount of direct exposition, that Matthew Arnold's method of criticism was not an isolated product of the nineteenth century, but that he belongs to one of the great families of human intelligence, which begins with Cicero, the father of them all, and passes through Erasmus and Boileau and Shaftesbury and Sainte-Beuve. These are the exemplars—not complete individually, I need not say—of what may be called the critical spirit: discriminators between the false and the true, the deformed and the normal; preachers of harmony and proportion and order, prophets of the religion of taste. If they deal much with the criticism of literature, this is because in literature more manifestly than anywhere else life displays its infinitely varied motives and results; and their practice is always to render literature itself more consciously a criticism of life. The past is the field out of which they draw their examples of what is in conformity with nature and of what departs from that norm. In that field they balance and weigh and measure; they are by intellect hesitators, but at heart very much in earnest. They are sometimes contrasted to their detriment with the so-called creative writers, yet they themselves stood each among the first writers of his day, and it is not plain that, for instance, Tennyson, in any true estimation, added more to the intellectual life of the world than Matthew Arnold, or Lucretius than Cicero, though their method and aim may have been different. The more significant comparison at least is not with the so-called creative writers, but with the great fulminators of new creeds—between Matthew Arnold and the Carlyles and Ruskins and Huxleys of his day; between Shaftesbury and, let us say, Rousseau; Boileau and Descartes; Erasmus and Luther; Cicero and St. Paul. Such a contrast might seem at first to lie as much in efficiency as in quality. In the very nature of things the man who seizes on one deep-reaching idea, whether newly found or rediscovered, and with single-hearted fervour forces it upon the world, might appear to have the advantage in power over the man of critical temper, who weighs and refines; who is for ever checking the enthusiasm of the living by the authority of the dead; and whose doctrine, even though in the end he may assert it with sovereign contempt of doubters, is still the command to follow the well-tried path of common-sense. Better the half-truth that makes for action and jostles the world out of its ruts, men cry, than such a timid search for the whole truth as paralyses the will, and may after all prove only an exchange of depth for breadth. That might appear to be the plain lesson of history; yet I am not so sure. Is there not a possibility that in our estimate of these powers we are a little betrayed by the tumult of the times, just as we are prone in other things to mistake bustle for movement? The critical spirit, as it has been exercised, may have its limitations and may justly be open to censure, but I doubt if its true reproach will turn out in the end to be a lack of efficiency in comparison with the more assertive force of the reformers. I am inclined to believe, for instance, that the balancing spirit of Erasmus is really more at work among us to-day than that of the dogmatic and reforming Luther; that Cicero's philosophy, though they would gape to hear it said, is really more in the hearts of the men you will meet in the street than is the theology of St. Paul. This may be in part because the representatives of the critical spirit, by their very lack of warping originality and by their endeavour to separate the true from the false, the complete from the one-sided, stand with the great conservative forces of human nature, having their fame certified by the things that endure amid all the betrayals of time and fashion. I know the deductions that must be made from that kind of fame. Cicero, it will be said, when in his *De Finibus* he brought together the various experiences of antiquity in regard to the meaning and values of life, weighing the claims of Stoic and Epicurean and the others, may have stood for something more comprehensive and balanced than did St. Paul with his new dogma of justification by faith. Yet St. Paul's theory of justification by faith, though it may be losing for us its cogent veracity, was the immediate driving force of history and a power that remade the world, while Cicero's nice discussion remained a luxury of the learned few. In one sense that is indisputably true; and yet, imprudent as it may sound, I question whether it is the whole truth. When I consider the part played by Stoic and Epicurean philosophies in the Renaissance and the transcendent influence of Cicero's dissertations upon the men of that day; when I consider that the impulse of Deism in the eighteenth century, as seen in Shaftesbury and his successors, was at bottom little more than a revival of this same Stoicism, as it had been subdued to the emotions by Cicero and mixed with Epicureanism; that Shaftesbury was, in fact, despite his worship of Epictetus, almost a pure Ciceronian; and when I consider that out of Deism sprang the dominant religion and social philosophy of our present world—when I consider these and many other facts, I question whether Cicero, while he certainly represents what is more enduring, has not been also, actually and personally, as dynamic an influence in civilisation as St. Paul, though the noise, no doubt, and the tumult have been around the latter. We are still too near Matthew Arnold's day to determine the resultant of all the forces then at work, yet it would not be very rash even now to assert that his critical essays will be found in the end a broader and more lasting, as they are a saner, influence than the exaggerated æstheticism of Ruskin or the shrill prophesying of Carlyle or the scientific dogmatism of Huxley. No, if there is any deduction to be made to the value of criticism, it is not on the side of efficiency. It is well to remember Matthew Arnold's own words. "Violent indignation with the past," he says, "abstract systems of renovation applied wholesale, a new doctrine drawn up in black and white for elaborating down to the very smallest details a rational society for the future—these are the ways of Jacobinism. . . . Culture [it is his word here for criticism] is always assigning to system-makers and systems a smaller share in the bent of human destiny than their friends like."

Perhaps it is a secret inkling of this vanity of the critic in its widest bearing, besides a natural antagonism of temper, that leads so many to carp against him and his trade. The inveterate hostility of "creative" writers to criticism is well known, and has been neatly summed up by E. S. Dallas in *The Gay Science:*

> Ben Jonson spoke of critics as tinkers, who make more faults than they mend; Samuel Butler, as the fierce inquisitors of wit, and as butchers who have no right to sit on a jury; Sir Richard Steele, as of all mortals the silliest; Swift, as dogs, rats, wasps, or, at best, drones of the learned world; Shenstone, as asses, which by gnawing vines first taught the advantage of pruning them; Burns, as cut-throat bandits in the path of fame; Walter Scott, humorously reflecting the general sentiment, as caterpillars.

The droll thing about it is that every one of these critics of criticism was so ready to act himself as butcher or ass or caterpillar. It is a common trick of the guild. For a modern instance, turn to Mr. Horace Traubel, the shirt-sleeved Boswell of Walt Whitman, and you will find pages of conversation recorded in which the seer of Camden belabours the professors of criticism and in almost the same breath exercises the art upon his brother poets with delightful frankness and at times rare penetration. But this ancient feud of the gentlemen of the pen is a special form, due in part to special causes, of the hostility that so often manifests itself against the critical spirit in general. The man of system and the man of unhesitating action are likely to feel something like contempt for the mind that balances and waits. The imperial Mommsen felt this contempt, and showed it, in his treatment of Cicero; it is rife even yet in the current tone of condescension toward Erasmus as compared with Luther, to which Matthew Arnold replied by calling Luther "a Philistine of genius"; Warburton showed it in his sneers at Shaftesbury as the man of taste, and Cardinal Newman has, with splendid politeness, echoed them; Matthew Arnold was equally feared and despised in his own lifetime, and

it is an odd fact that you will to-day scarcely pick up a piece
of third-rate criticism (in which there is likely to be anything
at work rather than the critical spirit), but you will come upon
some gratuitous fling against him. Most bitter of all was Henry
Sidgwick's arraignment of "The Prophet of Culture" in *Mac-
millan's Magazine* for August, 1867. There if anywhere the
critical spirit was stabbed with its own weapon. You will recall
the image of the pouncet-box:

> Mr. Arnold may say that he does not discourage action, but
> only asks for delay, in order that we may act with sufficient
> knowledge. This is the eternal excuse of indolence—insufficient
> knowledge. . . . One cannot think on this subject without recall-
> ing the great man who recommended to philosophy a position
> very similar to that now claimed for culture. I wish to give Mr.
> Arnold the full benefit of his resemblance to Plato. But when we
> look closer at the two positions, the dissimilarity comes out: they
> have a very different effect on our feelings and imagination; and
> I confess I feel more sympathy with the melancholy philoso-
> pher looking out with hopeless placidity "from beneath the
> shelter of some wall" than with a cheerful modern liberal, tem-
> pered by renouncement, shuddering aloof from the rank exha-
> lations of vulgar enthusiasm, and holding up the pouncet-box of
> culture betwixt the wind and his nobility.

Such an onslaught on our prophet of culture as a languid and
shrinking dilettante was fair enough in the heat of controversy
and was at least justified by its own art, if not by certain affections of its victim's style; but I protest against accepting it as
essentially true. Any one might perceive that Matthew Arnold
had beneath the irony and suavity of his manner a temper of
determined seriousness; that, like the bride of Giacopone di
Todi in his sonnet, his Muse might be young, gay, and radiant
outside, but had

a hidden ground
Of thought and of austerity within.

It would be interesting in this respect to continue the comparison of Arnold and Shaftesbury, and to show how near to-

gether they stood in their attitude toward nature and society and in their religion, and how profound was their own enthusiasm beneath their hostility to the sham or undisciplined enthusiasms of the day. Lord Shaftesbury might say that we have "in the main a witty and good-humoured religion," as Matthew Arnold might ridicule the sourness of the Nonconformists and the bleakness of the reformers in whose assemblies any child of nature, if he shall stray thither, is smitten with lamentation and mourning and woe; but there was solemnity enough, however we may rate their insight, in their own search for the God that sits concealed at the centre. Shaftesbury's creed became the formula of the deists. "Still ardent in its pursuit," the soul, he says, "rests not here, nor satisfies itself with the beauty of a part, but, extending further its communicative bounty, seeks the good of all, and affects the interest and prosperity of the whole. True to its native world and higher country, 'tis here it seeks order and perfection; wishing the best, and hoping still to find a just and wise administration. And since all hope of this were vain and idle if no universal mind presided; since without such a supreme intelligence and providential care the distracted universe must be condemned to suffer infinite calamities; 'tis here the generous mind labours to discover that healing cause by which the interest of the whole is securely established, the beauty of things and the universal order happily sustained." Matthew Arnold condensed that rhetoric into a phrase: "The stream of tendency, not ourselves, which makes for righteousness."

But the strongest evidence of their austerity of purpose is seen in those private notebooks which led me to couple their names together in this study of the spirit of criticism. This is not the time to deal at length with that sober and anxious self-examination of the noble Lord, as Shaftesbury's enemies of the Church were so fond of calling him. It is one of the important documents to show how completely Deism was a revival of pagan morality. It is, in brief, no more than a translation of the great maxims of antiquity into modern purposes: the inner record of a man seeking character in the two elements of attention $(\pi\rho\sigma\sigma\chi\acute{\eta})$ and the harmony of life (veræ numerosque modosque vitæ), and of a man who thought that this pursuit must be maintained unrelentingly. Of the two books it may seem strange that Matthew Arnold's, which consists merely of brief quotations without comment, should really open to us more intimately the author's heart than does the direct self-questioning of Shaftesbury's. Yet a book more filled with sad sincerity, a more perfect confession of a life's purpose, will scarcely be found than these memoranda. "I am glad to find," he wrote once in a letter to his sister, "that in the past year I have at least accomplished more than usual in the way of reading the books which at the beginning of the year I had put down to be read. . . . The importance of reading, not slight stuff to get through the time, but the best that has been written, forces itself upon me more and more every year I live." Now the *Notebooks* not only preserve some of these annual lists of books to be read, but show, in quintessential phrase, just what the books actually read meant to him. Some of the quotations are repeated a number of times, and if frequency of repetition can be taken as a criterion the maxim closest to Arnold's heart was the sentence, from what source I do not know: "*Semper aliquid certi proponendum est*—always some certain end must be kept in view." It is but an expansion of the same idea that he expresses in the words set down more than once from some French author: "A working life, a succession of labours which fill and moralise the days!" and in the beloved command of the *Imitation: "Cum multa legeris et cognoveris, ad unum semper oportet redire principium*—when you have read and learned many things, it is necessary always to return to one principle." That principle he sets down in aphorisms and exhortations from a hundred diverse sources—nowhere, perhaps, more succinctly than in the broken phrases of the stoic Lucan:

> servare modum, finemque tenere
> Naturamque sequi—
> Nec sibi, sed toti genitum se credere mundo—
> In commune bonus.[4]

He might well have applied to his own pursuit of culture the eulogy he quotes concerning another: "Study, which for most men is only a frivolous amusement and often dangerous, was for Dom Rivet a serious occupation consecrated by religion."

It was not a mere dilettante of sweetness and light who day by day laid such maxims as these upon his breast; it was not one who held up the pouncet-box of culture betwixt the wind and his nobility. Matthew Arnold, if any man in his generation, was by temperament a stoic for whom duty and submission and reverence made up the large part of life; and there is something of what we call the irony of fate in the thought that he who made σπουδαιότης, *high seriousness,* the test of great literature, should have suffered the reproach of levity. Yet, after all, fate is never quite blind in these things, and if criticism has thus drawn upon itself the censure of men like Sidgwick we may feel assured that in some way it has failed of the deeper truth. Those reproaches may in part be due to prejudice and revenge and the inevitable contrast of temperaments; they may err in ascribing to the critic a want of efficiency, as they may be wantonly perverse in denouncing him for frivolity; but they have a meaning and they cannot be overlooked. Now the future is often a strange revealer of secret things, and there is no surer way to detect the weak side of a leader than by studying the career of his disciples, or even of his successors.

You are familiar with the story of the concluding chapter of Pater's *Renaissance*—how it was withdrawn from the second edition of that book because the author "conceived it might possibly mislead some of those young men into whose hands it might fall"; and how it was restored, with some slight changes, to the later editions where it now stands. And you know the moral of that essay: that life is but an uncertain interval before the universal judgment of death, a brief illusion of stability in the eternal flux, and that "our one chance lies in expanding that interval, in getting as many pulsations as possible into the given time." And "of this wisdom," he concludes, "the poetic passion, the desire of beauty, the love of art for art's sake, has most; for art comes to you professing frankly to give nothing but the highest quality to your moments as they pass, and simply for those moments' sake." That philosophy of the Oxonian Epicurus and its scandal in a very un-Epicurean land are familiar enough; but perhaps we do not always stop to think how plausibly this doctrine of crowning our moments with the highest sensations of art flows from Matthew Arnold's definition of criticism as the disinterested endeavour "to know the best that is known and thought in the world, irrespectively of practice, politics, and everything of the kind."

The next step from Pater's Epicureanism, and so by a further remove from Arnold's criticism, brings us to one whose name, unfortunately, must always be mentioned with regret, but who is more significant in the development of English letters than is sometimes allowed. At the time when Paterism, as a recent writer has said, was "tripping indelicately along the Oxford High and by the banks of the Cherwell," a young votary of the Muses from Dublin came upon the scene, and began to push the doctrine of Pater as far beyond what the master intended as Pater had gone beyond Matthew Arnold. This is the young man who "would occasionally be seen walking the streets carrying a lily or a sunflower in his hand, at which he would gaze intently and admiringly." He had fashioned himself deliberately to pose as the head of a new sect of "æsthetes," as they styled themselves, who expanded Arnold's excluded tribe of Philistines to embrace all the sober citizens of the world. The fate of Oscar Wilde is still like a fresh wound in the public memory. What I wish to call to your mind is the direct connection (strengthened no doubt by influences from across the Channel) between Pater's philosophy of the sensation-crowded moment and such a poem as that in which Wilde attempted to concentrate all the passionate moments of the past in his gloating revery upon *The Sphinx*. He was himself not unaware of the treachery of the path he had chosen; the sonnet which he prefixed to his book of poems is sincere with the pathos of conscious insincerity, and is a memorable comment on one of the tragic ambitions of a century:

> To drift with every passion till my soul
> Is a stringed lute on which all winds can play,
> Is it for this that I have given away
> Mine ancient wisdom, and austere control?
> .   .   .   .
> Surely there was a time I might have trod
> The sunlit heights, and from life's dissonance
> Struck one clear chord to reach the ears of God:
> Is that time dead? lo! with a little rod
> I did but touch the honey of romance—
> And must I lose a soul's inheritance?

The answer to the poet's query he was himself to write in *The Ballad of Reading Gaol*:

> Silently we went round and round
>   And through each hollow mind
> The Memory of dreadful things
>   Rushed like a dreadful wind,
> And Horror stalked before each man,
>   And Terror crept behind.

This Memory of dreadful things is the too logical end, step by step, of the philosophy of the sensation-crowded moment; the concealed suspicion of it in Matthew Arnold's definition of criticism was the justification, if any there be, of the contempt hurled upon him by some of his contemporaries.

It is necessary to repeat that such a derivation from Matthew Arnold is essentially unfair because it leaves out of view the real purpose and heart of the man. If we could not read his great moral energy in his *Essays*, as I trust we all of us can, and if we did not know the profound influence of his critical philosophy upon the better life of our age, we could still dispel our doubts by looking into the *Notebooks*, in which memory is not turned to dreadful things for the soul's disgrace, but is the guide and impulse to strong resolution and beautiful forbearance. Yet withal it remains true that the Epicureanism of Pater and the hedonism of Oscar Wilde were able to connect themselves in a disquieting way with one side of Matthew Arnold's gospel of culture; and it behooves us who come upon the heels of this movement and who believe that the critical spirit is still to be one of the powers making in the world for right enjoyment, it behooves us to examine the first definition of culture or criticism—the words had about the same meaning as Arnold used them—and see whether something was not there forgotten. The fault lay not in any intrinsic want of efficiency in the critical spirit, nor in any want of moral earnestness in Matthew Arnold or Shaftesbury: that we have seen. But these men were lacking in another direction: they missed a philosophy which could bind together their moral and their æsthetic sense, a positive principle besides the negative force of ridicule and irony; and, missing this, they left criticism more easily subject to a one-sided and dangerous development.

To the nature of that omission, to the *porro unum necessarium,*[5] we may be directed, I think, by the critical theory of the one who carried the practice, in other respects, to its lowest degradation. In Oscar Wilde's dialogue on *The Critic as Artist,* one of the most extraordinary mixtures ever compounded of truth flaunting in the robes of error and error assuming the gravity of truth, you will remember that the advocate of criticism at the height of his argument proclaims the true man of culture to be him who has learned "the best that is known and thought in the world" (he uses Matthew Arnold's words), and who thus, as Matthew Arnold neglected to add, "bears within himself the dreams, and ideas, and feelings of myriad generations." The addition is important, how important, or at least how large, may be seen in the really splendid, if somewhat morbid, passage in which the idea is developed. Let me quote at some length:

> To know anything about oneself, one must know all about others. There must be no mood with which one cannot sympathise, no dead mode of life that one cannot make alive. Is this

impossible? I think not. By revealing to us the absolute mechanism of all action, and so freeing us from the self-imposed and
trammelling burden of moral responsibility, the scientific principle of Heredity has become, as it were, the warrant for the
contemplative life. It has shown us that we are never less free
than when we try to act. It has hemmed us round with the nets
of the hunter, and written upon the wall the prophecy of our
doom. We may not watch it, for it is within us. We may not see
it, save in a mirror that mirrors the soul. It is Nemesis without
her mask. It is the last of the Fates, and the most terrible. It is
the only one of the Gods whose real name we know.

And yet, while in the sphere of practical and external life it
has robbed energy of its freedom and activity of its choice, in
the subjective sphere, where the soul is at work, it comes to us,
this terrible shadow, with many gifts in its hands, gifts of strange
temperaments and subtle susceptibilities, gifts of wild ardours
and chill moods of indifference, complex multiform gifts of
thoughts that are at variance with each other, and passions that
war against themselves. And so, it is not our own life that we
live, but the lives of the dead, and the soul that dwells within
us is no single spiritual entity, making us personal and individual, created for our service, and entering into us for our joy.
. . . It can help us to leave the age in which we were born, and
to pass into other ages, and find ourselves not exiled from their
air. It can teach us how to escape from our experience, and to
realise the experiences of those who are greater than we are.
The pain of Leopardi crying out against life becomes our pain.
Theocritus blows on his pipe, and we laugh with the lips of
nymph and shepherd. In the wolfskin of Pierre Vidal we flee
before the hounds, and in the armour of Lancelot we ride from
the bower of the Queen. We have whispered the secret of our
love beneath the cowl of Abelard, and in the stained raiment
of Villon have put our shame into song. We can see the dawn
through Shelley's eyes, and when we wander with Endymion
the Moon grows amorous of our youth. Ours is the anguish of
Atys, and ours the weak rage and noble sorrows of the Dane. Do
you think that it is the imagination that enables us to live these
countless lives? Yes: it is the imagination; and the imagination is
the result of heredity. It is simply concentrated race-experience.

Now, this theory of race-experience, as Oscar Wilde formulated it, lends itself, no doubt, to an easy fallacy. I am aware of

the rebuke administered to one who was by the range of his
knowledge and by his historic sense much more justified in
such a presumption than was Oscar Wilde. "Is it not the strang-
est illusion," exclaimed the biographer of Renan, "to believe
that the mere reading of the Acts of the martyrs is sufficient
to give us their soul, to transfer to us in its real intensity the
ardour which ravished them admist their tortures? . . . Those
who have lost all the energy of living and acting may, if they
choose, shut themselves up in this kingdom of shadows; that is
their affair. But that they should proclaim theirs as the true life,
is not to be conceded to them." Séailles was right. These men,
whether it be a paradox-monger like Oscar Wilde or a great
scholar like Renan, should have laid to heart the favourite
maxim of Matthew Arnold, *semper aliquid certi proponendum
est:* true culture has always before its eyes a definite end and
is for self-discipline not for revery. Nor am I unaware that the
theory as expressed by Oscar Wilde, is mixed up with his own
personal taint of decadence. One thing at least is certain: that
the way of the true critical spirit is not to free us, as he boasts,
from "the self-imposed and trammelling burden of moral responsibility." His avowal in the same dialogue that the sole aim
of art is to produce the "beautiful sterile emotions" so hateful
to the world, his shameless vaunt that "there is nothing sane
about the worship of beauty," his whole philosophy of the ego
as above the laws of society, cannot be severed from the memory of dreadful things in which his own song ended: such a
philosophy is in fact a denial of the validity of that very race-
experience out of which he attempts to derive it. In this respect again he should have remembered the maxim of Matthew Arnold: "A working life, a succession of labours that fill
and moralise the days." The aim of culture is not to merge the
present in a sterile dream of the past, but to hold the past as
a living force in the present. In omitting these aspects of criticism Pater and, to a greater extent, Oscar Wilde fell into extravagance far more deleterious to culture than was any omission or incompleteness on the part of Matthew Arnold.

Nevertheless, with all its false emphasis and its admixture of personal error, that positive and emotional reassumption of the past, that association of the contemplative life (the βίος θεωρητικός) with the rapture of memory, contains the hint of a great truth which must be grasped and properly exercised if criticism is to confirm itself against such hostility as has hitherto kept it on the defensive. I would not say even that the mysticism, out of which Oscar Wilde's critical theory really springs, though expressed in the modish language of scientific evolution, is essentially perverse. For in a very true sense the past of mankind, by the larger race-memory and particularly by that form of it which we call literature, abides as a living reality in our present. We suffer not our individual destiny alone but the fates of humanity also. We are born into an inheritance of great emotions—into the unconquerable hopes and defeated fears of an immeasurable past, the tragedies and the comedies of love, the ardent aspirations of faith, the baffled questionings of evil, the huge laughter at facts, the deep-welling passion of peace. Without that common inheritance how inconceivably poor and shallow would be this life of the world and our life in it! These recorded emotions are, indeed, not for us what they were in actuality, nor by sitting at our own ease with memory can we enter into the exact emotions of the martyr at the stake and the hero in his triumph. These things are now transmuted into something the same and different, something less and greater. The intensity of the actual moment they cannot possess, but on the other hand with this loss of separate reality they are associated with life as a whole, and in that unity of experience obtain, what they lacked before, a significance and design. They bear in a way the same relation to practical life as that life bore to the ideal world out of which it arose and into which it is continually passing. And thus this larger memory, in its transmuting and unifying power, may not unmeaningly be regarded as the purpose of activity, and literature may not too presumptuously be cherished as the final end of existence. Some such mystery as this was hinted in the Greek and Gnostic doctrine of the *logos*, the Word, and in the Hindu name for the creator as *vâcas pati*, Lord of the

Word. And if such a theory sounds too absurdly metaphysical for the ears of prudent common-sense, consider that Homer, no philosopher of empty phrases surely, meant nothing very different when he judged of actions by their fame in future story. To him the warring of armies for ten long years and the desolation of Troy was for no other purpose than that the inner life of the race might be enriched by memory:

> Thus the gods fated, and such ruin wove
> That song might flourish for posterity.

And in this theory of memory criticism has an important office. We are beginning to hear a good deal these days about the French metaphysician, M. Henri Bergson, of whom Prof. William James has avowed himself a willing disciple, and whose disquisitions on *Matière et mémoire* and *L'Évolution créatrice* are perhaps more talked of than any other recent books of philosophy. I do not pretend to pronounce on the full scope of his theories, but his conception of the function of memory is rich with applications to the matter we have in hand. Our consciousness, that is to say our very self, is not, he says, a thing born new with each moment, not a *mens momentanea*, but an uninterrupted stream of activity, and what we now feel is directly bound up with what we have felt before. Nor is this consciousness, on the other hand, a mere heaping together indiscriminately of perceptions and emotions, but it is an active faculty, or, I should prefer to say, the servant of some active faculty, that depresses this particular experience into the background and centres attention upon that other experience, thus by a process of criticism secreting the present, so to speak, out of the past. Such a philosophy finds a new and profound truth in the saying of Pascal: *"La mémoire est nécessaire à toutes les opérations de l'esprit—*memory is necessary to all the operations of the mind."

This notion of the active memory is, I am told by those who should know, mixed up in Bergson with a questionable metaphysic, yet in itself alone it should seem to be nothing more than the laborious expression of a very simple fact. We have all of us met now and then in our daily intercourse a man whose conversation impressed us immediately as possessing a certain ripeness of widom, a certain pertinency and depth of meaning. If we wished to characterise such a man a single word, we should perhaps say that he was essentially educated. We feel that he has within him some central force which enables him to choose consistently amidst the innumerable conflicting impulses and attractions and dissipations of life, that he moves forward, not at haphazard, but by the direction of some principle of conduct, and that he can be depended upon for counsel and comfort. Well, if you stop to analyse this quality of mind, which we will call education, you will discover in every case, I believe, that the determining trait is just the force of a critical memory. I do not mean by this the mere facility of recalling the emotions and events and spectacles which have come to a man with the years; for such undisciplined reminiscence may be but a shabby wisdom to the man himself, as it may be the very contrary of joy to his hearer. I mean rather the faculty of selection as well as of retention, the weighing of cause and effect, the constant and active assumption of the past in the present, by which the events of life are no longer regarded as isolated and fortuitous moments, but are merged into a unity of experience. Those in whom this faculty rules are commonly the possessors of practical wisdom, but there are others, a few, who by its virtue are raised into another kind of wisdom. With these men the selective, reconciling memory is associated, more or less consciously, with the Platonic reminiscence in such a manner that not only are the past and present of passing time made one but our ephemeral life is fitted into that great ring of eternity which Henry Vaughan saw as in a dream. So it is that to them the things which others behold as sudden unrelated facts are made shadows and types of the everlasting ideas; and with the accumulation of knowledge they grow ripe in vision,

> Till old experience do attain
> To something like prophetic strain.

And as our private memory is not a merely passive retention of sensations, so in literature the critical spirit is at work as a conscious energy of selection. The function of criticism, as thus understood, is far removed from the surrender to luxurious revery which the impressionists believed it to be; nor is the good critic, as Anatole France said, he who recounts the adventures of his soul amid masterpieces; he is rather one who has before him always the *aliquid certi,* the definite aim of a Matthew Arnold. He does not, like Oscar Wilde, seek by losing the present in the past to throw off "the self-imposed and trammelling burden of moral responsibility"; he is rather one whose life is "a succession of labours that fill and moralise the days"—not in the narrow didactic sense, it need scarcely be said, but in so far as his task is a continual weighing of values. But the critical spirit is also something deeper than Matthew Arnold perceived, or, at least, clearly expressed. The error of criticism in his hands, as in the hands of his predecessors, was that in the exercise of judgment it used the past too much as a dead storehouse of precepts for schoolmastering the present; it was not sufficiently aware of the relation of this faculty of judgment to the indwelling and ever-acting memory of things. Here is the one touch of insight needed, I think, to raise criticism, while not forgetting its special duty of discrimination and judgment, to a more independent and self-respecting *genre.* In its conscious creation of the field of the present out of the past it takes an honoured, if not equal, place by the side of those impulses, more commonly recognised as creative, which are continually adding new material for its selective energy. "Valuing is creating," said Nietzsche; "to value is the treasure and jewel among all things valued." The critical spirit is thus akin to that force of design or final cause in the Aristotelian sense, which we are beginning once more to divine as the guiding principle, itself unchanged, at work within the evolutionary changes of nature; and in so far as it becomes aware of

this high office it introduces into our intellectual life an element outside of alteration and growth and decay, a principle
to which time is the minister and not the master.

Literary criticsm is, indeed, in this sense only the specific
exercise of a faculty which works in many directions. All scholars, whether they deal with history or sociology or philosophy
or language or, in the narrower use of the word, literature, are
servants of the critical spirit, in so far as they transmit and
interpret and mould the sum of experience from man to man
and from generation. Might not one even say that at a certain
point criticism becomes almost identical with education, and
that by this standard we may judge the value of any study as
an instrument of education, and may estimate the merit of any
special presentation of that study? It is at least, in the existing
chaos of pedagogical theories, a question worthy of consideration.

[1]   This essay was written hurriedly as a lecture for the Women's Club of St. Louis
        in February, 1910, and then delivered at the Yale University Club, in New
        Haven, on February 12, and at Columbia University, May 3, the same year.
        More included it in his Seventh Series of *Shelburne Essays* (1910). The essay
        illustrates More's allegiance to Arnold's view that literary criticism must be
        fundamentally a criticism of life and that the critic's first responsibility is to
        evaluate what is before him by "the indwelling and ever-acting memory of
        things"—*great and significant things*, that is, by which the impressions of the
        moment are tempered by schooled judgment. While resembling Arnold's
        "touchstone" theory, More's doctrine goes beyond that of Arnold, whom he
        criticises for using the past too much as a "dead storehouse of precepts for
        schoolmastering the present." The critical imagination, he said, is but the force
        of the indwelling past linking to itself what is of equal value in the present.
        "Valuing," thus, "is creating" (More quotes Nietzsche), and literary criticism
        is only one exercise of a faculty which works in many directions. Such criticism
        adds an "outside" element of permanence to the scene of "alteration and
        growth and decay." More saw himself in the tradition of Cicero, Erasmus,
        Boileau, Shaftesbury, Sainte-Beuve, and Arnold, who interpreted, molded, and
        transmitted "the sum of experience from man to man and from generation to
        generation." The essay is a good place for the student of Morean criticism to
        begin.
[2]   *Matthew Arnold's Notebooks, with a Preface by the Hon. Mrs. Wodehouse, and
        a Portrait.* [Eleanor Mary Caroline (Arnold) Wodehouse Mansfield, baroness
        Sandhurst, ed.] London, 1902.

[3] Quoted by Aristotle: τὴν μὲν ϭπουδὴν διαφθείρειν γέλωϊι τὸν δὲγέλωτα ϭπουδῇ [More's note] Gorgias (485?-380? B.C.) was a Greek rhetorician and sophist from Leontini, Sicily.

[4] "To preserve measure, to hold fast to the end, and follow nature—To believe oneself born not for oneself alone but for all the world—good for the community of mankind." [More's trans.]

[5] Literally: "and furthermore one necessary thing."

Arthur Symons: The Two Illusions[1]

It is a saying of Joubert, as subtle as it is true, that the essence
of art is to be found in the union of *l' illusion et la sagesse,*—
illusion and, to extend the meaning of the French phrase somewhat, disillusion; and for one who cares to penetrate into the
secret influences of poetry on the human heart, no better
guide can be suggested than this brief sentence. But like all
such generalisations it is susceptible of a false application in
practice as well as a right one, a distinction which has been
newly and emphatically attested by the publication of the collected poems of Mr. Arthur Symons. For there is a true illusion
without which poetry cannot exist, without which it sinks to
the level of unimaginative prose or passes into the thin aridi-
ties of metaphysics. In its simplest form this illusion may, perhaps, he seen in the pastoral world of our Elizabethan poets,
in the *Lycidas* and *Comus* of Milton best of all; and the skill
to lend reality to these idyllic dreams might even seem one of
the surest tests of a poet's right to deal with the high illusion
of art. *Lycidas* springs from this theme just as much as the
youthful *Pastorals* of Pope, but what a chasm there lies between them! As the poet's thoughts and aspirations are lifted
up beyond the thoughts of common men, so he is able without
violating artistic illusion to carry his reader into ideal scenes
never beheld on this earth. The noble isolation of Milton's soul
schooled him to speak understandingly the ideal language of

Arcadia, and something within our souls responds to every word. But in the mouth of a worldling like Pope this language becomes a shallow affectation and conveys no illusion of reality to the reader.

And if you wish to see the power of poetic illusion exemplified in a more general form than the pretty deceptions of Arcadia, turn to any of the greater plays of Shakespeare, to *Hamlet*, which will make you believe for the space of a few hours that human life really revolves about such mystic musings and expresses itself in such rapt language as the mad Dane's, or to *The Tempest*, in which the poet has symbolised his own powers of enchantment in the wizard Prospero. And yet, side by side with this illusion, there must always in the greater poets run a note of disillusion,—a note subdued for the most part so as scarcely to be heard, but rising to the surface now and again with a strange quivering of mingled sadness and joy, of sadness for the fair enchantment it dispels, of joy for the glimpse it affords into something divine and very high. You may hear this note of disillusion many times in Shakespeare, clearest of all in *The Tempest*, where with a word Prospero puts an end to his fairy drama in the woods, and all the insubstantial pageant fades away.

For one acquainted with Oriental literature it is impossible to reflect on this illusion of art without recurring to the Hindu doctrine of Mâyâ, who is supposed to be the creative force of all this wonderful web of appearances that enwrap the spirit in their mesh and charm the spirit's attention by their mystery of beauty and seeming benevolence. To the Oriental, as often to the man of the West who considers the character of this illusion, Mâyâ assumes the form of the eternal-feminine unfolding her allurements before the masculine looker-on. So in the book of one of the two great philosophies of India the story of illusion and disillusion is told in this metaphor of the stage:

> Like as a dancing-girl to sound of lyres
> Delights the king and wakens sweet desires

For one brief hour, and having shown her art
With lingering bow behind the scene retires:

So o'er the Soul alluring Nature vaunts
Her lyric spell, and all her beauty flaunts;
  And she, too, in her time withdrawing leaves
The Watcher to his peace—'t is all she wants.

Now have I seen it all! the Watcher saith,
And wonders that the pageant lingereth:
  And, He hath seen me! then the Other cries,
And wends her way: and this they call the Death.

And when the play is seen, the illusion dispelled, and the dancing has disappeared, for a while the watcher waits in quiet,
seeming to live the old life, as a potter's wheel revolves a little
space after the potter's hand is still; but in reality the desire of
this world is ended and in his time he withdraws into the
untroubled peace of his nature. It is called Death; it is also
called the Awakening. It is a consummation of philosophy not
unmixed with joy, though it may seem empty to most Western
minds. It is even in another way the consummation of poetry,
for ever and anon, as we have seen, the true poet lifts for a
moment the very veil of illusion he is weaving and shows us
glimpses of what is beyond. And that is well. But suppose,
when the play is ended, there is no wisdom of self-knowledge
attained, no spiritual joy to take the place of the old lust of the
eyes, no royal watcher sitting serenely apart, but only some
poor outcast of the street, a brother in life to the painted
dancer on the stage—what then?

Now the story of such an illusion and such an awakening is
the theme of the poems which Mr. Arthur Symons has recently
collected and published in two volumes. In one group of these
poems the parallel to the Oriental conception of the dancing-
girl is so marked that the author would almost seem to have
had the impressing of this moral in his mind when he wrote
them. I refer to *The Dance of the Seven Sins, The Lover of the
Queen of Sheba,* and *The Dance of the Daughters of Herodias,*

in each of which the poet imagines the allurements of the world as dancing before the eyes of some tempted watcher.

> Is it the petals falling from the rose?
> For in the silence I can hear a sound
> Nearer than my own heart-beat, such a word
> As roses murmur, blown by a great wind.
> I see a pale and windy multitude
> Beaten about the air, as if the smoke
> Of incense kindled into visible life
> Shadowy and invisible presences;
> And, in the cloudy darkness, I can see
> The thin white feet of many women dancing,
> And in their hands . . .

That is the illusion of the world and of the desires of the world, daughters of Herodias dancing before the grey face of Herod. And as they dance they sing—

> "For are not we," they say, "the end of all?
> Why should you look beyond us? If you look
> Into the night, you will find nothing there:
> We also have gazed often at the stars.
> We, we alone among all beautiful things,
> We only are real: for the rest are dreams."

But the watcher grows weary of the long monotony of the scene:

> Have I now seen you as you are
> Always, and have I once admired
> Your beauty? I am very tired,
> Dancers, I am more tired than you.
> When shall the dance be all danced through?

It is the beginning of wisdom, you say, the cry of the Hindu watcher, "Lo, I have seen it all!" and yet—

> Wisdom is weariness to me.
> For wisdom, being attained, but shows

> That all things are but shadows cast
> On running water, swiftly past,
> And as the shadow of the rose
> That withers in the mirror glassed.

And that is the outcome—"Wisdom is weariness!"

> O bondslave, bondslave unto death,
> Might I but hope that death should free
> This self from its eternity!

It was, you see, a false illusion that could lead only to a false awakening; it is utterly different from the true illusion such as hovers over the pastoral world of *Lycidas* and works through the magic of Prospero, and the awakening from it is equally different from the disillusion of Shakespeare or of the Hindu philosopher. The true illusion does not confuse the things of the spirit with the things of the world. It knows that for a while the way of the spirit must lie through this ἄτης λειμῶνα, this meadowland of calamity, and its office is by a deliberate effort of the will to throw the glamour of light and joy and freedom on the objects by the roadside, so that the spirit may journey swiftly and pleasantly to its own upland home. And when its task is completed it leaves the spirit at rest with itself, without regret or further craving, filled with the consummation of peace that springs from experience and self-knowledge, while the world of the senses remains in memory only so far as this world shadows the spirit's own high desires. But the false illusion is an inner blindness and confusion; it is false because there enters into it no faith in the joy of things unseen, no knowledge even that such things exist; it is false because for the voice of the spirit it hears only the clamorous outcry of a man's lower personality springing from the desires of the body and the perceptions of the body, and is in the end one with what is desired and perceived. At the first this false illusion is sweet, but soon it is troubled with the bitterness of satiety; and the awakening from it leaves only the emptiness of endless regret and self-tormenting. The false disillusion is a discovery

that the looker-on who masqueraded as the spirit is merely a
phantom of the body; it is a perception of the hollowness of the
old illusion without the power of escaping therefrom. The
watcher of the Oriental philosophers is one perfectly distinct
from this "self" that cries out to death for deliverance from its
own eternity. The disillusion of the flesh is perhaps the saddest
chapter in human experience.

Now the composition of Mr. Symons's two volumes is such
that we are able to trace the progress of his poetic mood from
the first illusion to its consummation in a false disillusion; and
this regular gradation we can follow with a precision which is
at least a striking proof of the author's sincerity. As stated in
the prefatory note, these volumes are made up of selections
from five previously published works, viz.: *Days and Nights*,
in 1889; *Silhouettes*, in 1892; *London Nights*, in 1895; *Amoris
Victima*, in 1897; and *Images of Good and Evil*, in 1899; to
which is added a sheaf of new poems, *The Loom of Dreams*.
In one respect the substance of these successive books is the
same; from beginning to end we are in a land of dreams—
dreams always, whether fair or gloomy, or the haunting
remembrance of dreams. The introductory poem of the first
book is a sonnet that describes the delicious sense of drowning
in the gulf of opium, and in like manner the last poem of all
closes with these words in the mouth of Faustus:

> When Helen lived, men loved, and Helen was:
> I have seen Helen, Helen was a dream,
> I dreamed of something not in Helen's eyes.
> What shall the end of all things be? I wait
> Cruel old age, and kinder death, and sleep.

But if the substance of all these poems is woven on the same
loom of dreams, there is still, as I have said, a profound change
in their colour and texture as we proceed. Passing over the first
book, from which only a few disconnected poems have been

chosen, and these evidently written before the author had arrived at maturity of self-consciousness, we come to the collection entitled *Silhouettes*, which will probably appeal to the largest circle of readers although they can hardly be called the strongest specimens of Mr. Symons's work. Yet even these poems can never attain to any wide popularity, nor can they ever have much weight with practical intelligences that shun the evanescent world of revery where the real and the unreal meet and blend together in indistinguishable twilight. For this atmosphere is one of indulgent brooding; their warp and woof are of the stuff of dreams woven by a mind that turns from the actual issues of life as a naked body cowers from the wind. The world is seen through a haze of abstraction, glimmeringly, as a landscape looms misty and vague through the falling, fluttering veil of the rain. Indeed it is noteworthy, how many of the poems descriptive of nature or of the London streets are drenched with rains and blown by gusty winds:

> The wind is rising on the sea,
> The windy white foam-dancers leap;
> And the sea moans uneasily,
> And turns to sleep and cannot sleep.
>
> Ridge after rocky ridge uplifts
> Wild hands, and hammers at the land,
> Scatters in liquid dust, and drifts
> To death among the dusty sand.
>
> On the horizon's nearing line,
> Where the sky rests, a visible wall,
> Grey in the offing, I divine
> The sails that fly before the squall.

And human nature is viewed through a like mist, a mist of tears over laughter, as it may look to one who dreams deliberately while the heart is young and the haunting terror of the awakening seems still something that can be held aloof at his own sweet will. Love is the constant theme, not the great passion of strong men that smites and burns through the world, but the lighter play of emotions that dally and wanton over their own flowering beauty. And these women, to whom the poet's love goes out, girls of the dancing hall and the street, still young and very fair, are only a Western reading of that symbol of nature that dances before the watching soul of the Orient. Their faces steal into the heart with the witchery and insubstantiality of music:

> Across the tides of music, in the night,
> Her magical face,
> A light upon it as the happy light
> Of dreams in some delicious place
> Under the moonlight in the night.

They are not moral and they are not immoral, for they bear no relation to the claims of the soul; they are the figures of a fleeting illusion, a mere blossoming of the flesh yet undefiled:

> White girl, your flesh is lilies
> Under a frozen moon,
> So still is
> The rapture of your swoon
> Of whiteness, snow or lilies.
>
> Virginal in revealment,
> Your bosom's wavering slope,
> Concealment,
> In fainting heliotrope,
> Of whitest white's revealment,
>
> Is like a bed of lilies,
> A jealous-guarded row,
> Whose will is
> Simply chaste dreams: but oh,
> The alluring scent of lilies!

So new is the illusion as yet, so fresh this vision of dreams under the spell of white loveliness, that it passes unscathed through the fires of lust:

There with the women, haggard, painted, and old,
One fresh bud in a garland withered and stale,
She, with her innocent voice and her clear eyes, told
Tale after shameless tale.

And ever the witching smile, to her face beguiled,
Paused and broadened, and broke in a ripple of fun,
And the soul of a child looked out of the eyes of a child,
Or ever the tale was done.

The illusion is fair and wonderful; it revels in sweet fragrances and the unforgettable odours of shaken hair; even the artificiality of this desired beauty, its falsities of rouge and pearl-powder, seem but a touch of added spice to make its allurement more pungent. What though he who observes and translates this beauty into rhymes knows that it is only illusion? and what though he who reads and for a while surrenders himself to its sweet intoxication knows it is only illusion? Because the watcher in his real heart penetrates this illusion and knows that it must so soon slip back into the hideous reality, into the painted and haggard ugliness of the flesh that is only flesh and grows old, therefore he feels a greater tenderness for this "frail duration of a flower," and a wistfulness deeper than comes to one who has something of his own spiritual hope to throw over the vanishing loveliness. He is touched by the foreboding of "the little plaintive smile"—

And those pathetic eyes of hers;
But all the London footlights know
The little plaintive smile that stirs
The shadow in those eyes of hers.

And joined with this tenderness for what must pass away, there is an undercurrent of regret for his own joys that endure so little a space; there is even now, while dreams are the only reality to him, a troublous suspicion rising at intervals that the substance is slipping from his grasp, and this suspicion deepens

his regret for the actual past into regret for the evanescent
present shadow of things,—

> We are two ghosts that had their chance to live,
> And lost it, she and I.

The poignancy of this tenderness and regret is something a
little different from the sigh that runs through so much poetry
for passing things; it is the result of a foreboding, half welcome,
half dreaded, that the illusion of this beauty is a treachery, a
snare set by some unseen tempter to hold a man from his true
happiness. More than once Mr. Symons compares this illusion
to the smile of Leonardo's Mona Lisa, whose haunted meaning
no man, unless it be perhaps Walter Pater, has ever interpreted:

> Your smile is like a treachery,
> A treachery adorable;
> So smiles the siren where the sea
> Sings to the unforgetting shell.
>
> .   .   .   .
>
> Close lips that keep the secret in,
> Half spoken by the stealthy eyes,
> Is there indeed no word to win,
> No secret, from the vague replies
>
> .   .   .   .
>
> Of lips and lids that feign to hide
> That which they feign to render up?
> Is there, in Tantalus' dim cup,
> The shadow of water, nought beside?

The shadow of water, indeed, and nothing more. There lies
the pity of it all. Suppose the thirsty watcher of the play suddenly becomes aware that the pageant is insubstantial shadows, and that the cup of this world's delight which he longs to
raise to his lips is empty and holds only the shadow of water
—what then? And suppose that the watcher has no desire in
his heart save this one desire of the world's delight—what
then? That is the terrible disillusion of the flesh, a cruel mock-

ery of the true awakening; and for the man on whom it falls
—as it must some day fall on every man of insight, either the
false disillusion or the true awakening—there is nothing left
but the endless rage of endeavour to hold fast an illusion which
no longer deceives, or the sullen apathy of despair, or the
unthinking submission to his ever coarsening appetites. You
will hear the first note of this coming disillusion in the inevitable cry of satiety:

> For us the roses are scarce sweet,
> And scarcely swift the flying feet
> Where masque to masque the moments call;
>
> All has been ours that we desired,
> And now we are a little tired
> Of the eternal carnival.

With this word of weariness we pass from the book of *Silhouettes* to the *London Nights*, published only three years
later, and the change is as marked as it is significant. On the
light illusion, the shimmering web of dreams that spun themselves almost of their own accord, begins to fall the lengthen-
ing shadows of the actual world. The transient note of satiety
becomes more persistent, and an ever greater effort of the will
is required lest the fluttering curtain of illusion be blown away
and so discover the naked reality which the watcher dreads to
behold. The watcher begins to grow conscious that he is himself a part of that nature, weary a little and saddened by the
satiety which must continue—for how long?—its dance of
forced gayety.

> My life is like a music-hall,
> Where, in the impotence of rage,
> Chained by enchantment to my stall,
> I see myself upon the stage
> Dance to amuse a music-hall.
>
> .   .   .   .   .   .
> My very self that turns and trips,
> Painted, pathetically gay,

An empty song upon the lips
In make-believe of holiday:
I, I, this thing that turns and trips!

What we have to observe now is this "impotence of rage" spending itself in the effort to preserve the fading illusion, or at least to save some part of that illusion's pleasure. To accomplish this all the colours must be heightened and all the emotions sharpened, though by doing so the very daintiness and subtlety of impressions which formed the fascination of the illusion are stript away and the deprecated end is hastened.

Ah! no oblivion, for I feel
Your lips deliriously steal
Along my neck, and fasten there;
I feel the perfume of your hair,
I feel your breast that heaves and dips
Desiring my desirous lips,
And that ineffable delight
When souls turn bodies . . .

Yet even here we are far from the simple passion of the flesh, the passion, for example, of Catullus for his Lesbia, in which there is no talk of souls that turn into bodies but only the natural cry of a man of strong animal appetites and strong unperverted intellect. The morbidness and decadence of Mr. Symons's verse are shown, indeed, in this very hankering after food which to suit a jaded appetite must be unwholesomely spiced with appeals to what is called the soul. He shrinks instinctively from the outright passion of a Catullus, and chooses instead—what?

"Love is a raging fire,
Choose thou content instead;
Thou, the child of the dust,
Choose thou a delicate Lust."
"Thou hast chosen," I said
To the angel of pale desire.

In this same way he cannot pause to find comfort in the homely associations of a love that is less a passion than a quiet haven from the vexations of life. You will find in these volumes nothing corresponding, for example, to the gentle verses of Tibullus counting up the treasures of his love and pastoral content while the morning rain washes on the roof. On the contrary you will find an artificial passion which requires every conceivable stimulus to preserve it from passing into sheer disgust:

> Pallid out of the darkness, adorably white,
> Pale as the spirit of rain, with the night in her hair,
> Renée undulates, shadow-like, under the light,
> Into the outer air.
>
> Mournful, beautiful, calm with that vague unrest,
> Sad with sensitive, vaguely ironical mouth;
> Eyes a-flame with the loveliest, deadliest
> Fire of passionate youth;
>
> Mournful, beautiful, sister of night and rain,
> Elemental, fashioned of tears and fire,
> Ever desiring, ever desired in vain,
> Mother of vain desire.

The morbid unrest that troubles this pallid hot-house flower is the attraction most of all sought by the watcher—anything to break the monotony of the awakening which to him is death. Even the sense of shame is welcomed if only it will lend a little poignancy to this desire that grows chill, if only it will for a moment continue the illusion that something in the watcher stands apart from the play and is above it:

> I too have sought on many a breast
> The ecstasy of an unrest,
> I too have had my dreams, and met
> (Ah me!) how many a Juliet.
>   .   .   .   .   .   .
> O lost and wrecked, how long ago,
> Out of the drowning past, I know

> You come to call me, come to claim
> My share of your delicious shame.

And shame at least is ready at hand. Out of this ecstasy of unrest, this morbid curiosity, this terror of satiety, there does spring at last a love that is genuine in its way, a pale amorphous passion, for one whom he calls Bianca. It is a love the telling of which haunts the imagination (so, indeed, it was meant to do) as something not of this world or the other, a thing unclean not with the taint of the untroubled body, but of the body that tortures itself maddeningly to escape from its own insufficiency and masquerade as the soul.

> So the simplicity of flesh
> Held me a moment in its mesh,
> Till that too palled, and I began
> To find that man is mostly man
> In that, his will being sated, he
> Wills ever new variety.
> And then I found you, Bianca! Then
> I found in you, I found again
> That chance or will or fate had brought
> The curiosity I sought.
> Ambiguous child, whose life retires
> Into the pulse of those desires
> Of whose endured possession speaks
> The passionate pallor of your cheeks;
> Child, in whom neither good nor ill
> Can sway your sick and swaying will,
> Only the aching sense of sex
> Wholly controls, and does perplex,
> With dubious drifts scarce understood,
> The shaken currents of your blood;
> It is your ambiguity
> That speaks to me and conquers me.

And the conclusion of the tale is this—"So Bianca satisfies my soul!" It is better to draw the veil of silence over this scene of painfully-won illusion. There are things it were good for a man, even for a decadent poet, not to have written, and these poems to Bianca, with their tortuous effort to find the soul in the ambiguities and unclean curiosities of a swaying will are of them. They are a waste of shame.

The outcome of such an "ecstasy of unrest" is not difficult to foresee, and is the theme of the two following books of the collection, *Amoris Victima* and *Images of Good and Evil.* When the illusion is dispelled, when the ambiguity is found to be merely a deception of the flesh and the curiosity has spent itself in a vain endeavour to discern what does not exist, what can remain but the desolation of emptiness?

> Was not our love fatal to you and me?
> The rapture of a tragic ecstasy
> Between disaster and disaster, given
> A moment's space, to be a hell in heaven?
>
> .   .   .   .   .   .
>
> Hearken, I hear a voice, a voice that calls;
> What shall remain for him? sadly it cries:
> Desolate years, eternal memories.

And so the first poems in this book which he calls *Amoris Victima* are filled with regrets that at least come nearer than any others in the collection to showing the agony of a genuine passion broken and defeated by some infirmity of the lover's will:

> I am weary of living, and I long to be at rest
> From the sorrowful and immense fatigue of love;
> I have lived and loved with a seeking, passionate zest,
> And weariness and defeat are the end thereof.
>
> I have lived in vain, I have loved in vain, I have lost
> In the game of Fate, and silently I retire;
> I watch the moon rise over the sea, a ghost
> Of burning noontides, pallid with spent desire.

But this sigh of passionate regret for what seems the loss of a real happiness is but a transient note of honest self-deception. What follows is the bitter cry of the long struggle, resumed

half-heartedly, between illusion and disillusion. I do not wish
to dwell at length on this struggle, for it is not entirely pleasant
reading, however great its psychological interest may be.
Through it all runs the memory of the past, but a memory of
shame and not of simple regret:

> O rapture of lost days, all that remains
> Is but this fever aching in my veins.
>
> I do not know you under this disguise:
> I am degraded by my memories.

The thoughts that follow such memories are to the poet like
hideous Harpyes, beaked and taloned, that gather about him
in the darkness of his soul. And the desires that torture him are
the cruel voice of the flesh from which all illusion has been torn
away, save the persistent denial of relief that makes of their
disillusion a mere mockery of the true awakening:

> Ah! in those shell-curved, purple eyelids bent
> Towards some most dolorous accomplishment,
> And in the painful patience of the mouth,
> (A sundered fruit that waits, in a great drouth,
> One draught of living water from the skies)
> And in the carnal mystery of the eyes,
> And in the burning pallor of the cheeks;
> Voice of the Flesh! this is the voice that speaks
> In agony of spirit, or in grief
> Because desire dare not desire relief.

In the ocean of these degrading memories, haunting
thoughts, and impuissant desires, the poor soul (let us call it
soul) of the poet is tossed alternately from the exaltation of
terror to the depths of indifferent despair. He learns at last that
"to have fallen through dreams is to have touched hell!" As
with King Richard dreaming on Bosworth Field, shadowy images rising from what has been and clamorous of what is to be,
torment him with a power greater than any reality of life. The
body and substance of this terror is a vision of emptiness, of the

dark void, that must swallow up the watcher when the growing disillusion is made complete:

> And something, in the old and little voice,
> Calls from so farther off than far away,
> I tremble, hearing it, lest it draw me forth,
> This flickering self, desiring to be gone,
> Into the boundless and abrupt abyss
> Whereat begins infinity; and there
> This flickering self wander eternally
> Among the soulless, uncreated winds
> Which storm against the barriers of the world.

It is not strange that this outcast self should make the whole
world of God to be a shadow of its own mood, and that this
mood should assume the likeness of insomnia:

> Who said the world is but a mood
> In the eternal thought of God?
> I know it, real though it seem,
> The phantom of a haschisch dream
> In that insomnia which is God.

There, I think, is the last word to distinguish this false awakening from the true. From such an agony of insomnia there can
be but one relief, the repose of utter oblivion and the escape
from self in perfect death. Such in the end and nothing else is
the pleading cry of the disillusioned watcher.

But again this paroxysm of rebellion spends itself in a little
time, and in its place comes the sigh of lonely indifference and
impotence. And I know not which of these alternating moods
should remain as the last impression of this tragic history.
"There are grey hours when I drink of indifference," he says;
and "all things fade Into the grey of a twilight that covers my
soul with its sky." And again: "The loneliness of the sea is in my
heart, And the wind is not more lonely than this grey mind."
All the wonted rapture of the world fades into the grey of this
impotent listlessness:

> The clamours of spring are the same old delicate noises,
> The earth renews its magical youth at a breath,
> And the whole world whispers a well-known, secret thing;
> And I hear, but the meaning has faded out of the voices;
> Something has died in my heart: is it death or sleep?
> I know not, but I have forgotten the meaning of spring.

Always while reading these poems, which are the first full and sincere expression of decadence in English, with their light and fair illusion passing gradually into the terror of disillusion, I have heard running through my memory three lines of old John Ford which contain the very essence of the right illusion of art (for art, as we have seen, has its true and necessary illusion of joy as well as this false illusion of sadness); and involuntarily these lines would sound out as an echo or counter-tone to the painfulness of Mr. Symons's lament. They are like a breath of fresh air let into a murky chamber:

> Since my coming home I've found
> More sweets in one unprofitable dream
> Than in my life's whole pilgrimage.

There would be a world of significance in comparing this "coming home" with the wandering of that "flickering self" in the void places of despair.

And yet I would not leave the word despair as the last comment on these poems, which, no matter what their sadness and morbidity may be, stand quite apart from the ordinary versifying of the day. They have, whatever may be said, a great psychological interest for one who is curious to study the currents of modern thought. Mr. Symons impresses us as being absolutely sincere, as being the only genuine and adequate representative in English of that widespread condition which we call decadence. And sincerity in verse is a quality of inestimable value. But more than that: these poems are now and again so instinct with original perception of beauty and so lilted with cadences of sweetness, as to be remarkable in themselves apart from their psychological interest. Toward the end of the second volume, and in the little book of recent poems that close the collection, there forces its way at times, through the turbulent cries of dull desires and stinging regrets, a recurrent note of the first simple delight in nature,—a note which one would gladly accept as prophetic of a new life to arise out of the tragedy of despair. The repose for which the poet sighs in this last poem I would quote, is at least a better and more wholesome thing than the impious oblivion of his earlier craving:

REST

> The peace of a wandering sky,
> Silence, only the cry
> Of the crickets, suddenly still,
> A bee on the window-sill,
> A bird's wing, rushing and soft,
> Three flails that tramp in the loft,
> Summer murmuring
> Some sweet, slumberous thing,
> Half asleep; but thou, cease,
> Heart, to hunger for peace,
> Or, if thou must find rest,
> Cease to beat in my breast.

[1] It would be difficult to overestimate the importance of this essay for anyone desiring to have an understanding of More. The doctrine of *illusion* in More is, like that of the *imagination*, subordinate only to the two major conceptions dominating his writing, that of *dualism* and *teleologism*. It also reveals the influence that his studies in Hindu literature had on his thought. It is for this reason that the essay is placed third among the papers of this second section, after the summary statements of his critical principles. The essay first appeared under the title, "Arthur Symons, the Poetry of Illusion and Disillusion," in the *Independent*, April 17, 1902, and then was included in the First Series of *Shelburne Essays* (1904). It is strange that neither More nor anyone else has seen fit to reprint since.

Pope [1]

After all this, it is surely superfluous to answer the question that has once been asked, whether Pope was a poet, otherwise than by asking in return, If Pope be not a poet, where is poetry to be found? To circumscribe poetry by a definition will only show the narrowness of the definer, though a definition which shall exclude Pope will not easily be made.

When Dr. Johnson handed down that famous decision he had no means of foreseeing, and indeed would not have cared to see, the great romantic revival which was to ask a good many times whether Pope was a poet, and was to circumscribe poetry with innumerable definitions. Even so cautious and classical a critic as Matthew Arnold was reduced by his Wordsworthian fervour into saying that, "though they may write in verse, though they may in a certain sense be masters of the art of versification, Dryden and Pope are not classics of our poetry, they are classics of our prose." Probably the majority of readers of verse to-day, certainly the lagging "official critics," still talk of Pope in an offhand way as a great writer, perhaps, but as at bottom scarcely a poet at all. Yet there are signs that the sounder taste of the present, grown a little weary of the old romantic presumptions, borrowed from Germany, is tending rather to a truer estimate of the neo-classic school. A pleasant witness of this returning sanity may be found in the new life of Pope by Miss Symonds, [2] whose measured judgement shows by its very lack of originality—I mean nothing disparaging by the phrase—the new set of the tide. In the end criticism is

likely to settle down on the sentence of Joseph Warton, himself
one of the forerunners of romanticism: "In that species of
poetry wherein Pope excelled, he is superior to all mankind;
and I only say that this species of poetry is not the most excellent one of the art."

No doubt the character of the poet and the indecorous
squabbles in which his life was passed have had something to
do with the critical obloquy that has occasionally fallen upon
him. If you wish to hear the worst of him—and it is pretty bad
—you have only to read Professor Lounsbury's learned work,
in which the quarrel between Pope and Theobald over the
Text of Shakespeare is made the excuse for raking together half
the scandalous doings of the little bard.[3] Professor Lounsbury,
as an eminent and honest scholar, may show just a touch of
partiality for the able editor and poor poet against the slovenly
editor and great poet, but, with the best of allowances, his
exposition of Pope's treacheries and endless machinations
leaves the would-be moralist a sorry figure to contemplate.
Well, let us admit that in stooping to Truth, as he boasted, Pope
showed rather a magnificent contempt for the prosaic precepts of that goddess. As a claimant on eternity he was ready
to treat the periods of passing time most cavalierly, antedating
and postdating his satirical thrusts quite as it suited him. His
success in getting his correspondence published against his will
is perhaps the finest piece of double-dealing recorded in the
annals of literature. His ways with women were peevish or
bullying as occasion demanded, and his gallantries are with
difficulty separated from his slanders. All this can be admitted,
yet much is left to be said on the other side. Wit was a recognized warfare in those days, and the honours went too often
to the ablest and not to the most honourable; but the reverse
is also true that dishonour has now overtaken Pope, not because he was more treacherous than his rivals, but because he
was cleverer—time is likely to take this revenge on a man for
lying too successfully. Nor was Pope altogether without a sense
of rectitude in the warfare of wit. In an age of pensions and
time-serving, he remained true to a losing religious and politi-

cal creed. If, as seems probable, he for some reason accepted a thousand pounds from the Duchess of Marlborough, and then left for publication after his death a satire which he must have known would be applied to that lady, against the discredit of such a stroke must be balanced the fact that he refused to insert a flattering mention of Alderman Barber in his verse at the price of four or five thousand pounds. As the world goes, I count the credit here above the debit. And at any rate the dæmonic Duchess, if she read the lines and paid for their suppression, thereby acknowledged the strength of the satire, or, if she could have seen them only after her own slanderous *Characters* were posthumously printed, would have vailed to one who fought with her own weapons, and more dexterously, in the duel of politics and wit:

> But what are these to great Atossa's mind?
> Scarce once herself, by turns all womankind!
> Who, with herself, or others, from her birth
> Finds all her life one warfare upon earth:
> Shines in exposing knaves, and painting fools,
> Yet is whate'er she hates and ridicules. . . .

Outside of that warfare Pope had his admirable traits. His filial piety was scarcely less beautiful because he made poetical capital of it. His friendship, barring the grievous and deplorable feud with Addison, was with his real rivals to fame; and the correspondence of these men, though its frank moralizing may sometimes offend an age grown dull to the distinction between reflection and affectation, is one of the great documents of human nature. When Pope lay "dying of a hundred good symptoms," he said to the priest, after taking the last sacraments: "There is nothing that is meritorious but virtue and friendship, and indeed friendship itself is only a part of virtue." It was indeed so accounted to him. Warburton, possibly as much to affront the world as to elevate Pope, called him "one of the noblest works of God, . . . an honest man." And Spence, in his anecdotes of Pope's last moments and of Bolingbroke's tenderness, raises their friendship into something almost as beautiful as the faith that gave sanctity to the death-bed scenes of the previous century. No rearrangement can better the seeming disorder of Spence's memoranda:

> There is so much trouble in coming into the world, and so much uneasiness in going out of it, that—it is hardly worth [His Lordship's melancholy attitude that morning (the 21st), leaning against Mr. Pope's chair, and crying over him for a considerable time with more concern than can be expressed.]
>
> Ah! great God, what is man?—*The same.* [Looking on Mr. Pope, and repeating it several times, interrupted with sobs.]
>
> When I was telling his Lordship that Mr. Pope, on every catching and recovering of his mind, was always saying something kindly either of his present or absent friends, and that this in some cases was so surprising, that it seemed to me as if his humanity had outlived his understanding, Lord Bolingbroke said, "it has so!" and then added, "I never in my life knew a man that had so tender a heart for his particular friends, or a more general friendship for mankind."
>
> I have known him these thirty years, and value myself more for that man's love and friendship, than——(sinking his head, and losing his voice in tears.)—*The same.*[5]

It is well to keep this picture in mind when we read of the dark ways of Pope's wit. When all is said we come back to the estimate of Chesterfield, who knew mankind both in general and in particular better than most others of his age. "Pope," he declared, "was as great an instance as any he quotes of the contrarieties and inconsistencies of human nature; for notwithstanding the malignity of his satires, and some blamable passages in his life, he was charitable to his power, active in doing good offices, and piously attentive to an old bedridden mother."

I suspect that Pope's detractors for the most part would be indifferent enough to the blamable passages of his life—for it needs a rare literary detective to trace his winding course—were it not that his greatest poems have become to them what Johnson called one of his letters, "nothing but tedious malignity." The problem to-day is not so much to rehabilitate Pope's personal character—a dubious task—as to explain why his very greatness as a poet has aroused so much resentment; and the first step to this end is to make clear to ourselves wherein his greatness really lies. There are, of course, aspects of his work which ought to appeal to all lovers of verse without distinction, and which need no defence. Mr. Courthope, for instance, has made a strong case for the variety and beauty of the heroic measure in his hands; and it is certainly a dull taste that will not respond to the sweet felicity of that couplet in the *Rape of the Lock:*

> The meeting points the sacred hair dissever
> From the fair head—for ever and for ever;

or that will not feel the passion of Eloisa's solitary cry:

> Shrines! where their vigils pale-eyed virgins keep,
> And pitying saints, whose statues learn to weep!
> Though cold like you, unmoved and silent grown,
> I have not yet forgot myself to stone;

or admire the justness of that simile of the scholar's progress, which Dr. Johnson thought "perhaps the best that English poetry can show":

> So pleased at first the towering Alps we try,
> Mount o'er the vales, and seem to tread the sky,
> The eternal snows appear already passed,
> And the first clouds and mountains seem the last:
> But, those attain'd, we tremble to survey
> The growing labours of the lengthen'd way,
> The increasing prospect tires our wandering eyes,
> Hills peep o'er hills, and Alps on Alps arise!

But dexterously wrought as such gems may be, we shall have a feeble case for Pope if we rest his claims on work in this *genre;* magnificent as it is, it lacks the glamour, the last touch of magic, which even the little poets of another school could command in isolated passages. You will read through the meanderings of William Chamberlain's *Pharonnida*, lost in a tedious wonder at its aimless involutions, when suddenly you will be arrested by a far vista like this:

> Farewell, Florenza! when both time and place
> My separated soul hath left, to be
> A *stranger masked in immortality*,
> Think on thy murthered friend.

You will say that these outlooks into the skies were closed when Pope began to reign. Or you will pause in the elegies of Katherine Philips at such a couplet as this:

> A chosen privacy, a cheap content,
> And all the peace a friendship ever lent.

Pope wrote much, and well, of friendship, but just that note of contented unworldliness he never quite felt, or never sang. In the same way Pope has many brilliant descriptions of nature, but a single line of Thomas Tickell (his contemporary, whose translation of the first book of the *Iliad*, under Addison's care, was the source of a veritable Iliad of woes) will stir a chord of human sentiment that the poet of *Windsor Forest* could never touch:

> Brown fields their fallow sabbaths keep.

By his very supremacy as master of the new school Pope lost what Chamberlain calls

> the fantastic clew
> To a delight, which doth in labyrinths sit,
> None e'er beheld while they preserved their wit.

No one, I think, would be so narrow-minded as to rank Chamberlain or Katherine Philips or Thomas Tickell above Pope, yet to reach a fair estimate of Pope's greatness we must begin by admitting that even in these minor writers there is an occasional glimpse of divine mysteries of whose existence Pope seems not even to have dreamed. If this were all there could be no gainsaying those who deny him the title of poet altogether. But it is by no means all, and there are other large fields of the imagination which the romantic poets closed to us. Pope, as a matter of fact, has been dethroned as much for his great positive qualities as for his deficiencies. Admirers of Pope, therefore, are likely to feel a touch of impatience at the extravagant praise so often bestowed upon *The Rape of the Lock*, as if his consummate success in this filagree of the mock-heroic should be held up as an excuse for his failure in the more serious style. There is only one honest way to deal with him; we must treat him squarely as the poet of satire, and, unfortunately for his fame, the world has come to regard satire as scarcely poetry at all. If it is not poetry, then, indeed, Pope was but the fragment of a poet. There are, of course, special reasons why such a satire as the *Dunciad*, which by reason of its size and scope comes first to mind, should find few and painful readers. All great poems, even those most universal in their human appeal, require a fairly high-developed historic sense for their appreciation, and it is idle to suppose that the *AEneid* will mean much to those who have not trained themselves to live in the Latin world, or that *Paradise Lost* can ever be interesting except to the scholar. No long poem of the past is really popular; but the *Dunciad* demands for its comprehension an altogether exorbitant acquaintance with men and manners of a brief particular period. Thus, at the beginning of the second book, the hero is raised to his proud eminence of dulness:

> High on a gorgeous seat, that far outshone
> Henley's gilt tub, or Flecknoe's Irish throne,
> Or that where on her Curlls the public pours
> All-bounteous, fragrant grains and golden showers,
> Great Cibber sate.

It is excellent satire and parody combined, but without footnotes the allusions will fall pointless to all save those who are
deep in the recondite frivolities of the age.

And even after the necessary minute knowledge has been
acquired—and to the scholar this local habitation and name of
the *Dunciad* may have a special though somewhat artificial
attraction—there remains the fact that the current of historic
sympathy has set strongly away from Pope, and that most of
us in our hearts are stung by his ridicule as were his living
enemies. For that battle of the wits was no causeless or merely
bookish event, but was part of the great political war of the
land. It grew inevitably out of the ruinous divisions, as it
echoed the drums and tramplings, of the previous century; and
if ink now flowed instead of blood, the contest was hardly the
less venomous for that, or the consequences less serious. It all
goes back to that terrible mischance which in the days of the
Stuarts divided the imagination and the practical sense of England into irreconcilable camps, and separated the loyalty to
symbols of authority so far from the actualities of force. That
separation kept its character through the following century, if
it has not continued down to this day. Bolingbroke's vision of
the Patriot King was a reassumption of the faith of the Cavaliers, and as it was a product of the imagination divorced of
practical sense, we see its working out in the follies of George
III and the loss of an empire. Walpole's policy was essentially
a continuation of the empire of Cromwell, and as it failed to
make a place for the imagination in its practice, we see the
result in the gradual lowering of England's ideal life. At the
beginning of the eighteenth century England was the intellectual leader of Europe; at the end she followed at a distance. I
know of no more distressing fact in her history than the situation which, at the critical moment of 1714, set almost all the
notable men of letters on the losing side—all of them, I should
say, with the exception of Addison and Steele, for Defoe at
least served Harley and fell with him. Consider the consequences to literature of the coming of the Hanoverians: Harley

himself imprisoned and tried for his head; Bolingbroke frightened out of the country; Atterbury exiled; Swift confined to
Dublin; Parnell also kept in Ireland; Pope cut off from political
life and retired to Twickenham; Gay nursing the insult of an
offer to be gentleman-usher to the infant Princess Louisa; Prior
imprisoned for two years, and then sinking to a frowsy degradation; Arbuthnot removed from St. James's, and at the end
writing to Pope his pathetic plea for euthanasia. It was with no
mere poetic licence that Pope painted the new sovereignty:

> She mounts the throne: her head a cloud conceal'd,
> In broad effulgence all below reveal'd
> ('T is thus aspiring Dulness ever shines);
> Soft on her lap her Laureate son reclines.
> Beneath her footstool Science groans in chains,
> *And Wit dreads exile, penalties, and pains.*

There is personal spite aplenty in the *Dunciad,* innumerable
strokes of vicious retaliation and wanton offense—these faults
cannot be severed from the character of the author; but
beneath these motives of personal satire we shall miss the
whole meaning of the poem if we fail to see the passionate
warfare of the losing party of wit against the triumphant party
of practical common-sense. Picture to yourself one of the din-
ners at Lord Oxford's, the guests that met there and what they
stood for, or call up one of the more intimate companies in the
apartments of that great talker and gourmand, Dr. Arbuthnot,
at St. James's, and in comparison with these think of what
passed in the palace of George I and his son, or even in the
chambers of Caroline, and what these things meant to letters.
There is no doubt much to admire in the society that Caroline
affected, and an evening at St. James's, when the Queen and
perhaps Mrs. Clayton drew out the conversation of Berkeley
or Clarke or Butler is one of the things I like best to contemplate in those days, even though, as Chesterfield and Horace
Walpole unite in saying, the mistress of the palace only bewildered herself in metaphysical disputes which she did not com-

prehend. But the master of the palace, like his own master, Sir Robert, had, I know, "a contempt for *Belles Lettres*, which he called trifling," and the Queen herself, I remember, in place of the poets she frowned upon or neglected, showered her favours upon the sad thresher-poet, Stephen Duck, whom she made librarian of her grotto "Merlin's Cave," in Richmond Gardens. George called the grotto "silly stuff"; what he thought of the poor favourite who was patronized to suicide, I do not know. In the contrast of Queen Anne's reign with that of the Hanoverians lies the real meaning of the *Dunciad*, and therein is the excuse for its bitterness. The pity of it is that politically, at least as we contemplate affairs within a narrow range of years, the Hanoverians were right, and as they seem to us right, we are drawn away from sympathy, even of a literary sort, with the satire that exposed the intellectual bareness of the land.

But there is still a deeper cause of our distaste than the old echoes of faction and our political incompatibility. A great change has come upon us in our attitude towards human nature itself, and, curiously enough, Pope himself is one of the prime movers of this revolution which has carried us away from the very comprehension of his own principal works. For there is this strange paradox in the philosophy of Pope. On the one hand, we have his contemptuous treatment of mankind, as if his satires were no more than a long development of the text of Machiavelli that "all men are caitive [*cattivi*, captive to the base impulses of egotism], and are ever ready to use the malignity of their spirit, when they have free opportunity." On the other hand, in his *Essay on Man*, inspired by the dubious optimism of his friend Bolingbroke, we have the deistic conception of the world as the best possible creation and of men as naturally altruistic in desire and as needing only liberty from restraint to develop into unselfishness of action:

> All nature is but art, unknown to thee;
> All chance, direction, which thou can'st not see;
> All discord, harmony not understood;

> All partial evil, universal good:
> And, spite of pride, in erring reason's spite,
> One truth is clear, Whatever is, is right.

And deism, which, be it noted, was the express theme of the
philosophers and divines who hung upon the court of Caroline,
won the day, altering our whole conception of society and our
manner of judging the individual. We have in the course of the
last two hundred years acquired a kind of tenderness for
humanity, which causes us to shrink from the old theological
notion of absolute evil in the world, and also from the literature of the moralists which was based on the same belief. With
this tenderness, if it be not the source of the feeling, our individual sensitiveness has increased enormously, so that we take
in a quite personal way the attacks of moralist and satirist on
mankind in general. We can listen to the singing of the still sad
music of humanity with a delicate self-pity, but from the philosophy of a Rochefoucauld or a Machiavelli we start back as
if a hand were laid on a concealed sore. It is certainly true that
he who has imbibed deeply this modern humanitarianism with
its fashion of mutual flattery, will be repelled from the literature of which Pope's satires are so perfect an example; in those
attacks on the meanness and folly and dulness and venality of
the world he will suffer a kind of uneasiness, and, taking his
revenge by decrying them as a base form of art, will turn for
consolation to what Cowper calls the

> charity that soothes a lie,
> And thrusts the truth with scorn and anger by.

I would not say that Machiavelli expressed the whole truth,
any more than did the deists, but it may as well be recognized
that, without some lingering suspicion of the eternal deceitful-
ness of the heart and some malicious glee in the unveiling of
the deceit, no man shall feel at home in the old battle of the
wits. Only the absence of that suspicion and glee can account,
I think, for the common apathy towards Pope's masterpiece,

the *Epistle to Dr. Arbuthnot*, which is at once the prologue and the consummation of his satires.

For myself I will admit frankly that I have read the *Epistle* oftener, perhaps, than any other English poem except *Lycidas*, and that long familiarity with its lines has given me always a deepening admiration for its art. If it is not poetry, I do not know where poetry is to be found. That Pope's inspiration moves on a lower plane than Milton's—though his art is as flawless—I should be the last to deny. Yet in a way their themes, despite the great difference of their age and faith, have unexpected points of contact. Milton, like the poet of Queen Anne, wrote in the heat of battle, and with him, too, *fecit indignatio versus.*[6] He was moved by a sublime rage against those who, as he believed, were degrading the Church and fattening on her spiritual poverty, against the blind mouths who, for their bellies' sake, were creeping into the fold, and against their lean and flashy songs. In contrast to this contagion he draws in a picture the true beauty and peace of the shepherd's trade, and the sweet companionship of those who walk therein, singing together their eager Doric lays, as it were an image and foretaste of the heavenly societies and of the unexpressive nuptial song.

The gap from Milton's theme to Pope's may seem complete, yet in reality one is the true successor of the other, and nothing can better show the mischievous confusion resulting from the division in the Stuart days than the fact that the practical party which Milton represented—so far as he can be said to have represented anybody but himself—was now the people of Dulness, while the party of the imagination, as we see it in the writings of Swift and Pope, was divested of all the magnificences of morality. Yet if the *Epistle to Dr. Arbuthnot* lacks Milton's mighty impulse of religion and draws from lower springs of Helicon, it still has its great compensations. The indignation is as terrible, if its causes are more mixed. Here, even more ruinously than in the *Dunciad,* and without the longer poem's tediousness of obscure detail, the dreaded secret is revealed—

That secret to each fool, that he's an ass.

We may doubt what was the exact nature of that two-handed engine which Milton suspended against the enemies of Puritanism, but there is nothing ambiguous about the revenge of Pope, whether with one blade he hews down his open enemies or with the other attacks his pretended friends. From the opening appeal to the poet's old and faithful servant:

> Shut, shut the door, good John! fatigued I said;
> Tie up the knocker, say I'm sick, I'm dead.
> The Dog-star rages! nay, 't is past a doubt,
> All Bedlam, or Parnassus, is let out:
> Fire in each eye, and papers in each hand,
> They rave, recite, and madden round the land—

to the last fling at the hypocrites:

> One from all Grub-street will my fame defend,
> And, more abusive, calls himself my friend—

there mis a succession of lines of almost dazzling wit, and every line a stab. Thackeray, as the father of Pendennis and the half-ironical patron of the Grub Street of his own day, has some pretty words of abuse upon Pope for fixing in the public mind this notion of the snarling, starving attic-world of authorship. No doubt Pope has touched up the picture with high lights, but an acquaintance with the lesser literature of the day, and with the periodicals, not omitting Pope's own blackguardly *Grub Street Journal*, gives all the justification needed for the portrait. And here again we shall miss the point if we take this fury as purely personal. There were principles involved, though Pope himself, I dare say, never really knew the difference between his principles and his spite. Something more than personal hatred envenoms the deadly caricature of Lord Hervey and the desire to "flap this bug with gilded wings." With the culmination of the satire,

> Or at the ear of Eve, familiar toad,

should be read Jonathan Richardson's comment:

> I have heard that this lord had actually a seat managed be-
> hind the queen's hunting chaise, where he sat perched behind
> her close at her ear, but he could never stand it above three or
> four times. Besides the ridicule of his friends, folks hooted at
> him as the machine passed along.

The real animus of the attack is the relation of Hervey to
Caroline and the Hanoverian court, and all that this meant to
the intellectual and imaginative life of England. This, too, must
be the palliation for the portrait of Addison, though it may
scarcely excuse the author's shiftiness in regard to the date of
writing and publishing the lines. They must be quoted:

> Peace to all such! but were there one whose fires
> True genius kindles, and fair fame inspires;
> Blest with each talent, and each art to please,
> And born to write, converse, and live with ease:
> Should such a man, too fond to rule alone,
> Bear, like the Turk, no brother near the throne,
> View him with scornful, yet with jealous eyes,
> And hate for arts that caused himself to rise;
> Damn with faint praise, assent with civil leer,
> And, without sneering, teach the rest to sneer;
> Willing to wound, and yet afraid to strike,
> Just hint a fault, and hesitate dislike;
> Alike reserved to blame, or to commend,
> A timorous foe, and a suspicious friend;
> Dreading e'en fools, by flatters besieged,
> And so obliging, that he ne'er obliged;
> Like Cato, give his little senate laws,
> And sit attentive to his own applause;
> While wits and Templars every sentence raise,
> And wonder with a foolish face of praise—
> Who but must laugh, if such a man there be?
> Who would not weep, if Atticus were he!

Of the exquisite finish of these verses there can, I suppose, be no question, unless De Quincey's frivolous criticism is to be listened to. The other day, while they were fresh in my memory, a friend of mine who loves and gathers beautiful things was showing me his collection of Japanese swordguards; and as I looked at those wonderfully wrought plates of steel and considered their ancient place on the instruments of battle, it occurred to me that their craftsmanship was not unlike that which had gone into the making of this detached masterpiece of words. And it seemed to me that the rectitude and patience of the work in each case was one of the causes of their perpetual charm. I have a prejudice in favor of genius, an invincible feeling that true art is in some way based on truth. And so, whether this portrait of Addison was written, as Warburton declares, in 1815, because the Earl of Warwick, Addison's stepson, had warned Pope of Addison's jealousy and of his instigation of Gildon to publish a scurrilous pamphlet against his supposed friend, or because Pope believed Addison to be responsible for Tickell's rival translation of the *Iliad*, whatever may have been the devious ways of Pope in explaining and spreading abroad the satire—I am convinced that the portrait was not entirely without similitude. In some way the jealousies of Addison's trade had set free the deceitful spirit of egotism that hides beneath the fairest character. It must be remembered also that in the year when the satire was written, and when the circle of Pope was suffering in so many ways from the death of Queen Anne, Addison, as Chief Secretary to Ireland, was enjoying the fruits of his service to the Whigs. He was, I believe, the only man of great parts in pure literature who profited by the new régime. That, indeed, may be to his credit politically; it will help to explain, nevertheless, why Pope placed him, not among the dunces, for that would have been to stultify the writer, but among those who in the desperate battle of the mind followed the false standard—the one lost leader, when so many lesser and more ignoble men were faithful. I think Pope had loved, and did always admire, Addison. There is the true pathos of wit—and wit may have its tears—

a cry of grief from a very great bitterness and regret in the last line,

> Who would not weep, if Atticus were he!

If the emotion here be not genuine, we may as well shut our bosoms to every appeal of books.

But there is in this satire something besides sorrow for the perversion, or at least the failure, of a noble friend; it must be read in connection with Pope's own feeling of weariness, if not of degradation. By the side of this scorn of the dull and the base, runs the contrasted note of friendship, which was always the finest trait of his character. Nowhere else does he express the union that bound together this body of defeated wits with so fine a charm as in the lines to the genial, much-beloved physician:

> Friend to my life, which did not you prolong,
> The world had wanted many an idle song.

In comparison with that peaceful bond, of what profit was the long-protracted and in the end losing enmity which inspired his satire? What evil genius projected him into this hateful air of conflict?—

> Why did I write? What sin to me unknown
> Dipp'd me in ink, my parents' or my own?

To understand the *Epistle* we must read it as Pope's *apologia pro vita sua*, at once an excuse for the warfare in which his days had passed and an acknowledgement of their waste and bitter fruit. With a kind of childlike and, I think, utterly sincere regret he compares the quiet tenor of his father's life with the discordant ambitions of literature, and counts as the one indisputable blessing to himself the homely respect for that life which he had preserved against all the inroads of the world's malice:

> O friend! May each domestic bliss be thine!
> Be no unpleasing melancholy mine:
> Me, let the tender office long engage,
> To rock the cradle of reposing age,
> With lenient arts extend a mother's breath,
> Make languor smile, and smooth the bed of death,
> Explore the thought, explain the asking eye,
> And keep awhile one parent from the sky!
> On cares like these if length of days attend,
> May Heaven, to bless those days, preserve my friend,
> Preserve him social, cheerful, and serene,
> And just as rich as when he served a queen.

Not Goldsmith himself painted a sweeter picture of resignation and piety; and, whatever else may have been true of Pope, these lines also speak the truth of him.

It may seem that the beauty of these contrasted notes in Pope's greatest poem is lost to the world to-day, because one of them at least, the warfare of the wits, was a temporary thing, now long forgotten and of interest only to the special student. To a certain degree and in the matter of form, this is no doubt the case. Yet the warfare substantially is not ended, and shall not end while the differences of human nature remain unreconciled. Men in this living age, always a few, are still fighting for the rights of the mind against a dull and delusive materialism, for the freedom of the imagination against a prosaic tyranny, for a pure and patient ambition against the quick success of vanity and pliant cleverness, for the reality of human nature against a fatuous self-complacency. To these the triumphant satire of Pope is a perpetual encouragement, while his pathetic apology expresses for them the relief needed when success appears far away, or, even if near, not worth the cost in the humiliating wager of soul against soul. Nor is the theme of the *Epistle* without its more universal aspect. For after all life itself, not for the wit only, but for each man in his place, is a contest, and poetry, from the time when Homer portrayed his heroes battling with sword and fire on the banks of the Simois, and longing for the peace of hearth and kindred and friends across the seas, has been the expression, varying in form and instruments, of that inevitable fate. The presentation of this truth may in Pope be narrowed to a particular manner and time, it may assume ignoble images and speak too often in reprehensible language, nevertheless he who does not respond to the deep emotion and humanity underlying the *Satires* has travelled but a short way into the realm of letters; he has even, I dare assert, felt but a little of the great realities of man's life.

---

1   While More admired Milton and the Puritans of the seventeenth century, he also saw that the Civil War had divided "the imagination and the practical sense of England" into two camps. The triumphant Puritan influence continued into the eighteenth century under Sir Robert Walpole and the Hanoverian monarchs; the other, "the losing party of wit," headed by writers like Swift, Bolinboke, Arthbutnot, Gay, and Pope, fought back with the weapon of satire. The wits tried to keep before mankind the old truth that the human heart was deceitful and malignantly opportunistic; and yet, to counterbalance Puritan sentimentalism, they set up a religion of reason, Deism, which eventually smothered the "old theological notion of absolute evil in the world" with the belief that men needed "only liberty from restraint to develop into unselfishness of action." It was not alone because Pope symbolizes these contradictions that More found him significant, but because something of his "malicious glee" in unveiling deceit and dullness is needed amidst "the welter of humanitarian optimism" and the "clashing extremes of flattery and detraction applied to human nature" in the twentieth century. The essay first appeared in *The Nation* on June 30, 1910, then it was reprinted in the Tenth Series of the *Shelburne Essays (With the Wits)* in 1919. It is a good example of the way More handles the other subjects in the volume.

2   *Mr. Pope: His Life and Times,* by George Paston [Miss E.M. Symonds]. New York: G. P. Putnam's Sons, 1909. [More's note]

3   T. R. Lounsbury [1838–1915], *The First Editors of Shakespeare. Pope as Editor of Shakespeare; Pope, Theobald, and the Dunciad* (1906). Published in U. S. as *The Text of Shakespeare.*

4   The phrase, *"The same,"* indicates that the words are Lord Bolingbroke's. [More's note]

5   Joseph Spence [1699–1768], *Anecdotes. Observations, and Characters of Books and Men Collected from the Conversations of Mr. Pope and Other Eminent Persons of His Time.* First edition, 1820, posthumous, edited by S. W. Singer.

6   "Indignation gives birth to poetry."

Keats[1]

In its pleasures and its toils the case of the critic, I often think, is not unlike that of the adventurous traveller. Every author into whose life in turn he diverts his own is to him a new voyage of exploration. He comes back laden with memories, whether the land he has traversed be one in the highways of commerce and already trodden by many feet, or an island almost forgotten in far-off seas. Cities of men he visits, and walks in crowded streets, or sits by sheltered hearths. Again, it is a country of unpeopled solitudes, where things of loveliness waylay him, or monstrous forms startle and affright. There are recollections of homely comfort to reward his toil; and of high adventures, as when, like Balboa, he stands and looks out, the first of men, over the infinite unknown Pacific; and there are ways of terror where he wanders alone on desolate frozen coasts and, far as the eye can reach, sees only ruinous death. All these visions and remembered emotions he carries to his desk, counting himself blessed if some happy chance of language or some unusual quickening of the blood shall enable him to convey to others though it be but a small part of his experience. That good fortune, he feels, with all noble conquests, is reserved for the poets:

> Much have I travell'd in the realms of gold,
>   And many goodly states and kingdoms seen;
>   Round many western islands have I been
> Which bards in fealty to Apollo hold.
> Oft of one wide expanse had I been told

> That deep-brow'd Homer ruled as his demesne;
> Yet did I never breathe its pure serene
> Till I heard Chapman speak out loud and bold:
> Then felt I like some watcher of the skies
>   When a new planet swims into his ken;
> Or like stout Cortez when with eagle eyes
>   He stared at the Pacific—and all his men
> Look'd at each other with a wild surmise—
>   Silent, upon a peak in Darien.

It is the sonnet that to most people probably comes first to mind when Keats is named and his destiny remembered. There is about it the golden flush and wonder of youth—it was written in his twentieth year—and one catches in it also, or seems to catch, a certain quickness of breath which forebodes the rapture so soon quenched. The inspiration of unsoiled nature and of England's clear-voiced early singers is here mingled as in no other of our poets. And especially this inheritance of the Elizabethan age rediscovered in a later century will have a new significance to any one who has just gone through the poems in the volume edited by Mr. E. de Sélincourt.[2]

There is a good deal to commend in this scholarly edition of Keats; the text has been prepared with extreme accuracy, and the notes, properly placed at the end of the book, are thorough and apposite. Mr. de Sélincourt's interest has lain more particularly in the study of sources, and Keats, among the most derivative and at the same time original of English poets, offered him here a rich field. For one thing, he has exploded the silly myth of the Lemprière.[3] To that dictionary (still a serviceable book, be it said, in its own way) Keats no doubt owed his acquaintance with many details of antiquity, but most of his information and all of the colour and movement that made of those legends a living inspiration he got from the translations of Chapman and Sandys and from the innumerable allusions in Spenser and the other great Elizabethans. One might have surmised as much from his sonnet to Chapman's Homer without waiting for the present editor's erudition. To call him a Greek, as Shelley did explicitly and as Matthew Arnold once did by implication, is to miss the mark. "Keats was no scholar," says Mr. de Sélincourt aptly, "and of the literature in which the Greek spirit found true expression he could know nothing. But just as it was through his devotion to Spenser that he became a poet, so was it through his kinship, both in spirit and taste, with the Elizabethans, that he became the poet of ancient Greece."

I am inclined to think that the essential kinship of Keats to "The fervid choir that lifted up a noise of harmony," as he called them, rests upon something even deeper than similarity of language and poetic method or than "natural magic," that it goes down to that faculty of vision in his mind which, like theirs, beheld the marriage of the ideas of beauty and death. As an editor concerned with the minutiæ of the poet's manner, Mr. de Sélincourt may well be pardoned for overlooking this more essential relationship; his services are sufficiently great after every deduction. It is not a small thing, for instance, to find in the Glossary a careful tabulation of the sources from which Keats drew his extraordinary vocabulary, and from the first word, "a-cold," to see how constantly he borrowed from Shakespeare and Milton and the writers that lie between, and how deliberately he sought to echo "that large utterance of the early Gods." The curious thing is that in the end all this borrowing should produce the impression of a fine spontaneity. Just as we are discovering more and more in the spaciousness of the Elizabethans a literary inspiration from foreign lands, so the freedom of diction in Keats was in large measure the influence of a remote age—which may be taken as another lesson in the nature of originality. The effect is as if the language were undergoing a kind of rejuvenation and no dulness of long custom lay between words and objects. Wordsworth's endeavour to introduce the speech of daily use is in comparison the mere adopting of another artifice.

It is scarcely necessary to add that this spontaneity in a mind so untrained as Keats's often fell into license and barbarism. From the days of the first reviewers his ill-formed compound terms and his other solecisms have, and quite rightly, been ridiculed and repudiated. Sometimes, indeed, his super-grammatical creations have a strange quality of genius that rebukes criticism to modesty. Thus in the familiar lines:

> As when, upon a trancèd summer-night,
> Those green-robed senators of mighty woods,
> Tall oaks, *branch-charmèd* by the earnest stars,
> Dream, and so dream all night without a stir,
> Save from one gradual solitary gust
> Which comes upon the silence, and dies off,
> As if the ebbing air had but one wave—

it is not easy to justify "branch-charmèd" by any common linguistic process; and yet who does not feel that the spell of the passage, the very mystery of its utter beauty, is concentrated in that one lawless word? It is the keystone of a perfect arch. By a stroke of rarer insight Keats, when he came to rewrite the scene for the later *Hyperion,* left that phrase untouched, though he changed, and in changing marred, nearly all the rest. But if occasionally these unlicensed expressions add to the magic of his style, more often they are merely annoying blemishes. There is no beauty in such a phrase as "unslumbrous night," to take the first words that occur, no force in "most drowningly doth sing," and his elision (which occurs more than once) of perhaps into *p'rhaps* is of a sort to make even a hardened reader wince.

The fact is, Keats might learn from the Elizabethans almost every element of style except taste, and here where he most needed guidance they seemed rather to sanction his lawlessness. But there was a difference between their circumstances and his. When a language is young and expanding, the absence of restraining taste is not so much felt, and liberty is a principle of growth; whereas at a later stage the same freedom leads often to mere eccentricity and vulgarisms. So it is that in Keats's language we are often obliged to distinguish between a true Elizabethan spontaneity and a spurious imitation that smacks too much of his London surroundings. We resent justly the review of *Endymion* in *Blackwood's* in which the author

was labelled as belonging to "the Cockney School of Poetry";
we take almost as a personal affront the reviewer's coarse deri-
sion: "So back to the shop, Mr. John, stick to 'plasters, pills,
ointment boxes' "; yet there is a hideous particle of truth in the
insult which will forever cling to Keats's name. Great poets
have come out of London, but only Keats among the immortals
can be pointed at as "cockney."

There is, in fact, something disconcerting in the circumstances of the poet's early life. He was born in London in 1795.
His father, a west-countryman, probably with Celtic blood in
his veins, was employed in a livery stable, of which he afterwards became manager, marrying the owner's daughter. He
died when John was nine years old. The mother soon married
a Mr. William Rawlings, also stable-keeper, who apparently
had succeeded her first husband in the Moorgate business. She
lived but a few years, and the family of children, of which John
was the eldest, were left orphans. There was some money, and
though towards the end pecuniary troubles came upon him,
Keats was in this respect more fortunate than many others; he
never had to waste his powers by writing for bread. Between
the years of 1806 and 1810 he attended a fairly good school
kept by the Rev. John Clarke at Enfield. After this he was
apprenticed for five years to a surgeon at Edmonton, and then
went, as the phrase is, to walk the London hospitals. Meanwhile he had been studying other things besides the human
anatomy. Charles Cowden Clarke, the son of his schoolmaster,
one day memorable in the annals of literature, had read Spenser's *Epithalamium* to him, and lent him *The Faerie Queen* to
take home. It was letting the wind in upon a sleeping fire. Said
a friend in after days: "Though born to be a poet, he was
ignorant of his birthright until he had completed his eighteenth year. It was *The Faerie Queen* that awakened his
genius. In Spenser's fairyland he was enchanted, breathed in
a new world, and became another being; till enamoured of the
stanza, he attempted to imitate it, and succeeded. This account
of the sudden development of his poetic powers I first received
from his brothers and afterwards from himself. This, his earli-

est attempt, the *Imitation of Spenser,* is in his first volume of poems, and it is peculiarly interesting to those acquainted with his history."

There was no more walking of hospitals for Keats. His first volume of *Poems* was published in 1817, with the significant motto from Spenser:

> What more felicity can fall to creature
> Than to enjoy delight with liberty.

It contains the first project of *Endymion,* the *Epistles,* in which Keats unfurls the flag of rebellion against poetic "rules," and a group of sonnets, including that on *Chapman's Homer.* The next year appeared the true *Endymion,* which won him the abuse of the reviewers and the admiration of Shelley. Only two years later, in 1820, when he was not yet twenty-five, there followed that wonderful book which has assured to him the passionate desire of his life, a place "among the English Poets." No poet of England at that age, barely four or five at any age, had published such works as these,—*Lamia, Isabella, The Eve of St. Agnes, Hyperion,* and the great Odes. What else he wrote was only to be printed posthumously, including, among other poems, the revised *Fall of Hyperion,* the exquisite fragment on *The Eve of Saint Mark,* the haunting ballad of *La Belle Dame sans Merci,* and the Dramas. Over some of this later work there seems to be a flush of hectic impatience, the creeping on of that dread which he had expressed in a sonnet, written indeed as early as 1818, but not published until after his death:

> When I have fears that I may cease to be
>   Before my pen has glean'd my teeming brain,
> Before high-pilèd books, in charact'ry,
>   Hold like full garners the full-ripen'd grain;
> When I behold, upon the night's starr'd face,
>   Huge cloudy symbols of a high romance,
> And think that I may never live to trace
>   Their shadows, with the magic hand of chance;

And when I feel, fair creature of an hour!
　That I shall never look upon thee more,
Never have relish in the faery power
　Of unreflecting love!—then on the shore
Of the wide world I stand alone, and think,
Till Love and Fame to nothingness do sink.

It expresses the ever-present fear of his brief life, but it contains also, at the close, the nearest approach in Keats to that profounder vision of disillusion which separates the Elizabethans from him; it calls to mind what are, I think, the greatest lines of Keats's Italian contemporary, Leopardi:

Io quello　　　　　.
Infinito silenzio a questa voce
Vo comparando: e mi sovvien l' eterno,
E le morte stagioni, e la presente
E viva, e il suon di lei. *Così tra questa*
Immensità s' annega il pensier mio;
E il naufragar m' è dolce in questo mare.[4]

But Keats owed to Cowden Clarke something more than his intellectual awakening; it was through the same friend he was introduced to the circle of literary and artistic men in London who supported and stimulated him in his work. Chief among these in his early impressionable years were Leigh Hunt and the half-mad painter, B. R. Haydon, and unfortunately both of these advisers reinforced the natural qualities of his mind with what may be called a kind of bastard, or cockney, Elizabethanism. It is painful to follow that influence, as so much in Keats's life is painful. In his maturity he could see the weakness of these friends and speak of them dispassionately enough. Of Leigh Hunt he wrote to his brother George, then in America: *"Hunt does one harm by making fine things petty and beautiful things hateful.* Through him I am indifferent to Mozart, I care not for white Busts—and many a glorious thing when associated with him becomes a nothing." So much Keats could see, but never, even in his greatest works, could he quite free himself from that malign influence; for it had laid hold of a corresponding tendency in his own nature. He was never quite able to distinguish between the large liberties of the strong and the jaunty flippancy of the underbred; his passion for beauty could never entirely save him from mawkish prettinesses, and his idea of love was too often a mere sickly sweetness. Never after the days of *Endymion*, perhaps, did he write anything quite in the character of "Those lips, O slippery blisses"; but even in the volume of 1820 he could not be sure of himself. There are too many passages there like these lines in *Lamia:*

> He, sick to lose
> The amorous promise of her lone complain,
> Swoon'd, murmuring of love, and pale with pain.

Not a little of this uncertainty of taste was due to Leigh Hunt.

And in the same way Haydon confirmed Keats on another side of his cockney Elizabethanism. Haydon himself was a man of vast and undisciplined, almost insane, enthusiasms, and he undoubtedly did much to keep the ambitious longings of Keats in a state of morbid fermentation. It would be a curious study to trace the friendship and humorous rupture of these two men in Keats's letters and in those journals of Haydon where so many of the geniuses of the day are presented in startling undress. At first all is smoothness. Keats tells Haydon in a letter "that there are three things to rejoice at in this Age—The Excursion, Your Pictures, and Hazlitt's depth of Taste"—poor Hazlitt being supplanted in a sonnet on the same theme by Hunt,

> He of the rose, the violet, the spring,
> The social smile, the chain for Freedom's sake.

On his part the painter describes his friend as the ideal poet; "Keats was the only man I ever met," he wrote, "who seemed and looked conscious of a high calling, except Wordsworth." Then it is a letter from Haydon:

> I love you like my own brother. Beware, for God's sake, of the delusions and sophistications that are ripping up the talents and morality of our friend! [A kindly allusion to Hunt] . . . Do not despair. Collect incident, study character, read Shakespeare, and trust in Providence, and you *will* do, you must.

Which brings from Keats this exalted reply:

> I know no one but you who can be fully sensible of the turmoil and anxiety, the sacrifice of all what [*sic*] is called comfort, the readiness to measure time by what is done and to die in six hours could plans be brought to conclusions—the looking upon the Sun, the Moon, the Stars, the Earth and its contents, as materials to form greater things—that is to say, ethereal things —but here I am talking like a Madman—greater things than our Creator himself made!!

Later a coolness sets in, occasioned by a common habit of asking for money—Haydon, indeed, was thought by some to have sat to Charles Lamb as a model for Ralph Bigod, Esq., captain of the mighty "men who borrow"—and at the last a mutual estrangement. On hearing of Keats's death Haydon summed up his charcter thus:

> A genuis more purely poetical never existed. In fireside conversation he was weak and inconsequent, but he was in his glory in the fields. . . . He was the most unselfish of human creatures; unadapted to the world, he cared not for himself, and put himself to any inconvenience for the sake of his friends. He was haughty, and had a fierce hatred of rank; but he had a kind heart, and would have shared his fortune with any one who wanted it. [Keats, by the way, had quarrelled with Haydon over the repayment of a loan.] He had an exquisite sense of humour, and too refined a notion of female purity to bear the little sweet arts of love with patience. . . . He began life full of hopes, fury, impetuous, and ungovernable, expecting the world to fall at once beneath his powers. Unable to bear the sneers of ignorance nor the attacks of envy, he began to despond, and flew to dissipation as a relief. For six weeks he was scarcely sober, and—to show what a man does to gratify his appetites when

they get the better of him—once covered his tongue and throat as far as he could with cayenne pepper, in order to appreciate the "delicious coldness of claret in all its glory"—his own expression.

I should like to be as sure as are some others, of Keats's own time and of the present, that this is a distorted view of the man's failings; they may well be somewhat exaggerated, yet Haydon had for the most part a wicked penetration into character, and his words here ring remarkably true. Nor is it the only place in which he asserts that Keats was beaten down by the cruelty of the reviewers, leading us to think that Byron's cynical rhyme on the "fiery particle" "snuffed out by an article" may have contained just a grain of truth. And as for the cayenne pepper, is it much more than a childish illustration of the thought repeated in many a verse—to "burst Joy's grape against his palate fine"? After all this is but the frailer, and, so to speak ephemeral, side of Keats; unfortunately, his associations were not of a kind to help him to overcome the initial lack of training, by correcting his flaws of taste and egotistic enthusiasm, and by purging what I have called his Elizabethan spontaneity of its cockney dross. As Wordsworth wrote in his patronising way: "How is Keats? He is a youth of promise, too great for the sorry company he keeps."

The wonder of it is that he grew so rapidly, and that so large a part of the volume of 1820 should have attained the true and lofty liberties of the spirit. In many aspects he stands curiously apart from his age. One feels this in his attitude toward nature, which in his verse is still unsubjected to the destinies of mankind. With Wordsworth and Shelley, even with Byron, some thought of man's sufferings and aspirations rises between the poet's eye and the vision of Nature, but with Keats she is still a great primeval force, inhuman and self-centred, beautiful, and sublime, and cruel, by turns. One catches this note at times in the earlier poems, as in the largeness and aloofness of such a picture as this:

> On a lone winter evening, when the frost
> Has wrought a silence.

It speaks with greater clearness in the later poems—in the elfin call of the nightingale's song,

> The same that hath
> Charm'd magic casements, opening on the foam
> Of perilous seas, in faery lands forlorn;

and in the imagery, calling us back to times before man's feebler creation, of that "sad place" where

> Crag jutting forth to crag, and rocks, that seemed
> Ever as if just rising from a sleep,
> Forehead to forehead held their monstrous horns.

One has the feeling that the poet's mind is in immediate contact with the object described, and the imagination of the reader is shocked from self-complacency by a kind of sympathetic surprise. It is at bottom a mark of that unperverted and untheorised sincerity whose presence condones so many faults in the Elizabethan writers, and whose absence mars so many brilliant qualities in the contemporaries of Keats.

But more particularly I see this backward-reaching kinship of Keats in his constant association of the ideas of beauty (or love) and death. In the dramatists that association attained its climax in the broken cry of Webster, which rings and sobs like a paroxysm of jealous rage against the all-embracing power:

> Cover her face; mine eyes dazzle: she died young,—

but everywhere in them it is present or implied. Of their thirst for beauty there is no need to give separate examples; nor yet of their constant brooding on the law of mutability. They cannot get away from the remembrance of life's brevity:

On pain of death, let no man name death to me:
It is a word infinitely terrible.

But for the tedium of repetition one might go through
Keats's volume of 1820, and show how completely the pattern
of that book is wrought on the same background of ideas.
Perhaps the most striking illustration may be found in those
two stanzas which relate how Isabella in the lonely forest
unearths the body of her buried lover:

> She gazed into the fresh-thrown mould, as though
>   One glance did fully all its secrets tell;
> Clearly she saw, as other eyes would know
>   Pale limbs at bottom of a crystal well;
> Upon the murderous spot she seem'd to grow,
>   Like to a native lily of the dell:
> Then with her knife, all sudden, she began
> To dig more fervently than misers can.
>
> Soon she turn'd up a soilèd glove, whereon
>   Her silk had play'd in purple phantasies,
> She kiss'd it with a lip more chill than stone,
>   And put it in her bosom, where it dries
> And freezes utterly unto the bone
>   Those dainties made to still an infant's cries:
> Than 'gan she work again; nor stay'd her care,
> But to throw back at times her veiling hair.

Every age has its peculiar adaptation of this universal theme,
and chants in its own way the everlasting hymeneal of beauty
and death; but in these stanzas there is something that calls the
mind back to the poetry of Webster and Ford. This poignant
meeting of the shapes of loveliness and decay is the inheritance of the middle ages, which in England more especially
was carried over into the new birth and made gorgeous with
all the cunning splendours of the Renaissance. Keats did not
learn his art from the real antiquity. The Greeks, too, had their
version of the theme, and in the story of Persephone and Dis

gave it its most perfect mythological form. But its interest with them lay primarily in its ethical associations, and the Powers of beauty and death were minor agents only in the great moral drama moved by the supreme unwritten laws. No Greek could have so gloated over the purely physical contrast of ideas—"A skull upon a mat of roses lying"—or put into it the same hungering emotion, as did Keats in these stanzas that follow the forest scene in *Isabella:*

In anxious secrecy they took it home,
    And then the prize was all for Isabel:
She calm'd its wild hair with a golden comb,
    And all around each eye's sepulchral cell
Pointed each fringèd lash; the smearèd loam
    With tears, as chilly as a dripping well,
She drench'd away:—and still she comb'd, and kept
Sighing all day—and still she kiss'd, and wept.

Then in a silken scarf,—sweet with the dews
    Of precious flowers pluck'd in Araby,
And divine liquids come with odorous ooze
    Through the cold serpent-pipe refreshfully,—
She wrapp'd it up; and for its tomb did choose
    A garden-pot, wherein she laid it by,
And cover'd it with mould, and o'er it set
Sweet Basil, which her tears kept ever wet.

And she forgot the stars, the moon, and sun,
    And she forgot the blue above the trees,
And she forgot the dells where waters run,
    And she forgot the chilly autumn breeze;
She had no knowledge when the day was done,
    And the new morn she saw not: but in peace
Hung over her sweet Basil evermore,
And moisten'd it with tears unto the core.

To see how far Keats is from the spirit of Greece, we need only turn from this last stanza to the scene of Antigone, in the play of Sophocles, treading the last road for the love of one dead, and looking for the last time on the light of the sun and never again any more. She, too, bids farewell to the bright things of the world, the springs of Dirce and the grove of Thebes, but it is not in the language of Isabella.

The same music wrung from the transience of lovely things runs like a monotone through the other poems of Keats's great volume, but in a different key. The incongruity (as it appears, yet it lies at the bottom of human thought) intrudes even into *The Eve of St. Agnes,* with the opening image of the benumbed beadsman among the sculptured dead and with the closing return to the same contrast. In the Odes it is subdued to a musing regret—heard pensively in the *Ode to a Nightingale:*

> Darkling I listen; and, for many a time
>   I have been half in love with easeful Death,
> Call'd him soft names in many a musèd rhyme,
>   To take into the air my quiet breath;
>   Now more than ever seems it rich to die,
>   To cease upon the midnight with no pain,
>   While thou art pouring forth thy soul abroad
>   In such an ecstasy!
>   Still wouldst though sing, and I have ears in vain—
>   To thy high requiem become a sod;—

speaking with a still more chastened beauty in the *Ode on a Grecian Urn:*

> Heard melodies are sweet, but those unheard
>   Are sweeter; therefore, ye soft pipes, play on;
> Not to the sensual ear, but, more endear'd,
>   Pipe to the spirit ditties of no tone:
> Fair youth, beneath the trees, thou canst not leave
>   Thy song, nor even can those trees be bare;
>   Bold Lover, never, never canst thou kiss,
> Though winning near the goal—yet, do not grieve;
>   She cannot fade, though thou hast not thy bliss,
>   For ever wilt thou love, and she be fair!—

uttered with greater poignancy in the *Ode on Melancholy:*

> She dwells with Beauty—Beauty that must die;
> And Joy, whose hand is ever at his lips
> Bidding adieu; and aching Pleasure nigh,
> Turning to poison while the bee-mouth sips.

It is the secret, for those who can read that mystery, of what is to many his most perfect work, the ballad of *La Belle Dame Sans Merci.*

From these ideal poems one turns naturally to the letters in which the fever and unrest, the glimpses of philosophy, and the broken hopes of Keats's actual life are expressed with such pathetic earnestness. The picture that results is of a strong man fighting against what he calls, with some self-depreciation, "a horrid Morbidity of Temperament." There is much to lament in this revelation never meant for the public; but in the end the sense of the man's greatness, the feeling of his reliance on the divine call, outweighs the impression of his painful susceptibility, and of his struggles to free himself from "the mire of a bad reputation." He may write on one day: "My name with the literary fashionables is vulgar, I am a weaver-boy to them, a tragedy would lift me out of this mess"; but the truer Keats is to be found in his moments of proud independence: "I value more the privilege of seeing great things in loneliness than the fame of a Prophet." *Great things in loneliness!* These were to him, as almost every page of the letters would prove, *The mighty abstract Idea of Beauty* and the ever-present consciousness of death. The pity of it is that these relentless powers should have passed for him from the realm of reflection to the coarse realities of life, and that the experience of his few years (they were only twenty-five) should have been torn by them as by a warring destiny. It was inevitable that this contention should take the form of love; nay, from the beginning, in his flippant, half-frightened allusions to the other sex, one feels that he is laying himself open to the recrimination of the deity.

"I am certain," he says, "I have not a right feeling toward
women"; and again, with a kind of foreboding, he avows that
his idea of beauty "stifles the more divided and minute domes-
tic happiness." Through all the correspondence his thought
seems to be leaping on as if pursued by a dreaded Necessity;
one hears the footsteps of the spurned goddess behind him. So,
he was overtaken at last, and his brief story was made another
example of the ways of Nemesis. The letters in which he pours
out the agony of his love for Fanny Brawne resemble Hazlitt's
Liber Amoris more than anything else in literature. They have
the same uncontrolled passion, and the same unfortunate note
of vulgarity, due not so much to the exuberance of his emotion
as to the lack of any corresponding force in the woman. The
flaccidity of her temperament deprives the episode of tragic
ideality, and lowers it to the common things of the street. It
even changes his master-vision to something approaching a
sickly sentimentalism. "I have two luxuries to brood over in my
walks," he writes, "your Loveliness and the hour of my death.
O that I could have possession of them both in the same minute." It helped to kill the poet in him,—save for that last sonnet, his wild swan-song written on his journey to Rome and a
Roman grave:

> Bright star! would I were steadfast as thou art—
>   Not in lone splendour hung aloft the night,
> And watching, with eternal lids apart,
>   Like Nature's patient, sleepless Eremite,
> The moving waters at their priestlike task
>   Of pure ablution round earth's human shores,
> Or grazing on the new soft fallen mask
>   Of snow upon the mountains and the moors—
> No—yet still steadfast, still unchangeable,
>   Pillow'd upon my fair love's ripening breast,
> To feel for ever its soft fall and swell,
>   Awake for ever in a sweet unrest,
> Still, still to hear her tender-taken breath,
> And so live ever—or else swoon to death.

As it seemed to him in those evil days when disease had laid hold of his body, Death was the victor in the contention of Fate. "If I should die," he wrote to Fanny Brawne, "I have left no immortal work behind me—nothing to make my friends proud of my memory—but I have loved the principle of beauty in all things, and if I had had time I would have made myself remembered." And the epitaph which he composed for himself—how well it is remembered!—was carved on stone: "Here lies one whose name was writ in water." But to the world, not Death but eternal Loveliness carried the palm. We think of him as the Marcellus of literature, who could not break through the *fata aspera*,[5] and as one of "the inheritors of unfulfilled renown"; and still we know that he accomplished a glorious destiny. His promise was greater than the achievement of others.

And yet a word to avoid misunderstanding, for it is so easy in these voyages of criticism to bring back a one-sided report, and to emphasise overmuch the broad aspects of a land while neglecting the nicer points of distinction. Thus, in pointing out the kinship of Keats to the Elizabethans, we should not forget that he is, like all men, still of his own age. By his depth and sincerity he differs, indeed, from certain other writers of the century who deal with the same subjects—from William Morris, for example, whose *Earthly Paradise* runs on the strange companionship of love and death with almost a frivolous persistence; but he is still far from the brave furor and exultation of the great passages in Marlowe. Again he has more than once imitated the simplicity of William Browne—notably in the *Ode on a Grecian Urn* where the lines to the "bold lover" already quoted are evidently an echo of a passage in the *Pastorals:*

> Here from the rest a lovely shepherd's boy
> Sits piping on a hill, as if his joy
> Would still endure, or else that age's frost
> Should never make him think what he had lost.

(Which is itself borrowed from Sir Philip Sidney's "Shepherd boy piping as though he should never be old.") But who does not feel that the young beauty of Keats is different from that first careless rapture, which has gone never to be recovered? Perhaps the very fact that he is speaking a language largely foreign to his own generation adds a personal eagerness, a touch at times of feverish straining, to his song.

I have already intimated that side by side with the superb zest of beauty there is another note in the dramatists which Keats rarely or never attains. That note is caught in such lines as Ford's

> For he is like to something I remember
> A great while since, a long, long time ago;

and always when it is struck, a curtain is drawn from behind the fretful human actors and we look beyond into infinite space. On the other hand, there is but little in Keats of the rich humanity and high passions that for the most part fill the Elizabethan stage. The pathos of *Isabella* is the nearest approach in him to that deeper source of poetry. Keats himself was aware that this background was lacking to his work, and harps on the subject continually. He perceived dimly that the motto of his faith,

> "Beauty is truth, truth beauty,"—that is all
> Ye know on earth; and all ye need to know,

was but a partial glimpse of the reality. Had he been sufficiently a Greek to read Plato, he might have been carried beyond that imperfect view; even the piteous incompleteness of his own life might have laid bare to him the danger lurking in its fair deception. As it is, his letters are filled with vague yearnings for a clearer knowledge; he is, he says, as one "writing at random, straining after particles of light in the midst of a great darkness." Unfortunately, inevitably perhaps, when he came to put his half-digested theories into practice, he turned, not to the moral drama of the Greeks or to the passionate human nature of the Elizabethans, but to the humanitarian philosophy that was in the air about him; and, accepting this, he fell into a crude dualism. "I find there is no worthy pursuit," he writes, "but the idea of doing some good to the world. . . . I have been hovering for some time between an exquisite sense of the luxurious, and a love for philosophy."

It has been generally supposed that Keats abandoned his unfinished *Hyperion,* and started to rewrite it in the form of a vision, through dissatisfaction with the Miltonic inversions of language in the earlier draft and through the influence of Dante's *Commedia.* That view is demonstrably true in part, but I think the real motive for the change goes deeper. There is, in fact, an inherent contradiction in his treatment of the theme which rendered a completion of the original poem almost impracticable. The subject is the overthrow of the Titans by the new race of gods—Saturn succumbing to the arms of his own child and Hyperion, Lord of the Sun, fleeing before Apollo of the golden bow and the lyre; it is the old dynasty of formless powers, driven into oblivion by the new creators of form and order. That was the design, but it is easy to see how in the execution the poet's dominant idea overmastered him and turned his intended pæan on the birth of the new beauty into a sonorous dirge for the passing away of the old. Our imagination is indeed lord of the past and not of the future. The instinctive sympathy of the poet for the fallen deities is felt in the very first line of the poem, and it never changes. Consider the picture of Hyperion's home:

> His palace bright,
> Bastion'd with pyramids of glowing gold,
> And touch'd with shade of bronzèd obelisks,
> Glared a blood-red through all its thousand courts,
> Arches, and domes, and fiery galleries;
> And all its curtains of Aurorian clouds
> Flush'd angerly—

or consider the apparition of Hyperion himself:

> He look'd upon them all,
> And in each face he saw a gleam of light,
> But splendider in Saturn's, whose hoar locks
> Shone like the bubbling foam about a keel
> When the prow sweeps into a midnight cove.
> In pale and silver silence they remain'd,
> Till suddenly a splendour, like the morn,
> Pervaded all the beetling gloomy steeps,
> All the sad spaces of oblivion,
> And every gulf, and every chasm old,
> And every height, and every sullen depth,
> Voiceless, or hoarse with loud tormented
>   streams: . . .
> It was Hyperion;—

are there any words left in the poet's armory after this to describe the glory of Apollo? As a matter of fact, the third book in which he introduces the young usurper is distinctly below the other two in force and beauty, and Keats knew it and broke off in the middle. That was, probably, in September of 1819; about two months later he was engaged in reshaping his work into *The Fall of Hyperion,* which was also left unfinished and was not published until 1856. In its altered form the poem is cast into a vision. The poet finds himself in a garden of rare flowers and delicious fruits. These vanish away and in their place is "an old sanctuary with roof august," wherein is a mystic shrine and a woman ministering thereat. Her name had once been Mnemosyne, the goddess of memory, the mother of the Muses, but now she is called Moneta, that is to say, the guide or admonisher—alas, for all the change means! The poet cries to her for help:

> "High Prophetess," said I, "purge off,
> Benign, if so it please thee, my mind's film."
> "None can usurp this height," returned that shade,
> "But those to whom the miseries of the world
> Are misery, and will not let them rest."

But are there not others, cries the poet, who have felt the agony of the world, and have laboured for its redemption? Where are they that they are not here? And then:

> "Those whom thou spakest of are no visionaries,"
> Rejoin'd that voice; "they are no dreamers weak;
> They seek no wonder but the human face,
> No music but a happy-noted voice:
> They come not here, they have no thought to come;
> And thou art here, for thou art less than they.
> What benefit canst thou do, or all thy tribe,
> To the great world? Thou art a dreaming thing."

And thereupon, in a vision, she unfolds before his eyes the fall of Hyperion and the progress of humanity symbolised in the advent of Apollo. To compare this mutilated version with the poem Keats had written under the instinctive inspiration of his genius is one of the saddest tasks of the student of literature.

No, it was not any dislike of Miltonic idioms or any impulse from Dante that brought about this change in his ambition; it was the working of the ineluctable Time-spirit. His early associations with Leigh Hunt had prepared him for this treachery to his nature, but there was a poverty in the imagination of those cockney enthusiasts for progress which would have saved him ultimately from their influence. It was the richer note of Wordsworth, the still sad music of humanity running through that poet's mighty song, that wrought the fatal revolution. As early as May of 1818 he had written to a friend (and the passage is worthy of quoting at some length):

> My Branchings out therefrom have been numerous: one of them is the consideration of Wordsworth's genius . . . and how he differs from Milton. And here I have nothing but surmises, from an uncertainty whether Milton's apparently less anxiety for Humanity proceeds from his seeing further or not than Wordsworth: and whether Wordsworth has in truth epic passion, and martyrs himself to the human heart, the main region of his song. [After some wandering there follows the famous

comparison of human life to a large mansion of many apartments, which may be used as a key to the symbolism of the later
Hyperion, and then] We see not the balance of good and evil;
we are in a mist, *we* are now in that state, we feel the "Burden
of the Mystery." To this point was Wordsworth come, as far as
I can conceive, when he wrote *Tintern Abbey,* and it seems to
me that his genius is explorative of those dark Passages. Now if
we live, and go on thinking, we too shall explore them. He is a
genius and superior to us, in so far as he can, more than we,
make discoveries and shed a light in them. Here I must think
Wordsworth is deeper than Milton, though I think it has depended more upon the general and gregarious advance of intellect, than individual greatness of Mind.

The Fall of Hyperion is nothing less than the attempt of
Keats, against the native grain of his genius, to pass from the
inspiration of Milton and Shakespeare to that of Wordsworth.
The thought of the two poems, and of the living beauty of the
one and the disrelish of the other, brings up the remembrance
of that story, told by Edward FitzGerald from a Persian poet,
of the traveller in the desert who dips his hand into a spring
of water and drinks. By and by comes another who drinks of
the same spring from an earthen bowl, and departs, leaving his
bowl behind him. The first traveller takes it up for another
draught, but finds that the water which has tasted sweet from
his own hand is now bitter from the earthen bowl. He wonders;
but a voice from heaven tells him the clay from which the bowl
is made was once *Man,* and can never lose the bitter flavour
of mortality.

---

¹   This essay first appeared in the Book Section of the *Evening Post* for Dec. 9,
    1905; it was then included in the Fourth Series of *Shelburne Essays* (1906). No
    collection of essays by More would be complete without one on a Romantic
    figure. This on Keats gives the lie to the idea that More was incapable of
    appreciating any but literature in the classical vein.
²   *The Poems of John Keats,* Edited with an Introduction and Notes by E. de
    Sélincourt. New York: Dodd, Mead & Co., 1905. [More's note]

3   J. Lemprière (1765? - 1824), editor of *Bibliotheca Classica*, 1788.

4   "I anon
    That infinite silence with this voice compare:
And I remember the eternal one,
    The seasons of the dead, and this of care
About us and its sound. So as I wonder,
My thought in this immensity sinks under;
    And shipwreck in that sea is sweet to bear." [More's note]

5   "The calamitous fates."

The Praise of Dickens[1]

If it ever seemed that the popularity of Dickens was waning, certainly there is no such appearance to-day. Publishers have been vying with one another in putting out his works in attractive form, and now Messrs. Chapman & Hall have begun to issue the National Edition in forty volumes, including many pieces never before collected, and designed in every way to be definitive.[2] And all the while about his work there is going up a critical chorus of praise, mingling the long growl of Swinburne's bass, the flute-like melody of Mrs. Meynell, the jumping staccato of Mr. Chesterton, with I know not how many lesser notes. This indeed is well, if by chance it helps us to move more familiarly in the shadow world that Dickens evoked. But no one can read these panegyrists without observing a curious fact: they all erect some bogus enemy, whom they thereupon proceed to knock over. Just who this dark miscreant of criticism may be, does not appear, for at the present hour scarcely a dissentient voice can be heard. Is it possible they are protesting against a reservation in their own minds? And, again, one observes a tendency to laud Dickens by a kind of bravado for the very qualities in which he is weakest. So, for example, you may read Mrs. Meynell, herself a writer of exquisite English, in praise of Dickens as a stylist, whereas it used to be accepted for a truism that Dickens had no style, as, indeed, properly speaking, he has not. This is not to deny that he was a master of the clinging, inevitable epithet, or that he was a maker of memorable phrases, or even that his language for many purposes was abundantly efficient. But style—not the grand, or the vigorous, or the antithetic, or the florid, but style in itself—is something different from these qualities; it is rather that rare gift of words, that union of simplicity and freshness, which lends a charm to writing quite independent of the ideas or images conveyed. Some great writers have never acquired it—George Eliot did not; others of less genius have had it always at command, as did Mrs. Gaskell; while to the greatest it belongs as do all things else. Certainly, of style in this sense, Dickens was never the possessor. Take the opening words of his last work, when, if ever, he should have been master of his craft: "An ancient English Cathedral Tower? How can the ancient English Cathedral Tower be here! The well-known massive grey square tower of its old Cathedral? How can that be here!" It is not too much to say that the practical writer who could begin a book thus, was radically deficient in the niceties of language.

And the faults of this passage point to some of the factors that go to the making of style. Manifestly, there must be no false emphasis, no straining for effect beyond the needs of the time and place, no appearance of uneasiness, but quiet assurance and self-subordination. The law of style may be defined as the rule of Apollo: Nothing too much; it is the art first of all of dealing frankly with the commonplace and the trivial without being common or mean. And it does not end here. In the more important passages, where direct pathos or humour or strong emotion of any kind is expressed, other qualities may conceal the absence of style; but where elevation is to be attained without this immediate appeal, nothing can take the place of the law of fitness and balance. I was struck while reading *David Copperfield* with the comparison of a scene in that book with a similar scene in *Henry Esmond*. Both have to do with the coming of a son to the home of a buried mother, who in life had suffered cruel wrong and bereavement, and only in the grave had found peace. There is here no occasion for passionate tears, but only that pathos of reflection which subdues the heart and sweetens memory. To read the closing sentences of

Thackeray and Dickens side by side is a practical lesson in language:

> Might she sleep in peace—might she sleep in peace; and we, too, when our struggles and pains are over! But the earth is the Lord's as the heaven is; we are alike his creatures here and yonder. I took a little flower off the hillock and kissed it, and went my way, like the bird that had just lighted on the cross by me, back into the world again. Silent receptacle of death; tranquil depth of calm, out of reach of tempest and trouble! I felt as one who had been walking below the sea, and treading amidst the bones of shipwrecks.

So Esmond turns away from the burial ground of the convent at Brussels. The page in *David Copperfield* is almost as well known:

> From the moment of my knowing of the death of my mother, the idea of her as she had been of late had vanished from me. I remembered her, from that instant, only as the young mother of my earliest impressions, who had been used to wind her bright curls round and round her finger, and to dance with me at twilight in the parlour. What Peggotty had told me now, was so far from bringing me back to the later period, that it rooted the earlier image in my mind. It may be curious, but it is true. In her death she winged her way back to her calm untroubled youth, and cancelled all the rest.

The passage from Thackeray may be commonplace in thought and a little over-sweet in sentiment, but the language has an unmistakable charm; whereas it seems to me that any one who is not conscious of something discordant in the close of Dickens' paragraph, in the false cadences and in the impropriety of the word "cancelled," must be equally dull to the truer and finer harmonies of language. And this passage is thoroughly typical of Dickens in his moods of reflective elevation.

Not all the modern praise of Dickens, to be sure, displays this perversity, and, whatever may be said against Mr. Chesterton's ebullition of doubtful epigrams, at least he has avoided the

error of choosing the shortcomings of Dickens for commendation.[3] Rightly he lays stress on the superb irresponsibility of
Dickens' world, and the divine folly of his characters. "Dickens's art," he says, "is like life, because, like life, it is irresponsible. . . . Dickens was a mythologist rather than a novelist;
. . . the last of the mythologists, and perhaps the greatest." And
again he stresses rightly the democratic nature of his genius:
"Dickens stands first as a defiant monument of what happens
when a great literary genius has a literary taste akin to that of
the community. . . . His power, then, lay in the fact that he
expressed with an energy and brilliancy quite uncommon the
things close to the common mind." I am inclined to think that
in his analysis of this genuine, not condescending, democracy,
Mr. Chesterton has found the real key to most that attracts and
repels us in the novels; yet even here he has not quite escaped
the malign influence that lies in wait for the critic of Dickens.
Why must Mr. Chesterton imply on every page that great art
is always, like that of Dickens, democratic? It is, on the contrary, a simple statement of fact to say that in practically all the
living literature of the past the predominant note has been
aristocratic. Who, to take a single illustration, is not acquainted
with the outrageous contempt of the Elizabethan playwrights
for the multitude whose taste they were in part compelled to
conciliate? Walt Whitman knew this well enough, and divided
literature into two great epochs, the aristocratic of the past,
and the democratic which was to spring from his own example.
Tolstoy knows it, and finds Shakespeare merely tiresome.[4]

The currents of ruling opinion are, indeed, likely here to
introduce confusion into any mind, for the question is not
without complications. Mr. Chesterton, with his own pun-
gency of epithet, designates the democratic element in literature as the "pungent and popular stab," and finds that the
universal test of what may be called popular, of the people, is
whether it employs vigorously the extremes of the tragic and
the comic. Barring the loose use of the word "tragic," the
definition is excellent, and undoubtedly in the judgments of
the heart the people is right. From this source of power the

maker of books will sever himself only to his own great peril. The demand for simple uncontrolled emotions, for clear moral decisions meting out happiness to the good and misery to the evil, (which is something quite different from tragedy,) the call for immediacy of effect and the direct use of the material of life—all this is the democratic soil from which literature must spring. Without this it lacks sap and the comfort of sweet reality. We feel the partial want of such a basis in the French classical drama, splendid as the work of that courtly age otherwise is.

Yet there is an odd paradox connected with this emotional root of letters: while it alone gives life, it cannot keep alive. Racine has outlived and will long outlive all the merely popular dramas ever written; one can foresee a time when Milton will be more read than Bunyan; the enjoyment of Gray's poems already is wider and less artificial than the taste for ballads which sprang warm from the communal heart. The straightforward appeal to the passions, the pathos and humour of the moment, have a strange trick of becoming obsolete with the passing of time and the change of circumstance. What threw the Globe Theatre into spasms of tears and laughter is, I suspect, not always the part of Shakespeare that moves us most to-day. The preservative of letters, what indeed makes literature, is the addition of all those qualities that, for the sake of comparison, we may call aristocratic,—the note of distinction which is concerned more with form than with substance, the reflective faculty which broods over the problems of morality, the questioning spirit which curbs spontaneity, the zest of discrimination which refines broad effects to the *nuance,* the power of fancy which transforms the emotions into ideas. In a word, the aristocratic element denotes self-control, discipline, suppression.

Now discipline and suppression Dickens never acquired, whether in art or character. No writer of England ever underwent in his life so sharp a contrast of neglect and celebrity, and the effect of either condition upon him is equally significant. His father, it is well known, furnished a model for the glorious, but rather uncomfortable, Mr. Micawber; his mother apparently was a heartless woman. Out of the shifting, and sometimes shifty, scenes of his youth, one experience stands out—his apprenticeship in a blacking factory, which he was later to describe as David Copperfield's slavery in the bottling establishment of Murdstone & Grinby. In a bit of autobiography which he once confided to his friend Forster, he shows how painfully he remembered the waste and degradation of that time:

> No words can express the secret agony of my soul as I sank into this companionship; compared these every-day associates with those of my happier childhood; and felt my early hopes of growing up to be a learned and distinguished man crushed in my breast. The deep remembrance of the sense I had of being utterly neglected and hopeless; of the shame I felt in my position; of the misery it was to my young heart to believe that, day by day, what I had learned, and thought, and delighted in, and raised my fancy and my emulation up by, was passing away from me, never to be brought back any more; cannot be written. . . . From that hour until this at which I write, no word of that part of my childhood which I have now gladly brought to a close has passed my lips to any human being. I have no idea how long it lasted; whether for a year, or much more, or less. From that hour until this my father and my mother have been stricken dumb upon it. I have never heard the least allusion to it, however far off and remote, from either of them. I have never, until I now impart it to this paper, in any burst of confidence with any one, my own wife not excepted, raised the curtain I then dropped, thank God.

He learned much in those dismal days—the foul spots of London, the slime of the river, the inside of Marshalsea prison (where his father was), the pawnshops, and decayed lodging houses; but one thing he did not learn—the chastening of spirit that suffering is supposed to bestow. He came up from that descent into ignominious drudgery in a state of nervous exacerbation. The memory of it rankled in his breast, and he never forgave his mother for her willingness to abandon him to that base misery. In his art he would describe the spectacle of poverty with enormous gusto, but the dull, aching resignation at the core of it and its discipline he left for others to lay bare.

A few years of miscellaneous occupation followed, as schoolboy, lawyer's clerk, and reporter; and then, in 1834, at the age of twenty-two, he began to publish the *Sketches of Boz*. Two years later *Pickwick* opened its career in monthly numbers, and soon raised the author to an incredible pitch of popularity. Wealth came to him almost at a bound, while he was still little more than a boy, and overweening fame as it came to no other man, even in those days of sudden celebrity. And it cannot be said that the effect upon him was wholly agreeable. Magnanimous in many ways, no doubt he always remained, and lovable to a few people, even to Carlyle, who could write of him after his death as "the good, the gentle, high-gifted, ever-friendly, noble Dickens—every inch of him an honest man"; but it is true, nevertheless, that his vanity was brought by all this egregious adulation to a state of unwholesome irritability. Applause could not reach him quickly enough and loud enough, and in the end he was almost ready to give up authorship for the noisier excitement of public recitation. There are many accounts of his manner of reading, or, more properly, acting; it was emphatic, intense; if anything, over-dramatic, like his writing. "I had to go yesterday to Dickens's Reading," writes Carlyle; he "acts better than any Macready in the world; a whole tragic, comic, heroic, *theatre* visible, performing under one *hat*, and keeping us laughing—in a sorry way, some of us thought—the whole night." Alas, how sorry a way! It is not only the waste of so splendid talents that we regret, but there is something distressful in the very thought of this great man brutalising his face to the likeness of Bill Sykes, or mopping and mowing as Fagin, out of the mere craving for publicity. To me, at least, it is one of the many painful chapters in our literary annals. And I think he could not have so paltered with his genius if his characters had ever been other than the product of a stupendous dramatic egotism.

Neither suffering nor prosperity brought him the one gift denied at his birth, intellectual *pudor*, and the absence of that restraining faculty passed, as how could it help passing, into his work. We are permitted to-day to use the word gentleman only at our risk, and the saying has gone abroad that it is vulgar to speak of vulgarity. Nevertheless it is merely idle to conceal the fact, as is commonly done in recent criticism, that a strain of vulgarity runs through Dickens. It is not that his characters belong for the most part to low life, but rather that they do not all move in that sphere. For the grace and ease that are born of voluntary self-discipline he had no measure, and the image of the gentleman which springs from that source he had no power of evoking. He was, with one or two doubtful and insignificant exceptions, equally unqualified to create or to satirise such a character. In all his novels you will meet with no Henry Esmond or William Dobbin, no, nor any Major Pendennis or Marquis of Steyne, for these also are the result of discipline, however selfish its end may have been. Unfortunately you will come here and there upon some distorted shadow of them which only betrays where the master's cunning failed. I do not see why we should refuse the word vulgarity where it so eminently belongs.

To the same cause must be attributed the absence in Dickens of that kind of tragedy which involves the losing contest of a strong man with destiny and his triumph through spiritual discipline. His nearest approach to the tragic is in the character of Bradley Headstone, but even here the second element is wanting, and there is more of pain than of liberation in the breaking of that obstinate soul. It may be said that this is not the proper field of the novelist, inasmuch as genuine tragedy requires also an instrument of ideal elevation which lies scarcely within the reach of prose fiction. So far Dickens was saved by his limitations from an attempt that would have been at best but a questionable success. In place of tragic awe, he has given us tears. I know that much of his pathos has grown stale with time, as that emotion is strangely apt to grow; yet here and there it still touches us in his stories as freshly almost as when they first came to the reader in monthly instalments; and, after all, they are but of yesterday. Most of us may find Dora, the child-wife, anything rather than pathetic, but there are few who will withhold their tears from the death of Little Nell.[5] Here is no conflict, no bitter and triumphant self-suppression; it is the picture of perfect meekness and gentleness fading flower-like in the breath of adversity. At his best there is a tenderness in the pathos of Dickens, a divine tenderness, I had almost said, which no other of our novelists has ever found. Who has been able to harden his heart when Copperfield, after the shame of Emily, talks with Mr. Peggotty and Ham on the seashore? and when the old man, being asked whether they will desert the stranded boat that has been their home, replies?—

> Every night, as reg'lar as the night comes, the candle must be stood in its old pane of glass, that if ever she should see it, it may seem to say, "Come back, my child, come back!" If ever there's a knock, Ham (partic'ler a soft knock), arter dark, at your aunt's door, doen't you go nigh it. Let it be her—not you—that sees my fallen child!

And again there is the same touch of human delicacy when, in the presence of David, the broken girl, discovered at last, sinks in her uncle's arms: "He gazed for a few seconds in the face; then stooped to kiss it—oh, how tenderly!—and drew a handkerchief before it." The beauty of the gesture is all the finer because it follows the coarsely conceived and coarsely written interview with the impossible Rosa Dartle. Nor was Ham, the lover of the girl, without something of that great-hearted tenderness. His death, with his enemy's, in the storm may border on melodrama, but it cannot blunt the memory of his last message to Emily, his parting with David by the boat-house, and then—

> With a slight wave of his hand, as though to explain to me that he could not enter the old place, he turned away. As I looked after his figure, crossing the waste in the moonlight, I saw him

turn his face towards a strip of silvery light upon the sea, and pass on, looking at it, until he was a shadow in the distance.

These things came to Dickens at times, and they give him freedom of the company of the greatest.

But if his pathos too often failed from some fault of taste, his humour was incessant and sure. I do not mean the mere ludicrousness of situation—the amiable Mr. Pickwick caught at eavesdropping, or the dashing Mr. Winkle on horseback, although there is abundance of this, too, in Dickens that has not grown stale—but the deeper and more thoroughly English humour of character. He is a humourist in the manner of Ben Jonson and Smollett and Sterne and a long line of others—the greatest of them, some think, and, alas that it should be so, the last, for with his followers, of whom Gissing is a type, a new spirit of sympathy enters hostile to the old spontaneous joy. It was not for nothing that his favourite reading as a child and as a man was the great novel writers of·the eighteenth century. From their hands he received the art which his genius was to develop in a hundred ways. Humours, as Walpole observed, are native to England, being the product of a government which allows the individual to develop without restraint. Quite as often, I should say, they are in reality the escape in one direction of faculties otherwise pent up and oppressed—the exaggeration of some whim or eccentricity until the whole demeanour of a man is dominated by it. Their very essence, at least as they come to us in art, is the insolence of irrepressible life. Sometimes Dickens descends into mere parrot-like reiteration of a phrase, such as "Barkis is willin' " or "I never will desert Mr. Micawber," but more commonly he invents a wonderful variety in sameness.

In one particular, in what may be called the humour of trade, Dickens is supreme. Others have seen the fruitfulness of this theme. Indeed, as Hazlitt remarks, "the chief charm of reading the old novels is from the picture they give of the egotism of the characters, the importance of each individual to himself, and his fancied superiority over every one else. We like, for instance, the pedantry of Parson Adams, who thought a schoolmaster the greatest character in the world, and that he was the greatest schoolmaster in it." Or, if we come to Dickens' own day, there is such a pedantic humourist as the Gypsy, who communicated to Borrow the secrets of rat-catching, and "spoke in the most enthusiastic manner of his trade, saying that it was the best trade in the world and most diverting, and that it was likely to last for ever." These characters are common enough everywhere, but in Dickens they flourish with extraordinary exuberance. Who can name them all?—from old Jack Bamber, the lawyer's clerk in the *Pickwick Papers*, with his doddering delight in the mouldering chambers and sordid tragedies of the Inns, to Durdles, the stone-cutter in *Edwin Drood*, with his grotesque complacency "down in the crypt among the earthy damps there, and the dead breath of the old 'uns"—who can count them? What horror or pain or dull subjection can diminish their infinite zest in living? It has always seemed to me that Jasper's complaints about the cramped monotony of his existence and the need of subduing himself to his vocation were a species of treachery to the genius of his creator, a sign that the author's peculiar power was passing away, or, at least, suffering a change. Only when we come to Durdles do we recognise the real Dickens again, or to Sapsea enlarging gloriously on the education to be derived from auctioneering, or to Tartar fitting up his room like a ship's cabin so as to have a constant opportunity of knocking his head against the ceiling.

And this special quality of humour, shown by a man's exultation in his trade, leads to a trait of Dickens which might easily be overlooked. Commonly—always, I think, when most characteristic—he describes his people from the outside and not from within. Let us not be deceived by that "pungent and popular stab"; these emotions that touch us so quickly are not what the characters themselves would feel, but what Dickens, the great egotistic dramatic observer, felt while looking out upon them. This pathos is not the actual grief of one bewildered and crushed by circumstances; it is the yearning for tears, the γόου ΐμερος [6] of the strong, impregnable heart. Do you suppose that Smike ever knew in his own breast the luxury of sorrow he gave to his creator and still gives to the reader? His misery, I fear, was of a dumber, grimier sort.

And so with those characters that merge into the pedantry of humour, to repeat Hazlitt's happy phrase. It is the democracy of Dickens that called them into birth, no doubt, but something else entered into their composition in the end—the great joy of creation which made it impossible for the author to abide within their vexed circle. Possibly old Weller got such hilarious glee out of the misdoings of his wife and Stiggins as his words import, but what of a thousand weaker souls who hug the evil conditions of their lot? There is the ragged stoker in *The Old Curiosity Shop*, who nourishes a romantic comfort from his sympathy with the cinders and the roaring furnace that have been his whole existence. There is "No. 20," who became so inured to the Fleet that within its walls was freedom and all without was prison. And there is the sublime Quilp, almost the highest stroke of the master. He is brother to all the spooks and goblins of the credulous past, a pure creature of fairyland. His trade is malice, and the sheer exhilaration of evil never received a more perfect expression. Wickedness in him, losing its sullen despair, is turned to a godlike amusement. I cannot be persuaded that Mrs. Quilp really suffered on that memorable occasion when she sat up all night, while her crooked lord smoked and imbibed grog; the pleasure of watching his fantastic features must have counteracted all sense of fatigue. In fact, we are told that she loved him to the end. It was unpardonable in Dickens to bring him to that fear and death in the slime of the river. Here he was misled by that other democratic instinct which demands the punishment of the malefactor, and if Dickens in creating Quilp had at all entered into the reality of evil, this grewsome climax would have been appropriate. But Quilp, the gay magician of malice, who breathed fire and whose drink was boiling rum—to think of him perishing in the cold element of water! A mere novice could have contrived his taking off better. There is a description of him in his solitary lair that suggests his true end:

> Mr. Quilp once more crossed the Thames and shut himself up in his Bachelor's Hall, which, by reason of its newly erected chimney depositing the smoke inside the room and carrying none of it off, was not quite so agreeable as more fastidious people might have desired. Such inconveniences, however, instead of disgusting the dwarf with his new abode, rather suited his humour; so, after dining luxuriously from the public-house, he lighted his pipe, and smoked against the chimney until nothing of him was visible through the mist but a pair of red and highly inflamed eyes, with sometimes a dim vision of his head and face, as, in a violent fit of coughing, he slightly stirred the smoke and scattered the heavy wreaths by which they were obscured. In the midst of this atmosphere, which must infallibly have smothered any other man, Mr. Quilp passed the evening with great cheerfulness; solacing himself all the time with the pipe and the case-bottle; and occasionally entertaining himself with a melodious howl, intended for a song. . . . Thus he amused himself until nearly midnight, when he turned into his hammock with the utmost satisfaction.

That was the time and the scene for the catastrophe. In a wild burst of flame he and his guilty haunt should have disappeared forever, while his wife and accomplices looked on in terror, wondering if they beheld his distorted countenance still grimacing at them out of the ascending smoke. But it was notoriously the way of Dickens to bring his people to an impossible conclusion. Quilp he could drown, while of Micawber he made a dignified magistrate and of Traddles a prosperous lawyer.

So it is that the emotions in Dickens' work are quick to life, whereas the people are external to us, if not unreal; to make the inevitable comparison, we seem to have known Dickens' characters, Thackeray's we have lived. And this goes with the surprising diversity of judgments you may read in his admirers. Take the three critical studies that lie before me at the present moment—by Prof. A. W. Ward, Mr. Chesterton, and Gissing—and you will find them in a state of most bewildering disagreement. To Mr. Chesterton the epitaph of Sapsea on his wife is a bit of "beatific buffoonery," the true essential Dickens, whereas Gissing will none of it, and thinks it transcends the limits of art. Gissing can put no faith in Mr. Peggotty, whereas Professor Ward finds this whole episode of Emily and her uncle the most perfect part of the book. Only he would exclude Rosa Dartle, who to Mr. Chesterton is one of Dickens' "real characters." Gissing rejoices to see Pecksniff in the end "felled to the ground," whereas Mr. Chesterton deems the penalty one of the peculiar blemishes in Dickens' dénouements. And so on through the list. Most astonishing of all, both Gissing and Professor Ward find special beauty in that story of "Doady" and Dora which to most readers, certainly, is an utterly tiresome piece of mawkishness.

Now there has been no such divergence of opinion among the admirers of Thackeray or Scott or any other of the great novelists. And the reason for it in the case of Dickens is plainly this, that his characters are so constructed that they will not bear analysis. Probably most people would join in calling Sam Weller (unless that honour is reserved for old Weller) the finest conception in Dickens, as his humour is the least subject to the disillusion of repetition. And yet, can any one really believe, if to his peril he stops to reflect, that such a union of innocence and worldly knowledge ever existed in a single breast? These conflicting judgments mean simply that the critical faculty has been at its dissolving work, not steadily, but at intervals, destroying the illusion where it touched and leaving other parts untroubled. For there is a right and a wrong way to read, or at least to enjoy, Dickens, as I have in my own experience, if I may be allowed the egotism, emphatically discovered. A number of years ago, when I was living in the remote seclusion of Shelburne, about the only novels at my command were a complete set of Dickens in the village library. One day, being hungry for emotion, I started on these volumes, and read them through—read as only a starved man can read, without pause and without reflection, with the smallest intermissions for sleep. It was an orgy of tears and laughter, almost immoral in

its excess, a joy never to be forgotten. Well, I have been reading the novels again, slowly now, and weighing their effect—
and in comparison how meagre my pleasure is!

But the old way was the right way, I think, and he who opens
his Dickens must be ready to surrender himself unreservedly
to the magician's spell. And then, what a place is this into
which he is carried! Who, while the charm is upon him, for any
realism of art would exchange the divine impertinence of a
world inhabited by Mrs. Gamp, and Richard Swiveller, and the
Marchioness, and Mark Tapley, and Toots, and Mantilini, and
Mrs. Nickleby, and the fat boy—but the list is as endless as the
master's hand was indefatigable. "The key of the great characters of Dickens," says Mr. Chesterton, "is that they are all great
fools." If one were asked to sum up in a single phrase the effect
of all this mad variety of humours, one might call it the actual
evocation into life of that doctrine of Folly which Erasmus
taught in his *Stultitiæ Laus*, some four centuries ago. We see
the preacher in his pulpit, expounding his lesson in examples
that Holbein limned so astutely; we hear him contrast the
feeble generation of the calculators and the sane with the
large-hearted children of folly—poets and martyrs, whimsicals
and originals, and all those whom the world esteems mad, but
who follow who knows what divine deep-seated guidance:
"Quod si mortales prorsus ab omni sapientiæ commercio
temperarent, ac perpetuo mecum ætatem agerent, ne esset
quidem ullum senium, verum perpetuâ iuventâ fruerentur
felices." [7] And this should be the motto for all the *mystæ* who
have been sealed into the fellowship of that secret knowledge:
"Ut nihil est stultius præposterâ sapientiâ, ita perversâ pru-
dentiâ nihil imprudentius." Nothing, indeed, is more foolish
than the preposterous wisdom, nothing more imprudent than
the perverse prudence, which would withdraw a man from the
untroubled fruition of all that Dickens has so bountifully provided.

1   This essay appeared in the Book Section of the *Evening Post* for Dec. 8, and in *The Nation* for Dec. 13, 1906. It was then included in the Fifth Series of *Shelburne Essays* (1908). More here handles one of his favorite themes, that of contrasting the aristocratic spirit and the democratic spirit; and he was never clearer.

2   Published 1906–08. This edition includes a life of Dickens by John Forster, published first in 1872–74.

3   *Charles Dickens: A Critical Study*, by G. K. Chesterton. New York: Dodd, Mead & Co., 1906. [More's note]

4   There lies before me now a little book called *Tolstoy on Shakespeare* (Funk & Wagnalls Co.), containing three essays by Tolstoy, Ernest Crosby, and Bernard Shaw, respectively. The first reports thus on reading the greatest of Shakespeare's plays: "Not only did I feel no delight, but I felt an irrestible repulsion and tedium." The second, extolling the democracy of Milton, Shelley, and Burns, begins his destructive criticism: "But Shakespeare?—Shakespeare? where is there a line in Shakespeare to entitle him to a place in this brotherhood? Is there anything in his plays that is in the least inconsistent with all that is reactionary?" As for Mr. Shaw, it is well known that his complaint against the elder dramatist is chiefly because he was not like Mr. Shaw. But there is also in his hatred a touch of the same feeling that moves Tolstoy. One need not be a blind worshipper of Shakespeare to resent such small talk as this. And is it not time that somebody spoke the truth about Tolstoy? I do not mean the author of *Anna Karenina*, but the critic who makes the taste of an illiterate Russian peasant the criterion of art and who preaches the gospel of peace in the spirit of malignant iconoclasm. Why should we show respect for this portentous charlatanry? I cannot see that the sacrifices of Tolstoy's life absolve him from such a charge. Quite the best thing in Mr. Chesterton's book is the contrast between reformers such as Gorky, who write of *Creatures that Once were Men*, and Dickens, across all whose sketches of the unfortunate might be written the title, *Creatures that Still are Men*. [More's note]

5   Yet Mr. Andrew Lang, in his *Letters to Dead Authors*, vows he is no more touched by Little Nell than by her lacrimose sisters. [More's note]

6   "Yearning cry."

7   "If people would avoid contact with wisdom entirely and dwell continually with me, there would be no old age, but only the joy of perpetual youth." Desiderius Erasmus, *The Praise of Folly. A New Translation with Introduction and Notes*, by Leonard S. Dean. New York: Henricks House, 1946, p. 52.

Victorian Literature[1]

(The Philosophy of Change)

To write a history of English literature from 1837 to 1901, in all its ramifications from political economy to fiction, is a task to make any but the stoutest heart quail, and, whatever else may be said of Professor Walker's volume, it bears evidence of industrious reading and patient understanding.[2] Like most works of its kind it suffers somewhat from uncertainty of aim, being neither quite encyclopædic in completeness of detail nor sufficiently arbitrary in selection to deal effectively with ideas. But its arrangement by subjects and its inclusion of so much that is commonly rejected from literary history offer this great compensation that we are enabled to see the interworking of the various intellectual currents: Darwin and Tennyson, Malthus and Matthew Arnold, Spencer and Newman, thus appear as fellow labourers, moulding and expressing that subtle, evasive thing we call the spirit of the age. Evasive in a way that spirit is, as the inner forces of life must always be, yet there is one date and one book so preeminent that no one can go astray in seeking the centre of the manifold activities of Victorian thought. At the close of the reign—Professor Walker recalls the incident that every one will remember—a London daily paper asked its readers to send in lists of the ten books, English or foreign, which in their judgment were the greatest and most influential of the century past. The lists varied widely, save in one respect: in every list stood Darwin's publication of 1859, *The Origin of Species*.

One is not inclined to take these plebiscites very seriously, yet this was really an extraordinary event. I doubt if such an agreement on the preëminence of a contemporary book would have been possible in any country in any other age of the world; nor is the nature of the selection less remarkable than its unanimity. Probably not half the persons who named *The Origin of Species* had ever seriously read it, yet they all felt in some vague way that this book had struck the keynote of the century; their concurrence showed a certain lack of individual intelligence, but it was unmistakably significant. In Darwin's hypothesis, though they may not have comprehended its full bearing, they thought the mind of man had found at last that for which it had long been seeking—the perfect scientific formula: it looked to them as if a new and everlasting basis for truth had been laid. Descartes had reduced the physical world to a mechanical system, and Newton had formulated its mathematical laws. But Descartes had, theoretically at least, separated the sphere of the human spirit from his system, and to bring the living world, exclusive of man, within its control he had, by a gross violation of facts, denied to animals all reason and emotion and treated them as mere machines; while Newton in his laws merely ignored the whole organic creation. This extra-scientific field Darwin finally reclaimed. Evolution, indeed, was an old hypothesis, and long before Darwin's day had been brought into considerable prominence; but in the earlier romantic philosophers of France and Germany it had not been fortified by the patient unemotional accumulation of observed facts, and in the theory of Lamarck, the greatest of the scientific ante-Darwinians, it had not purged itself of various complications with some incalculable principle guiding the development of organic nature to a definite end. By the elimination of teleological and other foreign elements and by the authority of his vast patience Darwin raised evolution to the side of gravitation. As an equivalent of the mechanical law of motion in the inanimate world he gave precise expression to the absolute law of change in the animate, thus uniting inorganic and organic (including all that is man) in one universal scheme of science. The new law left no place for a power existing outside of nature and controlling the world as a lower order of existence, nor did it recognise a higher and a lower principle within nature itself, but in the mere blind force of variation, in the very unruliness to design or government, found the source of order and development. Chance itself was thus rendered calculable, and science reigned supreme through "all this changing world of changeless law." No wonder that men were a little dazed by the marvellous simplicity and finality of this formula, and were ready to exclaim, with a new meaning to the words:

> Let the great world spin for ever down the ringing
> grooves of change.

But like all other monistic theories of the reason, whether in science or metaphysics, Darwinism soon discovered within itself a principle of disintegration, and the ancient truth was again vindicated that any logical explanation of the world when carried to its conclusion is illogical. Fitness, in the new creed of evolutionary survival, meant adaptability to environment, but environment itself was produced by fitness, and the theory was thus seen to be revolving in a vicious circle. Fitness, which was to explain the mystery of order and apparent design, becomes, unless it is made relative to something outside of the things fit, a perfectly empty word, and the whole system falls to the ground. Against so illogical a theory Paley's simple argument for design in creation from the analogy of the watch is entirely valid. That syllogism may not prove the existence of a personal God, as Paley desired, or confirm the Thirty-nine Articles, but it does expose the inadequacy of holding that we can explain the origin of an orderly system of nature through any such hypothesis as the Darwinian law of flux and probability. Like other cosmical theories it may have little affirmative value, but it is strong to devour its rivals. As a matter of fact the insufficiency of Darwinism in its purest form has been pretty widely acknowledged by men of science themselves. In the recent celebration of Darwin's centennial two things were remarkable: the great reverence accorded to the memory of the man, and the fact that his successors are making desperate, and so far unaccepted, efforts to supplement or supplant the law of survival as the driving force of evolution. An unscientific skeptic might hint—his words will do no harm—that there is something paradoxical in this extreme reverence for Darwin undisturbed by this discontent with his chief hypothesis. The admiration is not due to the character of the man alone, for others have devoted their lives nobly and unreservedly to the search for scientific truth; it is rather the recognition of the fact that he at last was able to impose for a while on the world an hypothesis of life which was purely "causo-mechanical," and which eliminated everything divine and incalculable above or within nature. The discontent is a forced avowal that no such hypothesis is tenable. The additions to the Darwinian theory or the substitutes for it—and they are to-day almost as numerous as the great centres of biological study—are with one or two exceptions steps away from the sufficiency of the mere law of change which was to correspond to the law of motion in the inorganic sphere; some of the substitutes are, in fact, not far from the submission to teleological principles which are frankly beyond the scope of scientific formulation.

All this may seem rather remote from Victorian literature, but in fact it is, as the anecdote related by Professor Walker indicates, the very heart of the matter. Science has been, admittedly, the dominating intellectual force of the age, and the point of contact of science with literature is just this law of change. For it must not be forgotten that law, as it is understood in science, is a formulation of motion in the organic and of change in the inorganic realms as a power sufficient without any added principle of control to work out the ends of creation as we see them amplified in orderly recurrence and progress. Science and romanticism sprang up together and have grown side by side. In one respect they have embraced diverse, even hostile, temperaments—on this side the man who deals with facts and tends to a hard materialism or a dry intellectualism, on the other the man of sentiment who dreams and loses himself in futile revery. Yet it is a notorious, if paradoxical, fact that the effect of science on art and literature has been to reinforce a romantic impressionism, and that the man of scientific training when he turns to the humanities is almost always an impressionist. The reason is plain: he simply carries into art the law of change with which he has dealt in his proper sphere, and acknowledges no principle of taste superior to the shifting pleasure of the individual. In this he is typical of the age, for if the particular causo-mechanical theory of evolution promulgated by Darwin has proved untenable, evolution itself has remained as almost, if not quite, the universal creed of those who believe that some such hypothesis will ultimately be found adequate to explain all the processes of life. Men of science are only servants of the law of change in their special field of material observation, and it is easy to trace the working of the same belief in other regions of contemporary thought, most easy no doubt in philosophy which is nothing more than the effort of the reason to interpret in its own terms the common impulse and ambition of a period. There is a respectable school of idealists who hold to a theory of absolute unity and stability in which all the diversity and motion of the world are in some transcendental way absorbed. But these are not the regnant and effective teachers; they are so to speak the beautiful relics of a past creed. Pragmatism is the slogan of the hour, and there is a kind of truth in the remark thrown out recently in an English review that William James was the most influential leader in the spiritual life of the present generation. Now Pragmatism is just the culmination of what may be called the central philosophising of the past century. It has assumed various forms and has often been denied by its followers, but its general tendency is plain: it is at once romantic and scientific, an adventurous revolt against the dogmatic intellectualism in which science has involved itself and at the same time thoroughly evolutionary, even Darwinian, in theory. In the words of Professor Dewey[3]:

When he [Darwin] said of species what Galileo had said of the earth, *e pur si muove,* he emancipated, once for all, genetic and experimental ideas as an organon of asking questions and looking for explanations.

As a result we have the metaphysical conception "of a wide open universe, a universe without bounds in time or space, without final limits of origin or destiny"—in short, to use the elegant pragmatic diction borrowed from the police courts, "a universe with the lid off." No, continues our philosophical guide,

> Nature is not an unchangeable order, unwinding itself majestically from the reel of law under the control of deified forces. It is *an indefinite congeries of changes.* Laws are not governmental regulations which limit change, but are convenient formulations of selected portions of change followed through a longer or shorter period of time, and then registered in statistical forms that are amenable to mathematical manipulation.

I am not here attempting to controvert Pragmatism, though it may be worth while to hint in passing that the supercilious tone of its votaries is utterly unjustifiable until the causo-mechanical theory of evolution on which it is based has found some commonly accepted formulation among biologists, and to repeat what I have said elsewhere, that it is just as much a one-sided rationalisation of the data of experience as the contrary theory of idealism which Professor Dewey brushes aside contemptuously as "intellectual atavism." To the self-sufficiency of the pragmatist and idealist alike there is one reply: "There are more things in heaven and earth than are dreamt of in your philosophy."

Of the other manifestations of the law of change, I may speak even more briefly. In religion it is exhibited in the extraordinary influence of Cardinal Newman upon Brunetière and other French modernists who see, or think they see, in his "theory of development of doctrine" a means of reconciling Christian dogma with the scientific spirit of the age. The Cath-

olic theory of development as expounded by Newman meant
the slow grasping by human intelligence of great ideas which
were nevertheless "communicated to the world once for all by
inspired teachers"; it is a perception of change playing about
a fixed basis of unchangeable truth, with a growing tendency
to lay weight in this dualism upon the element of change. The
so-called "new theology" of Protestantism is more thoroughgoing and, virtually dispensing with the relation of mankind to
an immutable deity, discovers all of religion that is necessary
in the varying sympathy of man with his fellow man un-
regulated by any divine command or revelation.

Economics in its acceptance of the temper of the times has
undergone a strange but perfectly logical reversal. Synchro-
nously with the growth of the evolutionary theory arose the
economic doctrine of *laissez-faire,* culminating in the Manchester school which held that a world of economic order
would develop mechanically from the free play of individuals
upon one another without the intervention of any govern-
mental and, so to speak, external regulation of competition. It
was the perfect counterpart to the Darwinian notion of the
survival of the fittest amidst the accidental and competitive
variation of individuals.[4] Such a theory was pragmatic with a
vengeance, and brought its pragmatic penalty of social disease
and rebellion. In its place has arisen the socialistic creed, which
for the struggle of individuals sets up the warfare of classes and
a foreordained democracy, and which bears roughly to the
Manchester school the same relation that some of the aspects
of "orthogenesis" bear to Darwinism. It is withal as con-
vincedly evolutionary as was its predecessor,—however much
it may threaten revolution in practice,—and as impatient of
any law of control outside of material forces, only these forces
have assumed a social instead of an individualistic form. Both
self-developing individualism and self-developing socialism
are the children of the law of change, and the admixture of
humanitarian sympathy in both is really only another aspect of
the same principle.

The theory of education has naturally gone along with these

economic and philosophic innovations. Thus, the elective system in its present form is plainly a late-born offspring of the individualistic doctrine of *laissez-faire*. The whole shift of emphasis from the classics and humanities to scientific or quasi-scientific studies is a revulsion from the old notion that the experience of life in its essential phases is permanent and has once for all been expressed, to the conception of man as completely immersed in the *indefinite congeries of changes* which we call nature. We sometimes blame the teachers of Latin and Greek for certain disquieting weaknesses that have shown themselves in the recent results of education; as a matter of fact their only fault has been the lack of sufficient insight and strength to stem the tide of custom; by endeavouring to bring classical instruction into conformity with the spirit of the age they have largely forfeited its distinct virtue and have so far rendered it superfluous. If Greek affords no discipline corrective of the influence of science and different from that of the languages in which modern tendencies are expressed, the study of it is merely an enormous waste of time.

These things are the commonplaces of criticism and will scarcely be disputed. I have thought it worth while to bring them together in these brief statements, because in this way we get a clearer perception of the principle that has been everywhere and busily at work in the imaginative product of the nineteenth century and of our own day. Poetically the sources of Victorian literature go back to Wordsworth, who is emotionally the father of us all. No doubt the originating power of Wordsworth has in one sense been exaggerated, or at least misunderstood, for his return to nature is no new thing but a logical outgrowth of the philosophy of Rousseau and beyond him of the natural religion of the English deists. Yet there is withal a difference between the deistic and the romantic spirit toward nature as profound as it is hard to define. Almost the precise Wordsworthian note may be heard now and then in the poets and philosophers of the early eighteenth century, but in general one feels that their absorption of humanity in nature was by a conscious and clear process of elimination. The higher part of man, all that we associate with the mystic and indefinable, was plainly omitted from the deistic union of the human and the natural, and there was consequently no confusion in their ideas. You may walk in the meadow land of their new world with a feeling of ease and comfort, unperturbed by the intrusion of alien and higher cravings, but rather with the assurance that at will, if the moment of dissatisfaction comes, you may lift your eyes away from its homogeneous beauty to an utterly different region. In Wordsworth's sphere, on the contrary, you are caught as it were in a web of illusion, from which there is no escape save by a violent rupture. When his fervid soul, dismayed by the outcome of the Revolution, turned for solace to the quiet of the fields and the sublimity of the hills, he carried into that communion all the enthusiasm which an earlier age had reserved for the religion of the supernatural and which the deists in their satisfaction with natural religion had deliberately and completely shut out from their consciousness. In thus obliterating the distinctions of the reason Wordsworth introduced into the worship of nature the great pathetic fallacy which was to bewilder the minds and hearts of poets for an indefinite period.

And inevitably as science, becoming aware of the sway of change in nature, tried to formulate this power in terms of a causo-mechanical law, so poetry attempted to give it expression in human emotion. If any one thing is learned from such a survey of the poets of the past age and of to-day as we get in Professor Walker's volume, it is the constant immanence of this philosophy of change, manifesting itself in both the form and the substance of our verse. Walt Whitman is taken by many to be the most significant poet of America, not on account of his mere democracy, but because his democracy was part and parcel of his proclamation of the philosophy of change and motion. The universe to his eyes was a strange motley procession of shifting forms, at which he gazed undismayed, calling upon no passing appearance to stay for an instant and deliver its meaning. To William Morris also the world was a swift-moving succession of forms, glinting now with iridescent colours and breathing entranced melodies, with always the haunting fear in the observer's mind that if for one moment they should pause in their headlong flight they would vanish irrevocably into the void: life is many-hued, intricate motion; rest is death. And the evocation of Swinburne was essentially the same unintermittment flux of phenomena, though with him it took the special form of dissolving the earth into endless impressions of blowing wind and billowing water, with no solid ground beneath the feet. In Browning the new philosophy took the disguise of a buoyant revelling in the mere conflict and tumult of life without any formal restraint upon its multiform activity. His joyous acceptance of the world and his optimistic assurance that all things will of themselves work out right have passed with many for spiritual insight, whereas in reality his appeal to the present is due to his blind courage in waiving the critical check of the spirit of permanence. So one might go on enumerating the major poets of the age, but the repetition would only add tedium to the argument, and, indeed, I have already touched on this point many times in my essays on individual writers.

There is of course another aspect of Victorian poetry which must not be ignored. As no age, even the most self-satisfied, is entirely itself, but carries with it the memory of all that has gone before, so these singers of the flux are troubled at times by echoes of a past experience. Now and again a line, a note, will slip in that recalls the old desire of changeless rest and of the consummation of peace. It might even be more exact to say that the poets of the century as a whole do not so much give utterance to the unhesitating acceptance of the official philosophy as they express its ever growing predominance. And thus the most characteristic voices among the Victorians were just the two, Tennyson and Matthew Arnold, who felt most poignantly and sang most clearly, though in diverse ways, the transition from the old to the new. In Tennyson the two fields lay curiously side by side, and it is the sign of a certain lack of hardness in his mental fibre that he never seemed to perceive their mutual antagonism. At one moment he is the conscious laureate of science and evolution and of a self-evolving change moving to some far-off divine event; at another he is the prophet of insight, singing the mystery of the timeless, changeless spirit. Matthew Arnold's intelligence was too well-knit to suffer any such disruption of its powers. With him the error was deeper, yet more logical. Emotionally he was about equally susceptible to the prevailing currents of his day and of the past, and their intimate fusion produced a strange uneasiness of mind and heart, leaving him at home neither in this world nor the other. He looked abroad and saw nothing but change, and it seemed to him as if the permanent things that his soul craved were themselves in a state of transition. So it was he made his famous complaint, which is in a way the confession of his generation, at the Grande Chartreuse:

> Wandering between two worlds, one dead,
> The other powerless to be born,
> With nowhere yet to rest my head,
> Like these, on earth I wait forlorn.

But if this confusion in Matthew Arnold, or parallelism in Tennyson, of the past and the present is characteristic of Victorian poetry, the victory in the end is coming overwhelmingly to the new philosophy. If any one writer represents the thought of those who are most deeply immersed in the spirit of the passing day, it is George Meredith, and there is no poet or prosewriter in English who more speaks and exalts the belief in humanity as completely involved in the process of natural growth. This I suspect, rather than any perversity of wit, is the true reason, that the few who have not yet utterly bent the knee to the time-spirit are at once attracted by his subtlety of superficial observation and repelled by the absence of those deep underlying emotions which they have learned to expect in great literature. He has written out his reading of life in *The Woods of Westermain,* and the heart of his reading is at the end of his glorification of Change as the wondrous renovator and revealer:

> Change, the strongest son of Life,
> Has the Spirit here to wife.

Perhaps we do not often enough consider the profound innovation that such a sentiment indicates, nor look unflinchingly
into the great gulf that is separating our little space of time
from all that has preceded. Innumerable poets of the past have
reflected on the law of mutability and on its part and meaning
in human destiny, and their testimony, until this moment of
ours, has been almost universally that which Spenser sang so
exquisitely well in the unfinished book of *The Faerie Queene:*

> What man that sees the ever-whirling wheele
> Of *Change*, the which all mortall things doth sway,
> But that therby doth find, and plainly feele,
> How MUTABILITY in them doth play
> Her cruell sports, to many mens decay?

No doubt there is much to admire in our modern poets, with
the great name of Tennyson at their head, who have bowed
down in the temple of the idol of Mutability. They have many
traits of beauty and strength; they tease us with subtle appeals
to the heart and brain; they write from a wide and complicated
experience, and their concern over "the hopeless tangle of the
age" gives them often an air of profundity; yet withal they
leave us doubting whether there is in them the solid stuff to
endure. Some deeper satisfaction or assurance is wanting to
their work, and they themselves seem in a way transitional and
transitory, as their themes and their very rhythms spring from
the spirit of change. If any one thing may be called certain in
criticism, it is that the quintessence of poetical emotion, the
very kernel of the bitter-sweet passion of life and the world,
arises from the simultaneous perception in man's destiny of
the ever-fleeting and of that which is *contrayr to mutabilitie.*
The contrast takes a thousand forms and conceals itself under
many obscure disguises, but always, if you search deeply, you
will discover its presence in the passages of verse, or even of
prose, that stir in the reader's heart the lasting response of art.

If illustrations are necessary, the most familiar are the best. Thus Andrew Marvell, in the poem inscribed *To His Coy Mistress,* starts suddenly from the contemplation of her several charms to that never-forgotten outcry:

> But at my back I always hear
> Time's wingèd chariot hurrying near,
> And yonder all before us lie
> Deserts of vast eternity.

In those lines, more perhaps than anywhere else in English, the coming together of change and changelessness, the conflict between the passionate desire of ephemeral beauty and the motionless depths of man's eternal nature, rises to a sublimity that is closer to fear than to pleasure. Oftener it speaks the language of regret or wistful playfulness, as in Waller's inimitable descant on the old, old theme:

> Go, lovely Rose!
> Tell her that wastes her time and me—

where the sting of the pathos is due to a kind of pretty condescension of the spirit to the transitory symbols of time. When I consider all the richness of emotional content that must go out of poetry with the loss in our consciousness of anything "stayed upon the pillars of eternity," I am filled with concern for the future of letters. Already the impoverishment of Victorian literature in this respect is notable, and even where the contrast between the two spheres of our nature is implied it comes generally with a significant assimilation of the higher to the lower; as in the well-known couplet of William Cory's *Mimnermus in Church*:

> But oh, the very reason why
> I clasp them, is because they die.

The Victorian age, even more than others, was a time of transition. It has passed, and one thing at least is sure: we shall have no great literature again until we have looked once more within our own breasts and learned that there is something in human nature besides an *indefinite congeries of changes.* As it is now the very mould and *genre* of the higher emotion have been lost. It is almost inconceivable, for example, that a true tragedy should be composed to-day; for the tragic character, whether it be Antigone breaking herself magnanimously in the name of the unwritten eternal laws against the edicts of Creon, or Œdipus bruised and blinded by his ignorance of the divine purpose but caught up after years of submission into mystic fellowship with the gods, or Hamlet musing undecided while he listens to the fateful voices—everywhere the tragic mood depends on the unresolved conflict in human motives between the universal and the particular, the changeless law and the temporal passion. It even seems that, with the disappearance of the greater form, there is passing away the ambition to write greatly. And naturally. For if the performance of a work of art is due to its fit expression of the permanent in human desire and experience, what room is there for the long hope, or what impulse to sacrifice present popularity for enduring fame, when the very notion has become discredited of any principle contrary to ceaseless change?

I have been concerned here primarily with literature, but obviously the destiny of literature is bound up with that of the practical world. If the disregard of permanence means formlessness and the absence of the higher emotion in letters, it means the same thing in society; nor under the existing worship of change, whether economic theory follows the individualism of Cobden or the collectivism of Karl Marx, can there be any escape for civilisation from the present dominance of material forces. Relax those brutal bulwarks against the inrush of ungoverned change and the result is simple anarchy. Nor is there real hope from the mitigating influence of that humanitarian sympathy which has accompanied the growth of scientific intellectualism; for such sympathy is but another aspect of the same absorption in change, being an attempt of the individual to flow, so to speak, in the direction of every emotional impact from the world. It contains no power of resistance or principle of restraint, but tends on the contrary to make man a more helpless prey of the ever-encroaching flood. The only salvation is in the recognition of some superior guiding and dividing law of just rule and right subordination, in the perception, that is, of something permanent within the flux.

There is need of firm hearts and clear brains to bring us out of this slough of indifference, but unfortunately the strong men are too often paralysed by a curious superstition of words. The saying has gone abroad that strength means joy in change and that he who would question change is reactionary and effeminate; and so in the name of progress and virility we drift supinely with the current. If by reactionary is understood only the man who shudders at all innovation and who cries out for some impossible restoration of the past, the charge is well made. Such a man in the social realm corresponds to the metaphysician who would deny the existence of change and the many for an exclusive and sterile idealism of the one. But reaction may be, and in the true sense is, something utterly different from this futile dreaming; it is essentially to answer action with action, to oppose to the welter of circumstance the force of discrimination and selection, to direct the aimless tide of change by reference to the co-existing law of the immutable fact, to carry the experience of the past into the diverse impulses of the present, and so to move forward in an orderly progression. If any young man, feeling now within himself the power of accomplishment, hesitates to be called a reactionary, in this better use of the term, because of the charge of effeminacy, let him take courage. The world is not contradicted with impunity, and he who sets himself against the world's belief will have need of all a man's endurance and all a man's strength. The adventurous soul who to-day against the reigning scientific and pragmatic dogma would maintain no vague and equally one-sided idealism, but the true duality of the one and the many, the absolute and the relative, the permanent and the mutable, will find himself subjected to an intellectual isolation and contempt almost as terrible as the

penalties of the inquisition, and quite as effective in producing
a silent conformity. If a man doubts this, let him try, and learn.
Submission to the philosophy of change is the real effeminacy;
it is the virile part to react.

[1]   This essay was published in *The Nation* for Oct. 6 and in the Book Section of
       the *Evening Post* for Oct. 22, 1910. More then included it in the Seventh Series
       of the *Shelburne Essays* (1910). A French translation by M. Louis J. A. Mercier
       came out in *Le Mouvement humaniste aux Etats-Unis* (1928). It has since been
       included in a volume of *American Critical Essays*, edited by More's fellow New
       Humanist, Norman Foerster, in 1930, and in *An Anthology of Contemporary
       English Prose*, edited by John C. H. Wu and M. C. Liang, published in Shang-
       hai, China, in 1940. The essay is another good example of More's ability to trace
       in present ills the effect of deep historial currents working in previous centu-
       ries.
[2]   *The Literature of the Victorian Era*, by Hugh Walker. Cambridge University
       Press. New York: G. P. Putnam's Sons, 1910. [More's note]
[3]   *The Influence of Darwin on Philosophy, and Other Essays in Contemporary
       Thought*, by John Dewey. New York: Henry Holt & Co., 1910. [More's note]
[4]   In theory, and in the practice of some individuals, the Manchester school of
       economics was mixed up with various philanthropic schemes. Throughout the
       century there is to be noted a fluctuation between the harshest egotism and
       the most sentimental sympathy; the two moods springing indeed from the
       same surrender to the philosophy of change and easily passing into each other.
       The compensation is doubtful, and as a matter of fact egotism will always under
       the stress of circumstances take the upper hand, unless controlled by some
       principle more foreign to itself than sympathy. As regards the relation of
       evolution to economics, it is well known that both Darwin and Wallace were
       led to the survival theory by the reading of Malthus. [More's note]

The Demon
of the Absolute[1]

From I. Standards

Luther once likened our human nature to a drunkard on horseback: prop him up on one side, and over he topples on the other. The simile is apt, and applies to taste as well as to morals. As soon as we are convinced that no absolute standard exists, forthwith we flop to the other extreme and swear that there are absolutely no standards at all; so hard is it to keep the middle path of common sense. And so behind the light-armed skirmishers of the press whom, to say the truth, no one takes very seriously, we have scholars like Mr. Spingarn, who, with the inverted sort of pedantry common today, teach a ready public that art is only expression and criticism only impression, and that no one need bother to hunt for standards of taste, which are not and never were. And worse than that, we have sober philosophers like Lord Balfour, arguing for pure relativity of taste on metaphysical grounds:

> That is for every man most lovable which he most dearly loves. That is for every man most beautiful which he most deeply admires. Nor is this merely a reiteration of the old adage that there is no disputing about tastes. It goes far deeper; for it implies that, in the most important cases of all, a dispute about either love or beauty would not merely be useless: it would be wholly unmeaning.

These men, I assert, and not the champions of reasonable standards of taste, are the veritable addicts of the Absolute and slaves of the Demon. They theorize very persuasively, but have their conclusions any relation to fact? Is it true that admiration so varies with time and place, and from individual to individual, that no common sense of beauty is discoverable which can be used as a basis of conversation and to which appeal can be made in argument? If my theme were the plastic arts, it would be sufficient to adduce the indisputable truth that the forms and pictures prized as lovely by the Orient do sooner or later obtain due recognition in the West, and *vice versa.* However it be with minor eccentricities, the supremely beautiful things in Greece and Italy and India and China are beautiful for all the world. But for our convenience we may look rather to the extraordinary absence of local and temporal barriers in lyrical poetry. When Simonides composed his epitaph for the Spartans who fell at Thermopylæ:

> O passer by, tell the Lacedæmonians that we lie here obeying their orders—

he used words that would carry the same poetic thrill to all men of all lands. Perhaps you will say that the emotion expressed by Simonides is so simple, the language so devoid of ornament or metaphor or fancy, that the couplet is scarcely to be reckoned as poetry. I think no one acquainted with the Greek would raise such an objection; but let it pass. Let us take one of the epigrams of the Anthology, written by a poet of no particular reputation and replete with the imagery of pagan superstition:

> Do thou, who rowest the boat of the dead in the water of this reedy lake, for Hades, stretch out thy hand, dark Charon, to the son of Cinyras, as he mounts the ladder by the gangway, and receive him. For his sandals will cause the lad to slip, and he fears to set his feet naked on the sand of the shore.

That is one of the trifles of art, yet its pathetic beauty could touch the heart of an American, Lafcadio Hearn, who had made his home in the far Orient, and who set by its side for comparison a *tanka* (a lyric confined to thirty-one syllables) of a Japanese governor on the death of his son:

> As he is so young, he cannot know the way. . . . To the messenger of the Underworld I will give a bribe, and entreat him, saying: "Do thou kindly take the little one upon thy back along the road."

Surely there is a common ground of feeling and taste even in these minor things, something that overleaps all estrangement of land and race and age. So, to come nearer home, Ben Jonson, "Saint Ben," as Herrick called him, Briton to the core of him, could cull a few phrases scattered through the very prosaic letters of Philostratus, and weave them into a song which, given the knowledge of the English tongue, will find an echo in the heart of any lover of beauty the world over:

> Drink to me only with thine eyes,
> And I will pledge with mine;
> Or leave a kiss but in the cup,
> And I'll not look for wine.
> The thirst that from the soul doth rise,
> Doth ask a drink divine:
> But might I of Jove's nectar sup,
> I would not change for thine.

And Goethe, alone amidst the trees and the mountains, in the wide silence of a summer night, once wrote in German what a Chinese, centuries ago and far away by the shores of the Yangtse River, might have expressed in his own metrical form:

> *Ueber allen Gipfeln*
> *Ist Ruh.* [2]

But we have no need to multiply examples. It is a simple fact, not a theory, that in the matter of taste there is still that which is not confined by the boundaries of space or nullified by the process of time, and which makes the whole world kin. This is not to say that we can lay down any absolute law of agreement;

but it does mean, emphatically, that certain standards of taste exist which approximate, more or less, to universality. It is a direct challenge to the veracity of those who would stop our mouths with the dictum that a debate about either love or beauty is not merely useless, but wholly unmeaning.

If only the henchmen of the press, who have been seduced by the prophets of the flux, would act consistently on the principle that there is no disputing about tastes! But this is the curious fact: just so surely as you meet with one of these relativistic critics, you will find him pretty soon uttering the most savage and exemplary judgements against those who disagree with him. This Mr. Powys, for instance, who is regarded as a model of adventurous and irresponsible sympathy, can slash about when he pleases with a cutting assurance which hints at a bowie-knife in his pocket, however he may eschew cosmic footrules. But the really test case is the great Anatole France, the flowing philosopher *par excellence,* from whom so many of our late-emancipated youth have borrowed their literary creed, to the effect that criticism is a continual adventure of the soul, a kind of freebooting romance for the curious and enlightened. Well, one day, in the course of his *Vie Littéraire,* Anatole France felt obliged to write about a certain novel, *La Terre,* which no amount of adventurous sympathy could make him like, which, in fact, he heartily disliked; and this is how he sums up his condemnation of the author: "He [M. Zola] has no taste, and I have come to believe that the want of taste is that mysterious sin spoken of by the Scripture, the greatest of sins, which alone will never be pardoned."

In other words, when Anatole France laid aside theory and spoke his real mind, he would judge as incisively as M. Brunetière or any other avowed doctrinaire; and admittedly he judges from a central principle of his nature, which he calls taste. How, indeed, could it be otherwise? Every man likes certain things and dislikes certain other things; more than that, every man likes a certain class of things and dislikes a certain other class of things, and praises or dispraises by a standard, whether he names it taste or refuses to acknowledge that it has a name.

II. Tradition

The simple truth is that every man, unless he be a dumb idiot, has a standard, more or less consciously chosen, by which he judges, and when the "irresponsibles" exhibit such fury at the sound of the word, they are merely throwing dust in our eyes to confuse the issue. The real question is not whether there are standards, but whether they shall be based on tradition or shall be struck out brand new by each successive generation or by each individual critic. And first of all is there in fact any discoverable tradition of taste, or do we deceive ourselves in imagining its existence?

The relativists, like Lord Balfour, point to the mistakes of criticism in the past, and particularly to its failure to recognize great works of original genius on their first appearance. They take a ghoulish glee in quoting the sentences of Jeffrey and Gifford and the other anti-romanticists of the early nineteenth century. And what, they ask, shall we expect of "official" criticism which says that *The Excursion* will never do, tells a certain young surgeon's apprentice named Keats to go back to his gallipots, and has no better description of Shelley's poems than "convulsive caperings of Pegasus labouring under colic pains"? Well, those much-maligned maligners are like the devil in one respect at least: they are not so black as they are painted. There were fools among them, no doubt; and our own feeble-minded are not all in asylums. But if those who take most delight in decrying Jeffrey, for instance, would condescend to read what they abuse, they would find that his taste was generally good, and that most, not all, of the things he condemned were worthy of condemnation. They might learn, too, that the despised Gifford's chief work, in *The Baviad* and *The Mæviad*, was to bring contempt upon the "namby-pamby madrigals" and "splay-foot doggrel," the "motley fustian, neither verse nor prose," of a horde of much-lauded poets now well forgotten. As Scott said, he "squabashed the Della Cruscans at one blow." I suspect that one of the things we most need in our own day is just a *Baviad* to pillory some of the lawless men who are trampling down the wild thyme of Parnassus.

I am far from saying that Gifford and his tribe were always judicious or generous. I do say, however, that where they failed it was precisely because they were not in the tradition, but pronounced sentence from the narrow and ephemeral point of view of the pseudo-classic, not the classic, school. Those who scold these errant critics as an illustration of the complete relativity of taste, forget that they do so by virtue of the validity of a larger tradition. It is with tradition as it is with standards: because tradition is not absolute and infallible, men are prone to cry out that there is no tradition. That is a habit deep-rooted in human nature, hard to eradicate. No intelligent man supposes that tradition is a scale fixed once and forever in all its *nuances* of valuation; but it is a simple matter of history, nevertheless, that a long tradition of taste does exist, wavering and obscure on its outskirts, growing steadier and more immutable as we approach its centre. Let us take a poet who stands in this central tradition and follow his fortunes, briefly by necessity, in general estimation. We shall see, I think, that the law of taste is the least changeable fact of human nature, less changeable than religious creeds, far less changeable than scientific theories. The advent of Christianity has left it untouched, and the waning of faith does not trouble it. The hypotheses of science —elemental spirits, antiphlogiston, corpuscular and undulatory explanations of light, atoms and ions and the continuum, catastrophism and natural selection—come and pass and come again, while the central tradition of taste is still the same. Wars and revolutions alter everything, but not this. It is like the sea:

> Man marks the earth with ruin, his control
> Stops with the shore.

If anything in history seems to be settled it is the position of Homer among the Greeks. To him they turned for the source of literature, the mirror of conduct, the fountain-head of all right thinking and all right speaking. He was the guide of the young, the philosopher of the middle-aged, the friend of the old. Not that his acceptance was absolute. Plato, though he could write of Homer in terms of adoration, also censured him harshly for his familiar treatment of the gods; and there was a crabbed grammarian named Zoilus, who won the epithet *Homeromastix*, scourge of Homer, for his systematic abuse of the poet. But these exceptions only prove that a solid fact need not be an absolute fact. And what Homer was to the Greeks, he continued to be to the Romans until the old civilization passed away.

With the coming of the Dark Ages—significant name—there is a change. The Greek language was almost forgotten in the West, and as a consequence the *Iliad* and *Odyssey* were little read. Nevertheless, the tradition was not lost, nor even totally eclipsed, and with the revival of learning it emerges once more, never again, let us hope, to be darkened. There were, however, several curious and, in part, contradictory currents in Renaissance criticism which for a while prevented the complete acknowledgement of Homer's literary supremacy. For one thing, owing to the language of the *AEneid* and to the ease with which Christian ideas could be read into various passages, Virgil had supplanted Homer through the Middle Ages as the master poet; and the scholars of the Renaissance, despite their pose of general rebellion, were too deeply involved in the spirit of the immediate past to escape its æsthetical restrictions without a long struggle. And the theory of the new criticism, with its insistence on the authority of reason and on the authority of age, tended to uphold the superiority of the Latin epic. These two principles of authority were clearly and definitely formulated by Scaliger in his *Poetice*, published in 1561, and were applied to the tradition of taste with childlike confidence. "Homer's genius," he says (*Poetice*, v, 2), "was the greatest; his art was of such a character that he seems rather to have happened on it than to have cultivated it. Wherefore there is no reason for surprise if I find in him a certain Idea of nature, but not art. . . . Then Virgil, having received art from Homer in this rude state, raised it by his selective study of nature and his judgement to the highest point of perfection. . . . As in the very circle of our life there are many things, yet few give pleasure,

and still fewer raise admiration; so many things would insinu-
ate themselves into the breast of the poet, but not all are to be
admitted. He who follows the example of Virgil prefers therefore to exclude an occasional good thing which might give
pleasure, rather than admit anything which can offer even the
suspicion of offence."

Here you will see how Scaliger applies to Homer and Virgil
the false notion of reason as a faculty superior to, and in a sense
hostile to, the creative imagination—the notion underlying
pseudo-classic art and pseudo-classic criticism, which, strange
as it may sound, is still confused with the true classic by some
of our belated scholars. It is easy to understand how such a
theory worked against the full and frank recognition of Homer
as an artist.

The other principle formulated by Scaliger was oddly inconsistent in its operation. Like the Renaissance scholars in general he was imbued with respect for authority as a power
synonymous with age. Now, in accordance with this law the
Iliad as the older poem ought to be the better, and this undoubtedly would have been Scaliger's avowed opinion were it
not that he stood committed to the greater regularity and art
of Virgil. Instead, therefore, of comparing Homer with Virgil
on the basis of authority by virtue of age, he switches aside and
makes his comparison between the *Iliad* and the *Hero and
Leander* of Musæus, really a late production of the sixth century after Christ, but by a confusion of its author with the
mythical Musæus held to be a work of the remote pre-Homeric
age. Scaliger was too sound a critic at heart not to see that the
actual matter of the *Hero and Leander* was relatively slight
and insignificant; but he had his hypothesis ready, like a true
philologian. He imagined that this poem was a mere *parergon*
of the mighty bard of antiquity and that the serious works of
Musæus and Orpheus and their coevals had been lost. "If Musæus," he says, "had written those things which Homer wrote,
we may suppose that he would have written them far better."
And as it is, "the style," if not the substance, "of Musæus is far
more polished and elegant than Homer's."

Now this triple judgement of Scaliger on Homer and Virgil and Musæus bears closely on the true nature of tradition. It shows, I think, that in his heart of hearts Scaliger was quite awake to the surpassing genius and art of Homer, but was seduced by current theories to express opinions not entirely in accord with his actual taste as determined by the criterion of pleasure. And one can follow this deflexion of expressed opinion right through the reign of pseudo-classicism. Let me illustrate what I mean by two familiar examples taken from English literature. One cannot read Pope's *Preface to the Iliad* without feeling his preference of the poet he was translating; yet so deeply ingrained in his mind was the Renaissance notion of the opposition between reason and inventive genius that he could not omit a formal comparison of the two ancient epics on the basis of this contrast. "No author or man," he says, "ever excelled all the world in more than one faculty; and as Homer has done this in invention, Virgil has in judgement. Not that we think that Homer wanted judgement, because Virgil had it in a more eminent degree; or that Virgil wanted invention, because Homer possessed a larger share of it; each of these authors had more of both than perhaps any man besides, and are only said to have less in comparison with one another. Homer was the greater genius, Virgil the better artist. In one we most admire the man, in the other the work." And so on. For our other illustration we may take the absurd wrangle that was the occasion of Swift's *Battle of the Books*. Does any one suppose that Sir William Temple and Boyle or any other champion of the *Epistles of Phalaris* got more satisfaction out of reading those frigid exercises in rhetoric than from the genuine masterpieces of Greek prose? Certainly they did not; yet because they believed these *Epistles* to be from the hand of the Sicilian tyrant and so endowed with the authority of primitive age, they did not hesitate to cross swords for them with the terrible Bentley himself. At least one of the false theories of pseudo-classicism, the sheer authority of age, was so damaged in that battle that it has had little force since then to deflect the straight line of tradition.

Homer was to come to his own with the revival of Romanticism, though here again the mischievous inheritance of the Renaissance can be seen at work. The romanticists were, and are, quite as convinced as any pseudo-classicist of the inherent hostility between reason and imagination, between judgement and genius; only they take the opposite side and bestow all their praises on imagination, as they understand it, and genius. Hence you will find a succession of scholars in the nineteenth century, particularly in Germany, who made much of the spontaneity and naiveté of the *Iliad*, likening it to the untutored ballads of the people, and comparing it in this respect favourably with the Æneid, which they were wont to belittle as a product of reflective judgement and conscious art. On the whole I am inclined to believe that the justice of tradition has come nearer to suffering a real perversion from these romantic sentimentalists than from the rationalists of the pseudo-classical school.

But withal the tradition still abides, and promises to abide. There are, of course, men today, like our late professional endower of libraries, who affect to look down on the *Iliad* as the work of a barbarous age. But if you investigate their opinion, you will find that it is warped by some extraneous theory, such as a crude pacifism which thinks it uncivic to enjoy a tale of fighting, or an equally crude evolutionism which measures excellence unflinchingly by the criterion of newness. And you will commonly find, moreover, that these faddists have not read the poem in the original, that is, properly speaking, have not read it at all, and so ought to be put out of court. The verdict of those who have a right to judge is almost without exception that in Homer we have the nearest approach to pure poetry, and that everything since is in a way derivative and secondary.

At any rate, I do not see how one can study the history of taste honestly without acknowledging this fact of the enduring permanence of the Homeric tradition. His place, you will observe, has not been absolutely fixed; it has deflected a little to this side and to that in accordance with the changing theories of criticism, but it has always moved close to a central point—like the North Star, which moves about at a slight distance from the axis of the sky. As we depart further and further from this core of tradition, our literary judgements become less certain and the probability of variation grows greater; but the central truth is not affected. Those who deny the validity of tradition are like watchers of the heavens who should set their eyes on the wandering planets of the ecliptic and from these alone should infer that there was no possibility of a Polar Star.

III. The Criterion

At this point a wary antagonist might break in with a seasonable objection. All this, he will say, is very well, but it scarcely touches the real issue. I will grant that standards do exist, in the sense that for all men certain works of art possess qualities which they instinctively or consciously use as a criterion of taste. I will even grant the existence in the past of those traditional standards on which you lay so much stress. But what is it to me though a hundred generations of mankind have united in acclaiming the merits of this or that poem; is that any reason why I should admire the same thing? The truth is that our relativists, who dwell with such satisfaction on the errors of authoritative criticism, are not so much concerned with disproving the existence of traditional standards as they are with establishing their own right to independence of taste.

Well, tradition does not *create* standards; to suppose that it did would be to fall into the pseudo-classical error of regarding age as a criterion of excellence. But tradition may be evidence that certain works of art embody qualities which it is very much our concern to appreciate, and which we have every reason to use as a criterion. To understand why this is so we must look a little into the nature of these criteria on which standards are formed. And here, luckily, we have the help of one who, as the first of romantic critics in English, ought to possess, and does possess, high credit among the relativists of today. "As it was my constant reply," Coleridge says in his

Biographia Literaria, "to authorities brought against me from later poets of great name, that no authority could avail in opposition to TRUTH, NATURE, LOGIC, and the LAWS OF UNIVERSAL GRAMMAR; actuated too by my former passion for metaphysical investigations; I laboured at a solid foundation, on which permanently to ground my opinions, in the component faculties of the human mind itself, and their comparative dignity and importance. According to the faculty or source, from which the pleasure given by any poem or passage was derived, I estimated the merit of such poem or passage. As the result of all my reading and meditation, I abstracted two critical aphorisms; . . . first, that not the poem which we have *read,* but that to which we *return,* with the greatest pleasure, possesses the genuine power, and claims the name of *essential poetry.* . . . Be it however observed, that I excluded from the list of worthy feelings, the pleasure derived from mere novelty in the reader, and the desire of exciting wonderment at his powers in the author."

Coleridge is verbose and wanders as usual, but his "solid foundation" resolves itself clearly enough into these four rules:

First: That the value of a work of art is not determined primarily by authority, but is a question of truth and nature.

Secondly: That our sense of truth and nature in a work of art is the pleasure we derive from it. To this notion, that the aim of art is to give pleasure, Coleridge returns frequently in the course of his rambling treatise.

Thirdly: Coleridge asserts that pleasures vary in value and importance by a criterion of permanence. For instance, other things being equal, we place a higher value on a poem which continues to interest us on a second or third perusal than on one which interested us a first time, but bores us a second time.

Fourthly: He asserts that pleasures vary also in value and importance by a criterion of quality, that is, in accordance with the faculty of the mind which is concerned.

Now to the first and second of these principles I do not see how the most truculent individualist can object; taken alone they might even appear to support the position for which he is contending. And the same thing, I suppose, might be said of the third and fourth principles, were it not for certain inferences which too patently can be drawn from them. In these inferences lies the very crux of the question at issue.

To take the third proposition: if it be true that pleasure is a criterion of value in a work of art, and if one element of comparison between two pleasures be their relative degree of permanence, if, that is to say, other things being equal, we instinctively prefer the pleasure that endures the longer, then is there not, on the face of it, a strong probability that the book which has been read with interest by a hundred generations of men, while other books have been read and forgotten, is the one which will maintain its interest for the individual reader, if he will give it a fair chance? At least the burden of proof rests upon those who would deny such an analogy.

Let me ask for indulgence if I speak from my personal experience. It was my custom for a number of years, while I enjoyed the schoolman's privilege of leisurely vacations, to pass my summers on the coast of Maine, and there each season, within sight and sound of Homer's eternal sea, to read through the *Iliad* and *Odyssey* alternatively, not indeed shedding tears like the captive of Calypso, who

> Day after day, from beach and rocky caves,
> Looked out upon the waste of untamed waves—

but filled with "the sober certainty of waking bliss," such as no other reading has ever afforded me. I do not give this experience as in any way peculiar to myself. On the contrary, Homer has kept his place in tradition just because he has offered this uncloying pleasure to all who are prepared to take it. Possibly some book written today might have the same power, but, considering the actual destinies of literature past and present, the chances are a million to one against it—*habent sua fata libelli.*[3]

Tradition, it is well to repeat, is not in itself a quality of excellence, but merely evidence of such qualities; and the question is still to be answered, why these poets—Homer and Virgil and Dante and Shakespeare and Milton and the other genuine classics—have attained their preeminence, and why they are able to afford us a permanence of delight such as we cannot get from ephemeral productions.

First of all they have this power, I think, because they appeal to what is universal in human nature, rather than to what is temporary and accidental. But this quality of universality needs to be defined, since it is of a double source, and in one of its aspects is the aim of a sort of art which can be called anything but classical. Men lose their differences and show the common ground of humanity when they rise to the height of their being and when they sink to its lowest substratum. There is a striking passage at the opening of the ninth book of the *Republic* in which Plato tells of the lawless desires that lurk in the breast of every man, even the most virtuous, silent by day when the man's will is awake, but sometimes in his sleep going forth to accomplish their filthy ends.[4] Yes, the beast is in all of us, and it is possible to attain a kind of universality by rousing it, and feeding it with suggestions, until it dominates the soul. This is the truth that the naturalists have learned. There is in fact a whole school of writers in Russia and Austria and Germany and Scandinavia who are trading on it systematically; and recently the same theory of art has begun to hold up its head in England and America. We have among us a growing number of pithecoid creatures, who know enough of art to understand that its appeal should be to the universal in human nature, but are not sufficiently educated to perceive that the true universal of art is of quite another order than the bestial. These naturalists forget that permanence of pleasure is a prime requisite of good art, or, remembering it, are blind to the fact that the pleasure derived from the inverted order of universality is of all kinds the quickest to cloy. This is not a matter of theory but of experience. Take Zola's *La Terre*, or any other of his novels in which the principle of naturalism was first worked out systematically, is it possible to imagine any normal man returning to such a book year after year, with ever-heightened enjoyment? Naturalism may conceivably fascinate by the shock of surprise, or may conceivably interest for a while by the intensity of the emotions it excites, but surprise and intensity are the least stable factors of pleasure, and, if they appeal to the animal within us, they pass quickly to satiety and from satiety to disgust. As Shakespeare's Friar Laurence said, in words that might be applied to naturalism long before Anatole France reviewed *La Terre*, it is but "the unreasonable fury of a beast":

> These violent delights have violent ends,
> And in their triumph die.

The universality of true art is of quite another order than this, and leads to the fourth of our criteria. It will be remembered that Coleridge, besides grading pleasures by the standard of permanence, distinguished them "according to the faculty or source" from which they were derived. Man, he would say, is not simple in his being, but dual; there is in all men the lurking beast, but there is also in all men a faculty of control whether you call this higher element reason or the divine or the supernatural. The error of the naturalist is to regard men as simple, or as natural in the sense of having no other nature than animal instincts. He seeks the universal there where, according to his imperfect psychology, it can alone be found, and the puppet world of his vision is like Cassio's: "I have lost the immortal part of myself, and what remains is bestial." The true artist, on the contrary, is aware indeed of the bestial in man, but sees also something else, and in that something else looks for the meaning of life.

I do not say that the artist, by this law of our double being, is restricted in his representation of nature to what is pure and innocent; very far from that. Homer and Shakespeare and Turgeniev, all the poets and dramatists and novelists in the great tradition, have not blenched before a world shaken, as the world we know is shaken, by passionate ambition and furious desire. Nor is the true artist one who takes upon himself the office of preacher, to rail unseasonably against the short-comings and vices of the life he is portraying; very far from that. Rather he is one who, by the subtle, insinuating power of the imagination, by just appreciation of the higher emotions as well as the lower, by the revelation of a sad sincerity, shall I call it, in his own soul, gives us always to feel that the true universal in human nature, the faculty by which man resembles man as a being different from the beast, is that part of him that is "noble in reason," the master and not the slave of passion. True art is thus humanistic rather than naturalistic; and its gift of high and permanent pleasure is the response of our own breast to the artist's delicately revealed sense of that divine control, moving like the spirit of God upon the face of the waters.

So far I seem to see my way clear. If you should ask me by what rhetorical devices or by what instrument of representation one poem or one work of art appeals more successfully than another to the higher faculty within us, how, for instance, Milton's *Paradise Lost* accomplishes this end better than Blackmore's *King Arthur*, though both poems were written with equally good intentions, I would reply frankly that the solution of this problem of the imagination may be beyond my powers of critical analysis. And, fortunately, I am not here concerned with artistic means but with artistic results. I could at least say to the questioner, with a good deal of assurance, that, if he would read honestly both *Paradise Lost* and *King Arthur*, however he might feel towards Milton's epic he would find his pleasure in Blackmore's epic less in kind and quality. No power on earth, not even the desire to rout an adversary, could make him read Blackmore a second time.

But there is still a difficulty. Why, if these criteria are inherent in human nature, are not they themselves universally acknowledged? Whence the obvious fact that the tradition of taste is so widely rejected today by those who make a boast of modernism? "I know," we can hear one of these gentlemen say, "that past generations of men pretended to find their fullest artistic satisfaction in Homer and Shakespeare and Milton and others of the illustrious dead; but I do not. I won't say much about Homer, since he is Greek to me; but Bernard Shaw gets more pleasure from his own plays than from Sophocles and Shakespeare and Racine rolled together, and so do I. And as for your Milton, I have heard college professors declare that no one now reads *Paradise Lost* except under compulsion, and I know that I and my friends are vastly more entertained by the meandering prose of Mr. Joyce's *Ulysses* than by all the formal epics ever composed. The past was in leading-strings, but we have suddenly grown alive and, I may add, honest."

Well, our sceptical friend is certainly honest, and he seems to be pretty wide awake; but is he educated? Now education embraces many things: it does not despise the most humble and utilitarian pursuits; it is largely occupied with the bare acquisition of knowledge; it aims to strengthen the muscles of the body and to tighten the fibres of the brain; but, above all, it is, or should be, a discipline of the soul in the appreciation of pleasure and pain. Do not suppose that such a discipline is a light or unimportant matter. If you will read the ninth book of Plato's *Republic* and the introductory books of the *Laws*, you will see how, to the eye of that keenly observant philosopher, the whole of human conduct, whether for good or for evil, is dependent on the right appreciation of pleasure and pain, and how deeply the welfare of the State is concerned with the education of youth in just this field. Teach a boy to take pleasure in things that are fine and pure and strong and of good repute, and you have prepared him for a life wholesome and happy in itself and useful to the community.

Certainly, at least, the standards of taste are involved in this discipline. That faculty of the soul which responds to the higher and more permanent pleasures of art is, no doubt, present in all men, and is thus potentially universal; but it may be, and commonly is, dormant until awakened by external stimulus. For the reason that its activity means a steady choice among our natural inclinations and impulses, demanding self-control and, in a way, self-abnegation, it comes to full fruition only by exercise that at first may be painful and repellent to the natural man. By nature men are prone to grasp at the nearest and easiest pleasure, and to shirk the labour necessary for the higher and more permanent pleasure. They are even inclined to question the reality of the higher and more permanent pleasure, until it has been forced upon their recognition by the experience of others. And just here is the function of tradition. The very essence of education is not to confirm the young mind in its natural temperament, in its tendency to pursue the present and easier pleasure, but to set before it the stirring example of those who have found their joy and consolation in the higher things, forcing it by a tender compulsion, painful perhaps at the moment, but leading gradually to the liberty of endless delight, to taste of these things for itself and to acquire the right to judge of them whether they be indeed full of pleasantness for the awakened soul. Education is the ability to judge. The educated man is he who has the right to pronounce on the standards of taste, because he has had experience of both the higher and the lower pleasures. I am not upholding any priggish or superhuman ideal. The educated man will not have lost his appreciation of the commoner things at their time and in their degree. He will enjoy the wholesome books that are of the moment and make no pretension to permanence or elevation; you will remember that our relativistic friends have even charged Mr. Root and Mr. Hughes, whether for honour or for dishonour, with finding a secret satisfaction in detective stories and penny-dreadfuls. But the educated man is one who has also been trained to know that highest and most enduring pleasure which is derived from the few great books selected and approved by the verdict of tradition. And in that power of enjoyment he will feel himself set free from his own petty limitations, and made a humble companion of those who share the heritage of time.

I suspect that these sticklers for the liberty of taste against the judgments of mankind are in the main simply uneducated; being untrained to feel the higher and more permanent pleasures of art, they grasp at any ephemeral work that offers an easy flattery of the lower elements of their nature, and swear there is nothing else. It may sound a bit paradoxical to reduce the rebellion against standards to so simple a matter as imperfect education, and indeed, that phrase does not tell the whole story. The merely uneducated man is likely to be indifferent to standards rather than actively hostile, or he may be a modest fellow who knows what he has missed, and would never think of raising his ignorance into a "cosmic footrule." There is a cause, a trait of character, behind the belligerence of ignorance. The belligerents themselves call it "irresponsibility of temperament" or the "spirit of romantic adventure," or may dignify it as a "philosophy of relativism"; but it has another name, which I rather hesitate to mention. In fact, I should not have courage to pronounce the invidious phrase at all, had it not been spoken long ago by those whose insight into human nature gave them the right to speak. Even Matthew Arnold, when he came to explain the common hostility to academic standards, thought it safer to take refuge behind a venerated authority, and quoted Spinoza's maxim that "the two great bans of humanity are self-conceit and the laziness coming from self-conceit"; and he might have appealed to a more ancient philosopher than Spinoza—to none other than Buddha, who also traced the origin of all evil, ethical and æsthetic, to this source. That, then, the spirit of indolence and conceit, is the animating cause behind the bitterness of those who proclaim against standards. It is the indolence, moral in some, intellectual in others, that revolts from such discipline as would enable a man to judge between the higher and the lower pleasure; it is the conceit that makes him cling tenaciously to his naked temperament as a better guide than the voice of tradition.[5] Standards there are, and all men judge by them; but there is a vast difference between the standards of education and those of a self-satisfied ignorance. Unfortunately, there is a theory abroad today, formulated and preached by a preposterous body of pedagogues, which professes to have found in this indolence and conceit the corner-stone of education.

That is the new thing, so far as there is anything new, in the world today; not indolence and conceit, which are as ancient as humanity, but the philosophy which justifies them under the title of absolute relativism. That is the present disguise of the Demon as he stalks abroad, instilling his venom into the innocent critics of the press.

[1]   More had preached, in season and out, since his earliest essays, that human reason, when divorced from day-to-day experience, ran to absurdities. It was in his later years, however, that he published in systematic form a statement which would not only sum up his whole thinking on the excesses of reason but provide at the same time a reasonable defense of permanent values in literature. That statement was to be the leading essay, "The Demon of the Absolute," in a book of the same title, and the first volume in the *New Shelburne Essays* (1928). In its position it served to give perspective to the rest of the essays in the collection, particularly the more polemical ones on twentieth-century literature, whose creators were saying, More felt, that man was an accident of nature and wholly explainable by the laws of natural science. It was because of this slavery to the "absolutes" emerging from empirical investigation, particularly in biology and chemistry, More said, that "modern vulgarians and witless aesthetes," like Anderson, Dos Passos, Lewis, Cabell, and Dreiser, felt free to roister around the privy holes of their own lubricity and solemnly pronounce such effusions "literature." What is here reprinted is a portion of the first three sections, which were adapted from a William Vaughan Moody Lecture delivered at the University of Chicago, April 26, 1917, and an article in the *Unpopular Review*, "Taste," read before the Middlesex Women's Club of Lowell, Massachusetts, Dec. 31, 1917.

[2]   "Beyond all the peaks there is rest."
[3]   "Books have their own destiny."
[4]   Pretty much all the truth of Freudianism can be found in the Platonic and Stoic theory of dreams. [More's note]
[5]   Anatole France, for example, was highly educated intellectually, and as a matter of fact his critical judgments are generally sound and in conformity with the great tradition. But his philosophy of life was tainted with moral indolence; which betrays itself in his literary productions and to some extent in his critical standards. [More's note]

PART III

Education and History

Natural Aristocracy[1]

In a certain New York club of authors and scholars, the conversation turned one evening, as it is so accustomed to turn, on the politics of the day; and some astonishment was caused when one of the circle, a distinguished student of sociology well known for his radical opinions, said with emphatic conviction that we were talking of little things, and that the one great question of the day was whether a democratic society could develop a natural aristocracy. By chance I had with me that night an excellent new book on *The Political Philosophy of Burke*, by Professor John MacCunn, late of the University of Liverpool,[2] and as we left the club I showed it to one of my fellow writers, with a word of commendation. "Ah," he said, handing it back unopened, "Burke! he's dead, is he not?" Well, Burke, I dare say, is dead for us, as so many other great memories have perished, and Lord Morley (plain John Morley then, a fairly practical statesman) was indulging in the usual enthusiasm of the biographer when, twenty-five years ago, he closed his luminous volume with the prophecy that "the historic method, fitting in with certain dominant conceptions in the region of natural science, is bringing men round to a way of looking at society for which Burke's maxims are exactly suited; and it seems probable that he will be more frequently and more seriously referred to within the next twenty years than he has been within the whole of the last eighty."[3] The historic method has an odd way of discrediting the authority of history, and certainly in the lustrum since Lord Morley's

predicted score of years the world of Lloyd George and Mr.
Roosevelt has not been referring abundantly to Burke's maxims. Yet, with the words of my radical sociological friend in my
ears, I could not help reflecting on the coincidence that Professor MacCunn, a writer thoroughly imbued with modern ideas,
should have led the whole of Burke's political philosophy up
to the same question of natural aristocracy. "For Burke's feet,"
he says, "were never on surer ground than when, as we have
seen, he argued that a civil society, by the very conditions of
social struggle and growth, must needs evolve 'a natural aristocracy, without which there is no nation.' " And then, being
sufficiently trained in the new historic method, he proceeds to
show how Burke entirely missed the real problem of society—
as if human nature had first sprung into existence with the
Reform Bill.

Of the urgency of the problem a reflective man will scarcely
doubt. The only thing, in fact, that might lead him to question
its urgency is its hoary antiquity. Plato wrestled with it when
he undertook to outline the ideal republic, and many of his
pages on the range of government through its five forms—
aristocracy, timocracy, oligarchy, democracy, and tyranny—
sound as if he had been reading yesterday's newspapers of
London and New York. In the orgy of misrule that brought
Athens to humiliation in the last years of the Peloponnesian
war he had seen oligarchs and timocrats tearing at each other's
throats like mad dogs; he had seen the triumph of the democratic party, and, knowing its instability, he had composed the
long dialogue of *The Republic* to show how, if possible, it might
be saved from impending tyranny. He wrote, so far as the
public was concerned, in a spirit of despair, almost as if foreseeing the domination of an Alexander and the cold despotism of
Rome; and in that saddened scepticism he was thinking more
of holding up the aristocratic idea of justice for any pious
seeker of the future than of creating an actual commonwealth.
Yet, however his application of the law of the individual to the
machinery of politics may appear at times fantastic, his argu-

ment never really gets far from the everlasting questions of government.

The oligarchy which he knew and described was what we should rather call a plutocracy. He had in mind a State in which, "instead of loving contention and honour [as under a timocracy], men become lovers of money and business, and they praise and admire the rich man, and confer office upon him, but despise the poor man." "And such a State," he adds, "will necessarily be not one but two States, one of the poor, the other of the rich, who are living in the same place and always plotting against each other." And when in such a society the disposers of wealth proceed from privilege to insolence and folly, and on the other side the many have lost the sense of reverence and have become aware of the sheer power of numbers, then the plutocratic State changes to the true democracy, the uncontrolled sway of the majority. The change is like that which comes to a rich young man who, forgetting the discipline of necessity, passes into the libertinism of indulgence. He will hearken to no word of advice; and if any one tells him there is a distinction among pleasures, that some are the satisfaction of gross and ignoble desires and others are the satisfaction of good and useful desires, he shakes his head in superiority, and swears that all pleasures are alike. So the oligarchical faction loses its power and position; and the democracy in its turn follows the same path, despising the constraint of authority and the guidance of experience, caught by the lure of indiscriminate pleasure. "The father comes down to the level of the son, being afraid of his children, and the son is on a level with his father, having no shame or fear of his parents. . . . So the schoolmaster fears and flatters his scholars, and the scholars despise their masters and tutors; and, in general, young and old are alike, the young competing with the old in speech and action, and the old men condescending to the young in their gay and easy manners, from dread of being thought morose and dictatorial."

Then arises the problem which confronted the State in Plato's day, as it did in Burke's, and which may not seem entirely irrelevant to the watcher of to-day: How shall the people be saved from themselves? How, indeed? To Plato, who beheld as in a vision the coming of Alexander and Cæsar, the actual historic answer was a gloomy picture of the change from licence to tyranny. His account of the impending fall can never lose its fresh interest:

> When a democracy which is thirsting for freedom has evil cupbearers presiding over the feast, then, unless her rulers are very amenable and give a plentiful draft, she calls them to account and punishes them, and says that they are cursed oligarchs. And loyal citizens are insultingly termed by her, slaves who hug their chains; she would have subjects who are like rulers, and rulers who are like subjects: these are the men whom she praises and honours both in private and public.
>
> By degrees the anarchy finds a way into private houses, and ends by getting among the animals and infecting them. Nor must I forget to tell of the liberty and equality of the two sexes in relation to each other. And I must add that no one who does not know would believe, how much greater is the liberty which the animals who are under the dominion of man have in a democracy than in any other State: for truly, the she-dogs, as the proverb says, are as good as their she-mistresses, and the horses and asses have a way of marching along with all the rights and dignities of freemen; and they will run at anybody who comes in their way if he does not leave the road clear for them; and all things are just ready to burst with liberty.
>
> The ruin of oligarchy is the ruin of democracy; the same desire magnified and intensified by liberty overmasters democracy—the truth being that the excessive increase of anything often causes a reaction in the opposite direction; and this is the case not only in the seasons and in vegetable and animal life, but above all in forms of government. The excess of liberty, whether in States or individuals, seems only to pass into excess of slavery. And so tyranny naturally arises out of democracy, and the most aggravated form of tyranny and slavery out of the most extreme form of liberty.
>
> Then come impeachments and judgments and trials of one another. The people have always some champion whom they set over them and nurse into greatness. This is he who begins

to make a party against the rich. After a while he is driven out, but comes back, in spite of his enemies, a tyrant full grown. Then comes the famous request for a body-guard—"Let not the people's friend," as they say, "be lost to them." (Jowett, condensed.)

One escape from this fatal declension Plato saw, that, by the working of the inner law of self-restraint or by some divine interposition, the people should, before it was too late, be turned to hearken to their natural leaders, and the State should thus develop from anarchy into a true aristocracy. The question, then or at any time, is not whether there shall be leaders but of what character these leaders shall be. There was the brawling tribe of demagogues and sycophants in the Athenian democracy, as there have been at other times of licencious upheaval. And the character of these men is always the same: they lead by flattery and by clamorous justification of the passing wave of desire. The aristocratic leaders whom Plato had in mind, and whom, for the confusion of posterity he called philosophers, were of the very opposite sort, being men who should guide by imposing their authority and experience on the impulsive emotions of the multitude. They should be politicians who might dare the displeasure of the people as Burke dared his constituents at Bristol: "The very attempt towards pleasing everybody discovers a temper always flashy, and often false and insincere. . . . I am to look, indeed, to your opinions; but to such opinions as you and I *must* have five years hence." They should be philosophers like John Stuart Mill who, facing the electors of Westminster and being asked whether he had ever said that English workingmen were "generally liars," replied simply, "I did." Such were to be the aristocrats of Plato's State, men of simple and rational desires, lords of their own souls and so masters of others. Nor should they govern for their own smaller profit. For, as Socrates says, "it is not to the injury of the servant that we think he ought to be governed, but because it behooves each of us to be governed by the divine wisdom, having that power within us if possible, or, if that be impossible, then by an external authority, so that we may all, following the same guidance, be brought into likeness one to another and into good will."

There is something at once strange and familiar in this political discussion, now more than two thousand years old. To it Plato brought all his wisdom, sometimes not disdaining sophistry, trying to show by what kind of education and by what arts of persuasion and illusion a natural aristocracy could be imposed and maintained. It was pretty much the same problem that confronted Burke at the time of the French Revolution, inspiring his earlier writings on that event with incomparable eloquence, and stinging him in the end almost to a frenzy of despair. Burke did not come to the question with so clear an intuition as the Greek, and in some ways his *Reflections*, despite their modern dress, are more remote from us than is Plato's *Republic*, because he dealt less with the universal aspects of human nature. And in so far as his practical reason was coloured by the peculiar circumstances of his own day, it has lost in direct application to the needs of another age. But he is not dead, despite my literary friend; wisdom is of longer life than the generations of mankind, and there is scarcely another book of modern times so full of political wisdom as Burke's *Reflections*.

And we must note, in the first place, that to Burke, as to Plato, it never occurred to think that society, even under the most lawless anarchy, could exist without leaders. "Power," he knew, "of some kind or other, will survive the shock in which manners and opinions perish." He knew too, and declared, that in the end he who made himself master of the army would overbear all other influences; but meanwhile he beheld the State of France under the sway of demagogues who were preparing the people for a carnival of blood and cruelty, and all his eloquence was exerted, and with extraordinary effect, to avert from his own country this plague of revolution. The *philosophes,* who had prepared the dogmas of popular flattery for the mouth of a Marat and a Robespierre, had intensified in him the natural British distrust of all application of abstract reasoning to government and the affairs of life; and he felt a profound aversion for those who would "lay down metaphysic propositions which infer universal consequences," and would then "limit logic by despotism." Being thus debarred from belief in a true philosophy by his experience of the false, yet having himself a mind that grasped at general principles, he turned to "the happy effect of following nature, which is wisdom without reflection, and above it." In that "discipline of nature" he looked for the genuine guidance of society, and one of the memorable passages of his works is that in which he describes the character of those who, themselves under this control, should be for others "men of light and leading":

A true natural aristocracy is not a separate interest in the State, or separable from it. It is an essential integrant part of any large body rightly constituted. It is formed out of a class of legitimate presumptions, which, taken as generalities, must be admitted for actual truths. To be bred in a place of estimation; to see nothing low and sordid from one's infancy; to be taught to respect one's self; to be habituated to the censorial inspection of the public eye; to look early to public opinion; to stand upon such elevated ground as to be enabled to take a large view of the widespread and infinitely diversified combinations of men and affairs in a large society; to have leisure to read, to reflect, to converse; to be enabled to draw the court and attention of the wise and learned wherever they are to be found;—to be habituated in armies to command and to obey; to be taught to despise danger in the pursuit of honor and duty; to be formed to the greatest degree of vigilance, foresight, and circumspection, in a state of things in which no fault is committed with impunity, and the slightest mistakes draw on the most ruinous consequences;—to be led to a guarded and regulated conduct, from a sense that you are considered as an instructor of your fellow-citizens in their highest concerns, and that you act as a reconciler between God and man;—to be employed as an administrator of law and justice, and to be thereby amongst the first benefactors to mankind;—to be a professor of high science, or of liberal and ingenuous art;—to be amongst rich traders, who from their success are presumed to have sharp and vigorous understandings, and to possess the virtues of diligence, or-

der, constancy, and regularity, and to have cultivated an
habitual regard to commutative justice—these are the circumstances of men that form what I should call a *natural* aristocracy, without which there is no nation.

Not many, even among the wisest of our own generation,
would fail to respond favourably to that glowing picture of
nature's aristocrats, but when we come to the means by which
Burke would ensure the existence and supremacy of such a
class, it is different. Despite some tincture of the so-called
"enlightenment," which few men of that age could entirely
escape, Burke had a deep distrust of the restive, self-seeking
nature of mankind, and as a restraint upon it he would magnify
the passive as opposed to the active power of what is really the
same human nature. This passive instinct he called "prejudice"—the unreasoning and unquestioning attachment to the
family and "the little platoon we belong to in society," from
which our affection, coincident always with a feeling of contented obligation, is gradually enlarged to take in the peculiar
institutions of our country; "prejudice renders a man's virtues
his habits, . . . through just prejudice his duty becomes a part
of his nature." Prejudice is thus the binding force which works
from below upwards; the corresponding force which moves
from above is "prescription"—the possession of rights and authority which have been confirmed by custom. In other words,
Burke believed that the only practical way of ensuring a natural aristocracy was by the acceptance of a prescriptive oligarchy; in the long run and after account had been taken of all
exceptions—and he was in no wise a blind worshipper of the
Whig families which then governed England—he believed
that the men of light and leading would already be found
among, or by reason of their preëminence would be assumed
into, the class of those whose views were broadened by the
inherited possession of privilege and honours.

He so believed because it seemed to him that prejudice and
prescription were in harmony with the methods of universal
nature. Sudden change was abhorrent to him, and in every
chapter of history he read that the only sound social develop-

ment was that which corresponded to the slow and regular growth of a plant, deep-rooted in the soil and drawing its nourishment from ancient concealed sources. In such a plan prejudice was the ally of the powers of time, opposing to all visionary hopes a sense of duty to the solid existing reality and compelling upstart theory to prove itself by winning through long resistance. And with the force of time stood the kindred force of order and subordination personified in privilege. "A disposition to preserve, and an ability to improve, taken together," would be Burke's standard of a statesman; "everything else is vulgar in the conception, perilous in the execution." In passages of a singular elevation he combines the ideas of Hobbes on the social contract with those of Hooker on the sweep of divine universal law, harmonizing them with the newer conception of evolutionary growth. "Each contract of each particular State," he says, "is but a clause in the great primeval contract of eternal society, linking the lower with the higher natures, connecting the visible and invisible world, according to a fixed compact sanctioned by the inviolable oath which holds all physical and all moral natures, each in their appointed place." And thus, too, "our political system is placed in a just correspondence and symmetry with the order of the world, and with the mode of existence decreed to a permanent body composed of transitory parts; wherein, by the disposition of a stupendous wisdom, moulding together the great mysterious incorporation of the human race, the whole, at one time, is never old, or middle-aged, or young, but, in a condition of unchangeable constancy, moves on through the varied tenor of perpetual decay, fall, renovation, and progression. Thus, by preserving the method of nature in the conduct of the State, in what we improve, we are never wholly new; in what we retain, we are never wholly obsolete."

If we look below these ideas of prejudice and privilege, time and subordination, for their one animating principle, we shall find it, I think, in the dominance of the faculty of the imagination. Nor did this imaginative substructure lying beneath all of Burke's writings and speeches, from the early essay on the *Sublime and Beautiful* to his latest outpourings on the French

Revolution, escape the animadversion of his enemies. Tom Paine made good use of this trait in *The Rights of Man*, which he issued as an answer to the *Reflections*. "The age of chivalry is gone," Burke had exclaimed at the close of his famous tirade on the fall of Marie Antoinette. "Now all is changed. All the pleasing illusions, which made power gentle, and obedience liberal, which harmonized the different shades of life, and which, by a bland assimilation, incorporated into politics the sentiments which beautify and soften private society, are to be dissolved by this new conquering empire of light and reason. All the decent drapery of life is to be rudely torn off. All the superadded ideas, furnished from the wardrobe of a *moral imagination.* . . ." To this Paine retorted with terrible incision. Ridiculing the lamentation over the French Queen as a mere sentimental rhapsody, he catches up Burke's very words with malign cunning: "Not one glance of compassion, not one commiserating reflection, that I can find throughout his book, has he bestowed on those who lingered out the most wretched of lives, a life without hope in the most miserable of prisons. It is painful to behold a man employing his talents to corrupt himself. Nature has been kinder to Mr. Burke than he has been to her. He is not affected by the reality of distress touching his heart, but by the showy resemblance of it striking his imagination. He pities the plumage, but forgets the dying bird."

Now there is an element of truth in Paine's charge, but there is distortion also. To say that Burke had no thought for the oppressed and the miserable is a wanton slander, disproved by abundant passages in the very *Reflections* and by his whole career. "If it should come to the last extremity," he had once avowed in Parliament, with no fear of contradiction, "and to a contest of blood, God forbid! God forbid!—my part is taken; I would take my fate with the poor, and low, and feeble." But it is the fact nevertheless, construe it how one will, that in the ordinary course of things Burke's ideas of government were moulded and his sentiment towards life was coloured by the vivid industry of his imagination, and that he thought the world at large controlled by the same power. I doubt if analysis can reach a deeper distinction between the whole class of minds to which Burke belongs and that to which Paine belongs than is afforded by this difference in the range and texture of the imagination.

And in this Burke had with him the instinct of his people, while in a way transcending it; for a good deal of what we regard as the British character depends on just the excess of imagination over a rather dull sensibility and sluggish intelligence. This, if we look into it, is what Bagehot signalized as the saving dulness of England and what Walpole meant by attributing to "the good sense [note the contrast of *sense* and sensibility] of the English that they have not painted better." It was this same quality that inspired Burke's great comparison of the French excitability with the British stolidity: "Because half a dozen grasshoppers under a fern make the field ring with their importunate chink whilst thousands of great cattle, reposed beneath the shadow of the British oak, chew the cud and are silent, pray do not imagine that those who make the noise are the only inhabitants of the field." In its higher working, when sensibility and intelligence are also magnified, the imagination, no doubt, is the source of the loftier English poetry and eloquence, but in the lower range, which we are now considering, it is rather a slow, yet powerful and endearing, visualization of what is known and familiar; it is the beginning of that prejudice for existing circumstances and actual relations which Burke exalted as the mother of content. And with content it produces a kind of egotistic satisfaction in the pomps and privileges which pass before the eye, giving to the humble a participation in things wherein they have no material share. In the baser nature this evokes a trait which we condemn as snobbishness; in the higher it results in a fine magnanimity: "He feels no ennobling principle in his own heart, who wishes to level all the artificial institutions which have been adopted for giving a body to opinion and permanence to fugitive esteem. It is a sour, malignant, envious disposition, without taste for the reality, or for any image or representation of virtue, that sees with joy the unmerited fall of what had long flourished in splendour and in honour." Thus, too, the imagination is an accomplice of time as well as of the law of subordination; indeed, its deepest and noblest function lies in its power of carrying what was once seen and known as a living portion and factor of the present, and there is no surer test of the quality of a man's mind than the degree in which he feels the long-remembered past as one of the vital and immediate laws of his being. So it is that the imagination is the chief creator and sustainer of the great memorial institutions of society, such as the Crown and the Church and the other pageantries of State, which are the very embodiment of prescription, as it were the soul of tradition taking form and awful authority among the living. How deeply Burke felt this prescriptive right of the imagination no one need be told; nor is it necessary to quote the familiar passages in which he likens the British monarchy, with its bulwark of nobility, to "the proud keep of Windsor, rising in the majesty of proportion, and girt with the double belt of its kindred and coeval towers," or calls on the Church to "exalt her mitred front in courts and parliaments." There is the true Burke; he knew, as Paine knew, that the support of these institutions was in their symbolic sway over the imaginations of men, and that, with this defence undermined, they would crumble away beneath the aggressive passions of the present, or would remain as mere bloodless vanities. He thought that the real value of life was in its meaning to the imagination, and he was not ashamed to avow that the fall and tragedy of kings, because they bore in their person the destiny of ancient institutions, stirred him more profoundly than the sufferings of ordinary men.

It is perfectly easy for a keen and narrow intelligence to ridicule Burke's trust in the imagination, but as a matter of fact there is nothing more practical than a clear recognition of its vast domain in human affairs—it was Napoleon Bonaparte who said that "imagination rules the world." Burke is not dead; his pages are an inexhaustible storehouse of inspiration and wisdom. But it is true nevertheless, that his ideas never quite freed themselves from their matrix, and that in his arguments the essential is involved in the contingent. Though he saw clearly enough the imperfections of the actual union of a prescriptive and a natural aristocracy, he was not able, with all his insight, to conceive the existence of the latter alone and by virtue of its own rights. He cried out that the age of chivalry was gone; he saw that the age of prescription, however it might be propped up for a time, was also doomed, not only in France but in his England as well, and with that away there was nothing for his imagination but an utter blank. As a consequence the problem of government for us to-day in its fundamental aspects is really closer to the exposition of the Greek philosopher two thousand years ago than to that of the modern English statesman. We have the naked question to answer: How shall a society, newly shaking itself free from a disguised plutocratic régime, be guided to suffer the persuasion of a natural aristocracy which has none of the insignia of an old prescription to impose its authority? Shall the true justice prevail, which by a right discrimination would confer power and influence in accordance with inner distinction; or shall that so-called justice prevail—for no man acknowledges open injustice — which recommends itself as equality of opportunity, but in practice, by confusing the distinctions of age, sex, and character, comes at last to the brutal doctrine that might makes right, whether that might be the material strength of money or the jealous tyranny of numbers?

Leaders there will be, as there always have been. Leaders there are now, of each class, and we know their names. We still call the baser sort a demagogue, and his definition is still what it was among those who invented the term: "a flatterer of the people." Or, if that description seems too vague, you will recognize him as one who unites in himself enormous physical and mental activity, yet who employs these extraordinary talents in no serious way for the comfort and sustenance of the higher life of the imagination, but for running about restlessly and filling the public mind with stentorian alarms. He is one who proclaims ostentatiously that the first aim of government "must always be the possession by the average citizen of the right kind of character," and then, in his own person, gives an example of identifying character with passion by betraying a friend and malignantly misinterpreting his words, as soon as that friend may be decried for balking the popular will—and balking the path of the decrier's ambition. He is one who has been honoured as the leader of a great political party, and then, as soon as he is dethroned from its leadership, denounces that same party as the tool of privilege and the source of corruption. He is one who, in proclaiming the principles of this new party, has constantly on his lips the magical word "justice," which he defines by the specious phrase "equality of opportunity," yet in the end identifies justice with the removal of all checks from government, to the end that the desire of the majority may be immediately carried out, whether right or wrong. For "it is impossible to invent constitutional devices which will prevent the popular will from being effective for wrong without also preventing it from being effective for right. The only safe course to follow in this great American democracy is to provide for making the popular judgment really effective."[4]

To this end our exemplary demagogue would take away every obstacle between the opinion of the moment and the enactment of that opinion into law. Hence the initiative and referendum. Above the legislators is the Constitution, devised in order that legislation upon any particular question may be made to conform essentially with what has been laid down on deliberation as the wisest general course of government. It is a check upon hasty action, and implies a certain distrust of the popular judgment at any moment when passion or delusion may be at play. Therefore our demagogue will denounce reverence for the Constitution as a fetich. Blithely ignoring the fact that Constitution-making and remaking is one of the pastimes of some States, and that even the Federal Constitution can be amended with none too great difficulty when the opinion of the people is really formed (as in the recent case of the election of senators), he will earnestly call upon the Constitutional Convention of Ohio "to provide in this Constitution means which will enable the people readily to amend it if at any point it works injustice"; and then, as if that provision were not sufficient to relax its mortmain, he will virtually abrogate its function of imposing any check whatsoever by adding "means which will permit the people themselves by popular vote, after due deliberation and discussion, but finally and without appeal, to settle what the proper construction of any constitutional point is"; and this construction is to be made, not legally, that is by an attempt to get at the actual meaning of the language used, but in accordance with the current notion of what is right.

But the full venom of his attack will be directed against the courts, because in them is impersonated the final sovereignty of unimpassioned judgment over the fluctuations of sentiment, and with it the last check upon the operations of the demagogue. The interpretation of the law in accordance with the conditions of life is to rest with the people. If necessary they are to have the power of recalling the judge who is recalcitrant to their views, and at the least they are to have opportunity to reverse any decision of the courts which seems to them wrong. In this way he thinks to ensure "an independent judiciary"! To enforce the need of the recall, he accuses the courts of "refusing to permit the people of the States to exercise their right as a free people." Thereupon he cites what he calls a "typical" case in New York, in which the judges declared a workingmen's compensation act unconstitutional. "In other words, they insisted that the Constitution had *permanently* cursed our people with impotence to right wrong and had *perpetuated* a cruel iniquity." This tirade, followed by the most inflammatory appeals to the emotions, was uttered in 1912,[5] at the very time when he was inveighing against the courts for perpetuating iniquity, the machinery was in train for amending the Constitution, and in less than two years that permanent curse was removed by the passage of a Constitutional law in full favor of the workingman. Such is the despotism of facts. And ever through these vituperative charges runs the high note of flattery: "If the American people are not fit for popular government, and if they should of right be the servants and not the masters of the men whom they themselves put in office."

The demagogue paints himself. In a word you may know him by this single trait: he is one who, in the pursuit of the so-called rights of humanity, has a supreme contempt for those

Unconcerning things, matters of fact;

one who, by means of an hypnotic loquaciousness, is constantly persuading the people that they have only to follow their first impulsive emotions to be right and safe, and that as a consequence every institution should be swept away which in their wiser, calmer moments they have created as a bulwark against their own more variable nature. To complete the picture we need to contrast with it Burke's portrait of the men of light and leading, with his sober statement of the law of liberty: "Men are qualified for civil liberty in exact proportion to their disposition to put moral chains upon their own appetites; in proportion as their love to justice is above their rapacity; in proportion as their soundness and sobriety of understanding is above their vanity and presumption; in proportion as they are more disposed to listen to the counsels of the wise and good, in preference to the flattery of knaves. Society cannot exist unless a controlling power upon will and appetite be placed somewhere, and the less of it there is within, the more there must be without. It is ordained in the eternal constitution of things, that men of intemperate minds cannot be free. Their passions forge their fetters." Or we may go further back and look upon Plato's portrait of the guides who have earned the right to persuade others to temperance by the diligent exercise of that virtue in their own lives.

But the most notable example of demagoguery to-day, is not a man, though he be clothed with thunder, but an institution. There are newspapers and magazines, reaching millions of readers, which have reduced the art to a perfect system. Their method is as simple as it is effective: always appeal to the emotion of the hour, and present it in terms which will justify its excess. Thus, in times when there is no wave of international envy disturbing the popular mind, our journal will print edifying editorials on brotherly love and laud the people as the great source of peace among nations. But let some racial dispute arise, as in the months preceding our Spanish war or the Italian raid on Africa, and this same journal will day after day use its editorial columns to inflame national hatred—and increase its circulation. On days when no sensational event has occurred, it will indulge in the prettiest sentimental sermons on the home and on family felicities. Nothing so moral; it will even plead in lacrimose type against the evil of allowing babies to lie in perambulators with their eyes exposed to the sun. But let the popular mind be excited by some crime of lust, and the same journal will forget the sweet obligations of home and wife,—

> That silly old morality,
> That, as these links were knit, our love should be—

and will deck out the loathsome debauchery of a murderer and his trull as the spiritual history of two young souls finding themselves in the pure air of passion; or some sordid liaison will be virtually lifted above marriage by the terms "affinity" or "heart-wife." And always, meanwhile, the people are to be soothed out of a sense of responsibility for errors and corruption by the skilfully maintained suggestion of a little group of men, entirely removed from the feelings and motives of ordinary humanity, sitting somewhere in secret conclave, plotting, plotting, to pervert the government. Our public crimes are never our own, but are the result of conspiracy.

These are the agencies that, in varying forms, have been at work in many ages. Only now we have formulated them into a noble maxim, which you will hear daily resounding in the pulpit and the press and in the street: "The cure of democracy is more democracy." It is a lie, and we know it is a lie. We know that this cry of the demagogue has invariably in the past led to anarchy and to despotism; and we know that to-day, were these forces unopposed, as happily they are not unopposed, the same result would occur—

> Our liberty reversed and charters gone,
> And we made servants to Opinion.

The remedy for the evils of licence is not in the elimination of popular restraint, but precisely in bringing the people to respect and follow their right leaders. The cure of democracy is not *more* democracy, but *better* democracy.

Nor is such a cure dependent on the appearance in a community of men capable of the light, for these the world always has, and these we too have in abundance; it depends rather on so relating these select natures to the community that they shall be also men in leading. The danger is, lest, in a State which bestows influence and honours on its demagogues, the citizens of more refined intelligence, those true philosophers who have discourse of reason, and have won the difficult citadel of their own souls, should withdraw from public affairs and retire into that citadel as it were into an ivory tower. The harm wrought by such a condition is twofold: it deprives the better minds of the larger sustenance of popular sympathy, producing among them a kind of intellectual *préciosité* and a languid interest in art as a refuge from life instead of an integral part of life; and, on the other hand, it tends to leave the mass of society a prey to the brutalized emotions of indiscriminate pleasure-seeking. In such a State distinction becomes the sorry badge of isolation. The need is to provide for a natural aristocracy.

Now it must be clearly understood that in advocating such a measure, at least under the conditions that actually prevail to-day, there is involved no futile intention of abrogating democracy, in so far as democracy means government by and of the people. A natural aristocracy does not demand the restoration of inherited privilege or a relapse into the crude domin-

ion of money; it is not synonymous with oligarchy or plutocracy. It calls rather for some machinery or some social consciousness which shall ensure both the selection from among
the community at large of the "best" and the bestowal on them
of "power"; it is the true consummation of democracy. And
again, it must be said emphatically that it is not an academic
question dealing with unreal distinctions. No one supposes that
the "best" are a sharply defined class moving about among
their fellows with a visible halo above them and a smile of
beatific superiority on their faces. Society is not made of such
classifications, and governments have always been of a more or
less mixed character. A natural aristocracy signifies rather a
tendency than a conclusion, and in such a sense it was taken,
no doubt, by my sociological friend of radical ideas who pronounced it the great practical problem of the day.

The first requisite for solving this problem is that those who
are designed by nature, so to speak, to form an aristocracy
should come to an understanding of their own belief. There is
a question to be faced boldly: What is the true aim of society?
Does justice consist primarily in levelling the distribution of
powers and benefits, or in proportioning them to the scale of
character and intelligence? Is the main purpose of the machinery of government to raise the material welfare of the masses,
or to create advantages for the upward striving of the excep-
tional? Is the state of humanity to be estimated by numbers,
or is it a true saying of the old stoic poet: *humanum paucis vivit
genus?* [6] Shall our interest in mankind begin at the bottom and
progress upward, or begin at the top and progress downward?
To those who feel that the time has come for a reversion from
certain present tendencies, the answer to this question cannot
be doubtful. Before anything else is done we must purge our
minds of the current cant of humanitarianism. This does not
mean that we are to deny the individual appeals of pity and
introduce a wolfish egotism into human relations. On the contrary, it is just the preaching of false humanitarian doctrines
that results practically in weakening the response to rightful
obligations and, by "turning men's duties into doubts," throws

the prizes of life to the hard grasping materialist and the coarse talker. In the end the happiness of the people also, in the wider sense, depends on the common recognition of the law of just subordination. But, whatever the ultimate effect of this sort may be, the need now is to counterbalance the excess of emotional humanitarianism with an injection of the truth—even the contemptuous truth. Let us, in the name of a long-suffering God, put some bounds to the flood of talk about the wages of the bricklayer and the trainman, and talk a little more about the income of the artist and teacher and public censor who have taste and strength of character to remain in opposition to the tide. Let us have less cant about the great educative value of the theatre for the people and less humbug about the virtues of the nauseous problem play, and more consideration of what is clean and nourishing food for the larger minds. Let us forget for a while our absorbing desire to fit the schools to train boys for the shop and the counting-room, and concern ourselves more effectively with the dwindling of those disciplinary studies which lift men out of the crowd. Let us, in fine, not number ourselves among the traitors to their class who *invidiæ metu non audeant dicere.*[7]

One hears a vast deal these days about class consciousness, and it is undoubtedly a potent social instrument. Why should there not be an outspoken class consciousness among those who are in the advance of civilization as well as among those who are in the rear? Such a compact of mutual sympathy and encouragement would draw the man of enlightenment out of his sterile seclusion and make him efficient; it would strengthen the sense of obligation among those who hesitate to take sides, and would turn many despondent votaries of fatalism and many amateur dabblers in reform to a realization of the deeper needs of the day. Nor is this an appeal to idle sentiment. Much is said about the power of the masses and the irresistible spread of revolutionary ideas from the lower ranks upward. The facts of history point in quite the other direction. It was not the plebs who destroyed the Roman republic, but the corrupt factions of the Senate, and the treachery of such patricians as Catiline and Julius Cæsar. In like manner the French Revolution would never have had a beginning but for the teaching of the philosophers and the prevalence of equalitarian fallacies among the privileged classes themselves. The Vicomtesse de Noailles spoke from knowledge when she said: "La philosophie n'avait pas d'apôtres plus bienveillants que les grands seigneurs. L'horreur des abus, le mépris des distinctions héréditaires, tous ces sentiments dont les classes inférieures se sont emparées dans leur intérêt, ont dû leur premier éclat à l'enthousiasme des grands."[8] And so to-day the real strength of socialistic doctrines is not in the discontent of the workingmen, but in the faint-hearted submission of those who by the natural division of society belong to the class that has everything to lose by revolution, and in the sentimental adherence of dilettante reformers. The real danger is after all not so much from the self-exposed demagogues as from the ignorant tamperers with explosive material. It is not so much from the loathsome machinations of the yellow press, dangerous as they are, as from the journals that are supposed to stand for higher things, yet in their interest in some particular reform, support whole-heartedly candidates who flirt with schemes subversive of property and constitutional checks; in their zeal for the brotherhood of man, deal loosely with facts, and in their clamour for some specious extension of the franchise, neglect the finer claims of justice. These men and these journals, betrayers of the trust, are the real menace. Without their aid and abetment there may be rumblings of discontent, wholesome enough as warnings against a selfish stagnation, but there can be no concerted drive of society towards radical revolution. For radical forces are by their nature incapable of any persistent harmony of action, and have only the semblance of cohesion from a constraining fear or hatred. The dynamic source or evolution must be in the perversion of those at the top, and anarchy comes with their defalcation. Against such perils when they show themselves, the proper safeguard is the arousing of a counter class consciousness.

It is a sound theorem of President Lowell's that popular

government "may be said to consist of the control of political affairs by pulic opinion." Now there is to-day a vast organization for manipulating public opinion in favor of the working-man and for deluding it in the interest of those who grow fat by pandering in the name of emancipation to the baser emotions of mankind; but of organization among those who suffer from the vulgarizing trend of democracy there is little or none. As a consequence we see the conditions of life growing year by year harder for those whose labour is not concerned immediately with the direction of material forces or with the supply of sensational pleasure; they are ground, so to speak, between the upper and the nether millstone. Perhaps organization is not the word to describe accurately what is desired among those who are fast becoming the silent members of society, for it implies a sharper discrimination into grades of taste and character than exists in nature; but there is nothing chimerical in looking for a certain conscious solidarity at the core of the aristocratical class (using "aristocratical" always in the Platonic sense), with a looser cohesion at the edges. Let that class become frankly convinced that the true aim of a State is, as in the magnificent theory of Aristotle, to make possible the high friendship of those who have raised themselves to a vision of the supreme good, let them adopt means to confirm one another in that faith, and their influence will spread outward through society and leaven the whole range of public opinion.

The instrument by which this control of public opinion is effected is primarily the imagination; and here we meet with a real difficulty. It was the advantage of such a union of aristocracy and inherited oligarchy as Burke advocated that it gave something visible and definite for the imagination to work upon, whereas the democratic aristocracy of character must always be comparatively vague. But we are not left wholly without the means of giving to the imagination a certain sureness of range while remaining within the forms of popular government. The opportunity is in the hands of our higher institutions of learning, and it is towards recalling these to their duty that the first efforts of reform should be directed. It is not my intention here to enter into the precise nature of this reform, for the subject is so large as to demand a separate essay. In brief the need is to restore to their predominance in the curriculum those studies that train the imagination, not, be it said, the imagination in its purely æsthetic function, though that aspect of it also has been sadly neglected, but the imagination in its power of grasping in a single firm vision, so to speak, the long course of human history and of distinguishing what is essential therein from what is ephemeral. The enormous preponderance of studies that deal with the immediate questions of economics and government inevitably results in isolating the student from the great inheritance of the past; the frequent habit of dragging him through the slums of sociology, instead of making him at home in the society of the noble dead, debauches his mind with a flabby, or inflames it with a fanatic, humanitarianism. He comes out of college, if he has learnt anything, a *nouveau intellectuel,* bearing the same relation to the man of genuine education as the *nouveau riche* to the man of inherited manners; he is narrow and unbalanced, a prey to the prevailing passion of the hour, with no feeling for the majestic claims of that within us which is unchanged from the beginning. In place of this excessive contemporaneity we shall give a larger share of time and honour to the hoarded lessons of antiquity. There is truth in the Hobbian maxim that "imagination and memory are but one thing"; by their union in education alone shall a man acquire the uninvidious equivalent in character of those broadening influences which came to the oligarch through prescription—he is moulded indeed into the true aristocrat. And with the assertion of what may be called a spiritual prescription he will find among those over whom he is set as leader and guide a measure of respect which springs from something in the human breast more stable and honourable and more conformable to reason than the mere stolidity of unreflecting prejudice. For, when everything is said, there could be no civilized society were it not that deep in our hearts, beneath all the turbulences of greed and vanity, abides the instinct of obedience to what is noble and of good repute. It awaits only the clear call from above.

1   *Aristocracy and Justice* (1915), the Ninth Series of the *Shelburne Essays*, is
     probably More's best known work. "Natural Aristocracy" is the first essay in the
     series and not only sets the tone for the whole volume but is the key to most
     of More's political and educational thought. The essay was first published in the
     Unpopular Review of April, 1914, then included in the Ninth Series the next
     year. Excerpts were reprinted in *The Great Tradition*, edited by Edwin Green-
     law and James Holly Hanford, 1919. The reader may wish to compare it with
     Irving Babbitt's *Democracy and Leadership* (1924).

2   John MacCunn, *The Political Philosophy of Burke*, London, 1913. The later
     quotation from this book is taken from p. 258.

3   John Morley, *Burke*, London, 1879. The quotation which follows is from p. 216
     of the 1936 reprint of Macmillan's New Pocket Edition.

4   The reference is to Theodore Roosevelt. The quotation is from Roosevelt's
     speech, "A Charter of Democracy," delivered before the Ohio Constitutional
     Convention at Columbus, Ohio, February 21, 1912. See *The Works of Theodore
     Roosevelt*, Vol. XVII (*Social Justice and Popular Rule*, 1910–1916), ed. Her-
     mann Hagedorn (New York: Charles Scribner's Sons, 1926), p. 123.

5   *Ibid.*, p. 143. See also pp. 198 ff.

6   "Mankind lives in its few."

7   Who "for fear of [arousing] hatred dare not speak out."

8   "Philosophy could have no more benevolent apostles than the great lords. The
     dread of evil custom, the contempt for hereditary distinctions, all of those
     feelings with which the lower classes are possessed as a result of their interests
     have owed their first outburst to the enthusiasm of the nobility."

Academic Leadership[1]

Any one who has traveled much about the country of recent years must have been impressed by the growing uneasiness of mind among thoughtful men.[2] Whether in the smoking-car, or the hotel corridor, or the college hall, everywhere, if you meet them off their guard and stripped of the optimism which we wear as a public convention, you will hear them saying in a kind of amazement. "What is to be the end of it all?" They are alarmed at the unsettlement of property and the difficulties that harass the man of moderate means in making provision for the future; they are uneasy over the breaking up of the old laws of decorum, if not of decency, and over the unrestrained pursuit of excitement at any cost; they feel vaguely that in the decay of religion the bases of society have been somehow weakened. Now, much of this sort of talk is as old as history, and has no special significance. We are prone to forget that civilization has always been a *tour de force,* so to speak, a little hard-won area of order and self-subordination amidst a vast wilderness of anarchy and barbarism that are continually threatening to overrun their bounds. But that is equally no reason for over-confidence. Civilization is like a ship traversing an untamed sea. It is a more complex machine in our day, with command of greater forces, and might seem correspondingly safer than in the era of sails. But fresh catastrophes have shown that the ancient perils of navigation still confront the largest vessel, when the crew loses its discipline or the officers neglect their duty; and the analogy is not without its warning.

Only a year after the sinking of the *Titanic* I was crossing the ocean, and it befell by chance that on the anniversary of that disaster we passed not very far from the spot where the proud ship lay buried beneath the waves. The evening was calm, and on the lee deck a dance had been hastily organized to take advantage of the benign weather. Almost alone I stood for hours at the railing on the windward side, looking out over the rippling water where the moon had laid upon it a broad street of gold. Nothing could have been more peaceful; it was as if Nature were smiling upon earth in sympathy with the strains of music and the sound of laughter that reached me at intervals from the revelling on the other deck. Yet I could not put out of my heart an apprehension of some luring treachery in this scene of beauty—and certainly the world can offer nothing more wonderfully beautiful than the moon shining from the far East over a smooth expanse of water. Was it not in such a calm as this that the unsuspecting vessel, with its gay freight of human lives, had shuddered, and gone down, forever? I seemed to behold a symbol; and there came into my mind the words we used to repeat at school, but are, I do not know just why, a little ashamed of to-day:

> Thou, too, sail on, O Ship of State!
> Sail on, O Union, strong and great!
> Humanity with all its fears,
> With all its hopes of future years,
> Is hanging breathless on thy fate! . . .

Something like this, perhaps, is the feeling of many men—men by no means given to morbid gusts of panic—amid a society that laughs over much in its amusement and exults in the very lust of change. Nor is their anxiety quite the same as that which has always disturbed the reflecting spectator. At other times the apprehension has been lest the combined forces of order might not be strong enough to withstand the ever-threatening inroads of those who envy barbarously and desire recklessly; whereas to-day the doubt is whether the natural champions of order themselves shall be found loyal to their trust, for they seem no longer to remember clearly the word of command that should unite them in leadership. Until they can rediscover some common ground of strength and purpose in the first principles of education and law and property and religion, we are in danger of falling a prey to the disorganizing and vulgarizing domination of ambitions which should be the servants and not the masters of society.

Certainly, in the sphere of education there is a growing belief that some radical reform is needed; and this dissatisfaction is in itself wholesome. Boys come into college with no reading and with minds unused to the very practice of study; and they leave college, too often, in the same state of nature. There are even those, inside and outside of academic halls, who protest that our higher institutions of learning simply fail to educate at all. That is slander; but in sober earnest, you will find few experienced college professors, apart from those engaged in teaching purely utilitarian or practical subjects, who are not convinced that the general relaxation is greater now than it was twenty years ago. It is of considerable significance that the two student essays which took the prizes offered by the Harvard *Advocate* in 1913 were both on this theme. The first of them posed the question: "How can the leadership of the intellectual rather than the athletic student be fostered?" and was virtually a sermon on a text of President Lowell's: "No one in close touch with American education has failed to notice the lack among the mass of undergraduates of keen interest in their studies, and the small regard for scholarly attainment."

Now, the *Advocate* prizeman has his specific remedy, and President Lowell has his, and other men propose other systems and restrictions; but the evil is too deep-seated to be reached by any superficial scheme of honours or to be charmed away by insinuating appeals. The other day Mr. William F. McCombs, chairman of the National Committee which engineered a college president into the White House, gave this advice to our academic youth: "The college man must forget

—or never let it creep into his head—that he's a highbrow. If it does creep in, he's out of politics."[3] To which one might reply in Mr. McComb's own dialect, that unless a man can make himself a force in politics (or at least in the larger life of the State) precisely by virtue of being a "highbrow," he had better spend his four golden years other-where than in college. There it is: the destiny of education is intimately bound up with the question of social leadership, and unless the college, as it used to be in the days when the religious hierarchy it created was a real power, can be made once more a breeding place for a natural aristocracy, it will inevitably degenerate into a school for mechanical apprentices or into a pleasure resort for the *jeunesse dorée* (*sc.* the "gold coasters"). We must get back to a common understanding of the office of education in the construction of society and must discriminate among the subjects that may enter into the curriculum by their relative value towards this end.

A manifest condition is that education should embrace the means of discipline, for without discipline the mind will remain inefficient just as surely as the muscles of the body, without exercise, will be left flaccid. That should seem to be a self-evident truth. Now it may be possible to derive a certain amount of discipline out of any study, but it is a fact, nevertheless, which cannot be gainsaid, that some studies lend themselves to this use more readily and effectively than others. You may, for instance, if by extraordinary luck you get the perfect teacher, make English literature disciplinary by the hard manipulation of ideas; but in practice it almost inevitably happens that a course in English literature either degenerates into the dull memorizing of dates and names or, rising into the O Altitudo, evaporates in romantic gush over beautiful passages. This does not mean, of course, that no benefit may be obtained from such a study, but it does preclude English literature generally from being made the backbone, so to speak, of a sound curriculum. The same may be said of French and German. The difficulties of these tongues in themselves and the effort required of us to enter into their spirit imply some degree of intellectual gymnastics, but scarcely enough for our purpose. Of the sciences it behooves one to speak circumspectly; undoubtedly mathematics and physics, at least, demand such close attention and such firm reasoning as to render them properly a part of any disciplinary education. But there are good grounds for being sceptical of the effect of the non-mathematical sciences on the immature mind. Any one who has spent a considerable portion of his undergraduate time in a chemical laboratory, for example, as the present writer has done, and has the means of comparing the results of such elementary and pottering experimentation with the mental grip required in the humanistic courses, must feel that the real training obtained therein was almost negligible. If I may draw further from my own observation I must say frankly that, after dealing for a number of years with manuscripts prepared for publication by college professors of the various faculties, I have been forced to the conclusion that science, in itself, is likely to leave the mind in a state of relative imbecility. It is not that the writing of men who got their early drill too exclusively, or even predominantly, in the sciences lacks the graces of rhetoric—that would be comparatively a small matter—but such men in the majority of cases, even when treating subjects within their own field, show a singular inability to think clearly and consecutively, so soon as they are freed from the restraint of merely describing the process of an experiment. On the contrary, the manuscript of a classical scholar, despite the present dry-rot of philology, almost invariably gives signs of a habit of orderly and well-governed cerebration.

Here, whatever else may be lacking, is discipline. The sheer difficulty of Latin and Greek, the highly organized structure of these languages, the need of scrupulous search to find the nearest equivalents for words that differ widely in their scope of meaning from their derivatives in any modern vocabulary, the effort of lifting one's self out of the familiar rut of ideas into so foreign a world, all these things act as a tonic exercise to the brain. And it is a demonstrable fact that students of the classics do actually surpass their unclassical rivals in any field where a fair test can be made. At Princeton, for instance, Professor West has shown this superiority by tables of achievements and grades, which he has published in the *Educational Review* for March, 1913; and a number of letters from various parts of the country, printed in the *Nation,* tell the same story in striking fashion. Thus, a letter from Wesleyan (September 7, 1911) gives statistics to prove that the classical students in that university outstrip the others in obtaining all sorts of honours, commonly even honours in the sciences. Another letter (May 8, 1913) shows that of the first semester in English at the University of Nebraska the percentage of delinquents among those who entered with four years of Latin was below 7; among those who had three years of Latin and one or two of a modern language the percentage rose to 15; two years of Latin and two years of a modern language, 30 per cent; one year or less of Latin and from two to four years of a modern language, 35 per cent. And in the *Nation* of April 23, 1914, Professor Arthur Gordon Webster, the eminent physicist of Clark University, after speaking of the late B. O. Peirce's early drill and life-long interest in Greek and Latin, adds these significant words: "Many of us still believe that such a training makes the best possible foundation for a scientist." There is reason to think that this opinion is daily gaining ground among those who are zealous that the prestige of science should be maintained by men of the best calibre.

The disagreement in this matter would no doubt be less, were it not for an ambiguity in the meaning of the word "efficient" itself. There is a kind of efficiency in managing men, and there also is an intellectual efficiency, properly speaking, which is quite a different faculty. The former is more likely to be found in the successful engineer or business man than in the scholar of secluded habits, and because often such men of affairs received no discipline at college in the classics the argument runs that utilitarian studies are as disciplinary as the humanistic. But efficiency of this kind is not an academic product at all, and is commonly developed, and should be developed, in the school of the world. It comes from dealing with men in matters of large physical moment, and may exist with a mind utterly undisciplined in the stricter sense of the word. We have had more than one illustrious example in recent years of men capable of dominating their fellows, let us say in financial transactions, who yet, in the grasp of first principles and in the analysis of consequences, have shown themselves to be as inefficient as children.

Probably, however, few men who have had experience in education will deny the value of discipline to the classics, even though they hold that other studies, less costly from the utilitarian point of view, are equally educative in this respect. But it is further of prime importance, even if such an equality, or approach to equality, were granted, that we should select one group of studies and unite in making it the core of the curriculum for the great mass of undergraduates. It is true in education as in other matters that strength comes from union and weakness from division, and if educated men are to work together for a common end they must have a common range of ideas, with a certain solidarity in their way of looking at things. As matters actually are, the educated man feels terribly his isolation under the scattering of intellectual pursuits, yet too often lacks the courage to deny the strange popular fallacy that there is virtue in sheer variety and that somehow well-being is to be struck out from the clashing of miscellaneous interests rather than from concentration. In one of his annual reports some years ago President Eliot, of Harvard, observed from the figures of registration that the majority of students still at that time believed the best form of education for them was in the old humanistic courses, and *therefore*, he argued, the other courses should be fostered. There was never perhaps a more extraordinary syllogism since the *argal* of Shakespeare's grave-digger. I quote from memory, and may slightly misrepresent the actual statement of the influential "educationalist," but the spirit of his words, as indeed of his practice, is surely as I give it. And the working of this spirit is one of the main causes of the curious fact that scarcely any other class of men in social intercourse feel themselves, in their deeper concerns, more severed one from another than those very college professors who ought to be united in the battle for educational leadership. This estrangement is sometimes carried to an extreme almost ludicrous. I remember once in a small but advanced college the consternation that was awakened when an instructor in philosophy went to a colleague—both of them now associates in a large university—for information in a question of biology. "What business has he with such matters," said the irate biologist: "let him stick to his last, and teach philosophy—if he can!" That was a polite jest, you will say. Perhaps; but not entirely. Philosophy is indeed taught in one lecture hall, and biology in another, but of conscious effort to make of education an harmonious driving force there is next to nothing. And as the teachers, so are the taught.

Such criticism does not imply that advanced work in any of the branches of human knowledge should be curtailed; but it does demand that, as a background to the professional pursuits, there should be a common intellectual training through which all students should pass, acquiring thus a single body of ideas and images in which they could always meet as brother initiates.

We shall, then, make a long step forward when we determine that in the college, as distinguished from the university, it is better to have the great mass of men, whatever may be the waste in a few unmalleable minds, go through the discipline of a single group of studies—with, of course, a considerable freedom of choice in the outlying field. And it will probably appear in experience that the only practicable group to select is the classics, with the accompaniment of philosophy and the mathematical sciences. Latin and Greek are, at least, as disciplinary as any other subjects; and if it can be further shown that they possess a specific power of correction for the more disintegrating tendencies of the age, it ought to be clear that their value as instruments of education outweighs the service of certain other studies which may seem to be more immediately serviceable.

For it will be pretty generally agreed that efficiency of the individual scholar and unity of the scholarly class are, properly, only the means to obtain the real end of education, which is social efficiency. The only way, in fact, to make the discipline demanded by a severe curriculum and the sacrifice of particular tastes required for unity seem worth the cost, is to persuade men that the resulting form of education both meets a present and serious need of society and promises to serve those individuals who desire to obtain society's fairer honours. Mr. McCombs, speaking for the "practical" man, declares that there is no place in politics for the intellectual aristocrat. A good many of us believe that unless the very reverse of this is true, unless the educated man can somehow, by virtue of his education, make of himself a governor of the people in the larger sense, and even to some extent in the narrow political sense, unless the college can produce a hierarchy of character and intelligence which shall in due measure perform the office of the discredited oligarchy of birth, we had better make haste to divert our enormous collegiate endowments into more useful channels.

And here I am glad to find confirmation of my belief in the stalwart old *Boke Named the Governour*, published by Sir Thomas Elyot in 1531, the first treatise on education in the English tongue and still, after all these years, one of the wisest. It is no waste of time to take account of the theory held by the humanists when study at Oxford and Cambridge was shaping itself for its long service in giving to the oligarchic government of Great Britain whatever elements it possessed of true aristocracy. Elyot's book is equally a treatise on the education of a gentleman and on the ordinance of government, for, as he says elsewhere, he wrote "to instruct men in such virtues as shall be expedient for them which shall have authority in a weal public." I quote from various parts of his work with some abridgment, retaining the quaint spelling of the original, and I beg the reader not to skip, however long the citation may appear:

Beholde also the ordre that god hath put generally in al his creatures, begynning at the moste inferiour or base, and assendynge upwarde; so that in euery thyng is ordre, and without ordre may be nothing stable or permanent; and it may nat be called ordre, excepte it do contayne in it degrees, high and base, accordynge to the merite or estimation of the thyng that is ordred. And therfore hit appereth that god gyueth nat to euery man like gyftes of grace, or of nature, but to some more, some lesse, as it liketh his diuine maiestie. For as moche as understandying is the most excellent gyfte that man can receiue in his creation, it is therfore congruent, and accordynge that as one excelleth an other in that influence, as therby beinge next to the similitude of his maker, so shulde the astate of his persone be auanced in degree or place where understandynge may profite. Suche oughte to be set in a more highe place than the residue where they may se and also be sene; that by the beames of theyr excellent witte, shewed throughe the glasse of auctorite, other of inferiour understandynge may be directed to the way of vertue and commodious liuynge. . . .

Thus I conclude that nobilitie is nat after the vulgare opinion of men, but is only the prayse and surname of vertue; whiche the lenger it continueth in a name or lignage, the more is nobilitie extolled and meruailed at. . . .

If thou be a gouernour, or haste ouer other soueraygntie, knowe thy selfe. Knowe that the name of a soueraigne or ruler without actuall gouernaunce is but a shadowe, that gouernaunce standeth nat by wordes onely, but principally by acte and example; that by example of gouernours men do rise or falle in vertue or vice. Ye shall knowe all way your selfe, if for affection or motion ye do speke or do nothing unworthy the immortalitie and moste precious nature of your soule. . . .

In semblable maner the inferior persone or subiecte aught to consider, that all be it he in the substaunce of soule and body be equall with his superior, yet for als moche as the powars and qualities of the soule and body, with the disposition of reason, be nat in euery man equall, therfore god ordayned a diuersitie or preeminence in degrees to be amonge men for the necessary derection and preseruation of them in conformitie of lyuinge. . . .

Where all thynge is commune, there lacketh ordre; and where ordre lacketh, there all thynge is odiouse and uncomly.

Such is the goal which the grave Sir Thomas pointed out to the noble youth of his land at the beginning of England's greatness, and such, within the bounds of human frailty, has been the ideal even until now which the two universities have held before them. Naturally the method of training prescribed in the sixteenth century for the attainment of this goal is antiquated in some of its details, but it is no exaggeration, nevertheless, to speak of the *Boke Named the Governour* as the very Magna Charta of our education. The scheme of the humanist might be described in a word as a disciplining of the higher faculty of the imagination to the end that the student may behold, as it were in one sublime vision, the whole scale of being in its range from the lowest to the highest under the divine decree of order and subordination, without losing sight of the immutable veracity at the heart of all development, which "is only the praise and surname of virtue." This was no new vision, nor has it ever been quite forgotten. It was the whole meaning of religion to Hooker, from whom it passed into all that is best and least ephemeral in the Anglican Church. It was the basis, more modestly expressed, of Blackstone's conception of the British Constitution and of liberty under law. It was the kernel of Burke's theory of statecraft. It is the inspiration of the sublimer science, which accepts the hypothesis of evolution as taught by Darwin and Spencer, yet bows in reverence before the unnamed and incommensurable force lodged as a mystical purpose within the unfolding universe. It was the wisdom of that child of Statford who, building better than he knew, gave to our literature its deepest and most persistent note. If anywhere Shakespeare seems to speak from his heart and to utter his own philosophy, it is in the person of Ulysses in that strange satire of life as "still wars and lechery" which forms the theme of *Troilus and Cressida*. Twice in the course of the play Ulysses moralizes on the cause of human evil. Once it is in an outburst against the devastations of disorder:

> Take but degree away, untune that string,
> And, hark, what discord follows! each thing meets
> In mere oppugnancy: the bounded waters
> Should lift their bosoms higher than the shores,

And make a sop of all this solid globe:
Strength should be lord of imbecility,
And the rude son should strike his father dead:
Force should be right; or rather, right and wrong,
Between whose endless jar justice resides,
Should lose their names, and so should justice too.
Then every thing includes itself in power,
Power into will, will into appetite.

And, in the same spirit, the second tirade of Ulysses is charged
with mockery at the vanity of the present and at man's usurpa-
tion of time as the destroyer instead of the preserver of continuity:

For time is like a fashionable host
That slightly shakes his parting guest by the hand,
And with his arms outstretch'd, as he would fly,
Grasps in the comer: welcome ever smiles,
And farewell goes out sighing. O, let not virtue seek
Remuneration for the thing it was;
For beauty, wit,
High birth, vigour of bone, desert in service,
Love, friendship, charity, are subjects all
To envious and calumniating time.

To have made this vision of the higher imagination a true
part of our self-knowledge, in such fashion that the soul is
purged of envy for what is distinguished and we feel ourselves
fellows with the preserving, rather than the destroying, forces
of time, is to be raised into the nobility of the intellect. To hold
this knowledge in a mind trained to fine efficiency and
confirmed by faithful comradeship is to take one's place with
the rightful governors of the people. Nor is there any narrow
or invidious exclusiveness in such an aristocracy, which differs
in this free hospitality from an oligarchy of artificial prescription. The more its membership is enlarged, the greater is its
power and the more secure are the privileges of each individual. Yet, if not exclusive, an academic aristocracy must by its
very nature be exceedingly jealous of any levelling process

which would shape education to the needs of the intellectual proletariat and so diminish its own ranks. It cannot admit that, if education is once levelled downwards, the whole body of men will of themselves gradually raise the level to the higher range; for its creed declares that elevation must come from leadership rather than from self-motion of the mass. It will therefore be opposed to any scheme of studies which relaxes discipline or destroys intellectual solidarity. It will look with suspicion on any system which turns out half-educated men with the same diplomas as the fully educated, thinking that such methods of slurring differences are likely to do more harm by discouraging the ambition to attain what is distinguished than good by spreading wide a thin veneer of culture. In particular it will distrust the present huge overgrowth of courses in government and sociology, which send men into the world skilled in the machinery of statecraft and with minds sharpened to the immediate demands of special groups, but with no genuine training of the imagination and no understanding of the longer problems of humanity. It will think that the dominance of such studies is one of the causes that men leave our colleges with no hold on the past, with nothing, as Burke said, "amidst so vast a fluctuation of passions and opinions, to concentrate their thoughts, to ballast their conduct, to preserve them from being blown about by every wind of fashionable doctrine." It will set itself against any regular subjection of the "fierce spirit of liberty," which is the breath of distinction and the very charter of aristocracy, to the sullen spirit of equality, which proceeds from envy in the baser sort of democracy. It will regard the character of education and the disposition of the curriculum as a question of supreme importance; for its motto is always, *abeunt studia in mores.*[4]

Now this aristocratic principle has, so to speak, its everlasting embodiment in Greek literature, from whence it was taken over into Latin and transmitted, with much mingling of foreign and even contradictory ideas, to the modern world. From Homer to the last runnings of the Hellenic spirit you will find it taught by every kind of precept and enforced by every kind of example; nor was Shakespeare writing at hazard, but under the instinctive guidance of genius, when he put his aristocratic creed into the mouth of the hero who to the end remained for the Greeks the personification of their peculiar wisdom. In no other poetry of the world is the law of distinction, as springing from a man's perception of his place in the great hierarchy of privilege and obligation from the lowest human being up to the Olympian gods, so copiously and magnificently set forth as in Pindar's Odes of Victory. And Æschylus was the first dramatist to see with clear vision the primacy of the intellect in the law of orderly development, seemingly at variance with the divine immutable will of Fate, yet finally in mysterious accord with it. When the philosophers of the later period came to the creation of systematic ethics they had only the task of formulating what was already latent in the poets and historians of their land; and it was the recollection of the fulness of such instruction in the *Nicomachean Ethics* and the Platonic Dialogues, with their echo in the *Officia* of Cicero, as if in them were stored up all the treasures of antiquity, that raised our Sir Thomas into wondering admiration:

> Lorde god, what incomparable swetnesse of wordes and mater shall he finde in the saide warkes of Plato and Cicero; wherin is ioyned grauitie with dilectation, excellent wysedome with diuine eloquence, absolute vertue with pleasure incredible, and euery place is so farced [crowded] with profitable counsaile, ioyned with honestie, that those thre bokes be almoste sufficient to make a perfecte and excellent gouernour.

There is no need to dwell on this aspect of the classics. He who cares to follow their full working in this direction, as did our English humanist, may find it exhibited in Plato's political and ethical scheme of self-development, or in Aristotle's ideal of the Golden Mean which combines magnanimity with moderation, and elevation with self-knowledge. If a single word were used to describe the character and state of life upheld by Plato and Aristotle, as spokesmen of their people, it would be *eleutheria*, liberty: the freedom to cultivate the higher part of a man's nature—his intellectual prerogative, his desire of truth, his refinements of taste—and to hold the baser part of himself in subjection; the freedom also, for its own perfection, and indeed for its very existence, to impose an outer conformity to, or at least respect for, the laws of this inner government on others who are themselves ungoverned. Such liberty is the ground of true distinction; it implies the opposite of an equalitarianism which reserves its honours and rewards for those who attain a bastard kind of distinction by the cunning of leadership without departing from common standards, for the demagogues, that is, who rise by flattery. But this liberty is by no means dependent on the artificial distinctions of privilege; on the contrary, it is peculiarly adapted to an age whose appointed task must be to create a natural aristocracy as a *via media* between an equalitarian democracy and a prescriptive oligarchy or a plutocracy. The fact is notable that, as the real hostility to the classics in the present day arises from an instinctive suspicion of them as standing in the way of a downward-levelling mediocrity, so, at other times, they have fallen under displeasure for their veto on a contrary excess. Thus, in his savage attack on the Commonwealth, to which he gave the significant title *Behemoth*, Hobbes lists the reading of classical history among the chief causes of the rebellion. "There were," he says, "an exceeding great number of men of the better sort, that had been so educated as that in their youth, having read the books written by famous men of the ancient Grecian and Roman commonwealths concerning their polity and great actions, in which books the popular government was extolled by that glorious name of liberty, and monarchy disgraced by the name of tyranny, they became thereby in love with their forms of government; and out of these men were chosen the greatest part of the House of Commons; or if they were not the greatest part, yet by advantage of their eloquence were always able to sway the rest." To this charge Hobbes returns again and again, even declaring that "the universities have been to this nation as the Wooden Horse was to the Trojans." And the uncompromising monarchist of the *Leviathan*, himself a classicist of no mean attainments, as may be known by his translation of Thucydides, was not deceived in his accusation. The tyrannicides of Athens and Rome, the Aristogeitons and Brutuses and others, were the heroes by whose example the leaders of the French Revolution were continually justifying their acts.

> There Brutus starts and stares by midnight taper.
> Who all the day enacts—a woollen-draper.

And again, in the years of the Risorgimento, more than one of the champions of Italian liberty went to death with those great names on their lips.

So runs the law of order and right subordination. But if the classics offer the best service to education by inculcating an aristocracy of intellectual distinction, they are equally effective in enforcing the similar lesson of time. It is a true saying of our ancient humanist that "the longer it continueth in a name or lineage, the more is nobility extolled and marvelled at." It is true because in this way our imagination is working with the great conservative law of growth. Whatever may be in theory our democratic distaste for the insignia of birth, we cannot get away from the fact that there is a certain honour of inheritance and that we instinctively pay homage to one who represents a noble name. There is nothing really illogical in this, for, as an English statesman has put it, "the past is one of the elements of our power." He is the wise democrat who, with no opposition to such a decree of Nature, endeavours to control its operation by expecting noble service where the memory of nobility abides. When, recently, Oxford bestowed its highest honour on an American, distinguished not only for his own public acts but for the great tradition embodied in his name, the Orator of the University did not omit this legitimate appeal to the imagination, singularly appropriate in its academic Latin:

> . . . Statim succurrit animo antiqua illa Romae condicio, cum non tam propter singulos cives quam propter singulas gentes

nomen Romanum floreret. Cum enim civis alicujus et avum et proavum principes civitatis esse creatos, cum patrem legationis munus apud aulam Britannicam summa cum laude esse exsecutum cognovimus; cum denique ipsum per totum bellum stipendia equo meritum, summa pericula "Pulcra pro Libertate" ausum, ... Romanae alicujus gentis—Brutorum vel Deciorum—annales evolvere videmur, qui testimonium adhibent "fortes creari fortibus," et majorum exemplis et imaginibus nepotes ad virtutem accendi.[5]

Is there any man so dull of soul as not to be stirred by that enumeration of civic services zealously inherited; or is there any one so envious of the past as not to believe that such memories should be honoured in the present as an incentive to noble emulation?

Well, we cannot all of us count Presidents and Ambassadors among our ancestors, but we can, if we will, in the genealogy of the inner life enroll ourselves among the adopted sons of a family in comparison with which the Bruti and Decii of old and the Adamses of to-day are veritable *new men*. We can see what defence against the meaner depredations of the world may be drawn from the pride of birth, when, as it sometimes happens, the obligation of a great past is kept as a contract with the present; shall we forget to measure the enlargement and elevation of mind which ought to come to a man who has made himself the heir of the ancient Lords of Wisdom? "To one small people," as Sir Henry Maine has said, in words often quoted, "it was given to create the principle of Progress. That people was the Greek. Except the blind forces of Nature, nothing moves in this world which is not Greek in its origin." That is a hard saying, but scarcely exaggerated. Examine the records of our art and our science, our philosophy and the enduring element of our faith, our statecraft and our notion of liberty, and you will find that they all go back for their inspiration to that one small people, and strike their roots into the soil of Greece. What we have added, it is well to know; but he is the aristocrat of the mind who can display a diploma from the schools of the Academy and Lyceum and from the Theatre of

Dionysus. What tradition of ancestral achievement in the Senate or on the field of battle shall broaden a man's outlook and elevate his will equally with the consciousness that his way of thinking and feeling has come down to him by so long and honourable a descent, or shall so confirm him in his better judgment against the ephemeral and vulgarizing solicitations of the hour? Other men are creatures of the visible moment; he is a citizen of the past and of the future. And such a charter of citizenship it is the first duty of the college to provide.

I have limited myself in these pages to a discussion of what may be called the public side of education, considering the classics in their power to mould character and to foster sound leadership in a society much given to drifting. Of the inexhaustible joy and consolation they afford to the individual, only he can have full knowledge who has made the writers of Greece and Rome his friends and counsellors through many vicissitudes of life. It is related of Sainte-Beuve, who, according to Renan, read everything and remembered everything, that one could observe a peculiar serenity on his face whenever he came down from his study after reading a book of Homer. The cost of learning the language of Homer is not small; but so are all fair things difficult, as the Greek proverb runs, and the reward in the case is precious beyond estimation.

[1]   "Academic Leadership" was the second essay in *Aristocracy and Justice*. Like its predecessor, it was originally written for the *Unpopular Review* where it saw light in July, 1914. Norman Foerster included it in his *Essays for College Men, Second Series* (1915).

[2]   Written, all this, before the European war. [More's note]

[3]   William Frank McCombs (1875–1921), New York attorney, who managed the national campaigns resulting in the nomination and the election of Woodrow Wilson as President in 1912. He was Chairman of the Democratic National Committee, 1912–16.

[4]   "Studies affect the habits and character." *Dictionary of Foreign Phrases and Classical Quotations*, Ed. Hugh Percy Jones, New and Revised Edition (Edinburgh: John Giant, Booksellers, Ltd., 1949). p. 1.

[5]   "One's mind reverts inevitably to that ancient state of affairs in Rome, when the Roman name was illustrious not only through individual citizens, but also through particular families. For when we consider that a man's grandfather

and great-grandfather held the highest office in a State, and that his father represented his country with the highest distinction at the court of Great Britain, and when we remember, finally, that the man himself gave all his strength to military service throughout a war, incurring extreme perils 'For the sake of Sweet Liberty.' . . . in these recollections we seem to be unrolling the annals of some Roman family,—of the Bruti or the Decii, annuals bearing witness to the fact that 'the strong are born to the strong,' and that by the examples and traditions of their ancestors the descendants are incited to distinguished achievement."—The honour was bestowed on the late Charles Francis Adams. [More's note]

Scholarship of Ideas[1]

"My case is probably by no means unique. After gradua-
ting with honors at———I obtained a position as teacher of
English in the school where I now am. My ambition is to
enter on a college career, but to do this I should have to go
back to the graduate school of my university, and I cannot
bring myself to undergo the gruelling process with such a
course means. As an undergraduate I was not alone in feeling that the work required for the doctor's degree seems to
be specially designed to eliminate all who have any imagination or any ideas."

We print this complaint because it is typical of an opinion
which comes to us from many sources and in many forms,
and which sooner or later must be reckoned with. It is in
accord with the avowal of at least one college president to
the effect that the recommendation of a certain eminent
and dominating scholar would be a detriment to a candidate for a place in his faculty; and it may have some bearing upon the conditions which have led a keen observer in
a large Western university to declare, whether rightly or
wrongly, that the grade of men now preparing themselves
for college teaching is distinctly inferior to what it was ten
or fifteen years ago. No one can converse widely with the
younger students over the country without having this attitude of revolt thrust forcibly upon his attention. The question is whether this discontent will be able to organize itself
and effect a wise reform or waste itself blindly and suffer

the graduate instruction in the English and modern language departments to go the way of the classics.

As for the classical men, they have taken account of their house, and, in alarm for their very existence, are making desperate efforts to throw off the shackles of pedantry with which they were bound and to introduce something into their curriculum besides linguistics and archaeology. It would be uncritical to attribute the present low state of the classics entirely, or perhaps even chiefly, to the narrow philological method of teaching which so long prevailed, but this method was undoubtedly a contributory cause, and the great difficulty now, when the error is acknowledged and larger views are cherished, is to find instructors who can put into practice what all, or almost all, so earnestly desire. Scholars breed their kind, and a bad system has an obstinate way of perpetuating itself. We are glad to print in this issue of *The Nation* the argument of one who has always stood for true scholarship, and who, certainly as much as any other one man in the country, has labored to save the classics from the sands of pedantry on the one side and the bog of dilettantism on the other.

This, in fact, is the dilemma—pedantry on the one side and dilettantism on the other—which always confronts a collegiate department, and which now faces English and the modern languages with peculiar acuteness. The problem is complicated by the observed psychological fact that these two extremes of scholarship tend to work together with a kind of tolerant contempt for each other, to the exclusion of the virile scholarship of ideas which is inimical to both and is opposed by both. Emerson was right in saying that an idea is a terrible thing to let loose upon the world—certainly upon the academic world. A department under the control of a philological tradition, if called to account for not teaching "literature," will by natural instinct look out for a mild and pleasant lecturer with whose taste it can sympathize in hours of languid relaxation and whom it can probably dominate without difficulty. Meanwhile,

Povera vai e nuda, filosofia. [2]

The remedy is not to transfer the emphasis from philology, using that word in its narrower sense, to "literature," using this word in its flabbier sense. The graduate school does not exist primarily for training the sensibilities, and the right graduate teacher is not one who can titillate the aesthetic nerve of the nice young poet. It is questionable whether the graduate school is properly used in any way for direct training in literary production. Skill in constructing a drama or writing a marketable short story is better acquired elsewhere. The graduate school is first and last a place for scholars, and the scholars who are now in charge may justly resent any move to put the aesthete and the amateur and the "literary" man in their chairs. Nor are they wrong in asserting that the most minute form of research—the relentless pursuit of some Anglo-Saxon vowel or the wild chase of some folk-tale through five mediaeval languages—has its own place and honor. These things should be done, but the other things—the larger study of life, what we call the scholarship of ideas—should not be left undone; they should rather lead and give the tone to the whole. It is a matter of emphasis, and unfortunately the present state of affairs would seem almost to justify the complaint of an old English divine, that "no sort of Men think so little for the most part as they that are ingaged in the Profest Study of Learning and Knowledge."

Scholarship of ideas may seem a vague programme to set before those who are in the brunt of actual teaching. Certainly not the least of the difficulties to be overcome is that laxity of training which begins in the kindergarten, and which follows the student all the way up in his career, compelling the teacher to whom he comes in the graduate school, as Professor Shorey points out so emphatically, to waste his time in elementary discipline.[3] Nevertheless, there are steps which lie clearly before the departments of English and modern languages, and will lead to immediate and practical reform. In the first place, they must free themselves from the ruck of mediaevalism, in which may be included much of the raking among the dregs of Elizabethan drama. Mediaeval studies are well in their way, but their dominance in the modern language field has done more perhaps, than any other one cause to lay an undue emphasis on philological research of the most desiccating type and to drive away men of large, humane ideas. In place of mediaeval phonetics and theme-chasing, a close alliance should be formed with the classics. One of the most significant warnings pronounced in many a year was the strong plea of Mr. Edward M. Shepard, speaking at the last meeting of the Modern Language Association, as a scholar and man of the world, for just this affiliation. From Athens and Rome, not from the Middle Ages, come the vital ideas of modern literature, the high association of letters and life, which we have so nearly lost from view. Such an alliance would at once introduce something more of actuality into the study of the classics and lend to modern languages the larger historical background, the sense of great currents of thought which have moulded and are still moulding the fate of mankind. He who, like the late Master of Balliol,[4] has in mind the creative ideas that have passed from that ancient time to these modern days is not likely to lose himself either in pedantic intricacies or in the *O Altitudo* of a precious aestheticism. Beauty and the motives of conduct will be wedded with him for the making of the true scholarship.

Another practical step is the escape from the present tyranny of the German doctorate. It may be that for many men the preparation of a thesis is the best training, as it apparently is for the teacher the easiest method of testing a student's proficiency. But the system is subject at least to grave abuses. Even supposing that the student has advanced far enough to devote to the special research needed for a thesis a year or two years of the time without heavy sacrifice in other directions, the emphasis laid on this kind of work tends to confuse the meaning of productive and creative scholarship and to establish wrong standards of excellence. It tends also to foster the peculiar sin of German scholarship which Professor Shorey

brands as inaccuracy, but which we should prefer to call lack
of mental integrity—the habit, that is, of erecting vast theories
on a slender basis of fact, and so clogging the paths of truth.
Only a huge illusion can hold that a student who by a satisfactory, even an admirable, thesis has added some small account
to the sum of knowedge is in any true sense of the word a more
creative mind than one who has thoroughly assimilated a wide
range of ideas and prepared himself to hand on the judgments
of time. At least along with the doctorate, we need to
strengthen and raise the master's degree as a symbol of large
assimilative study. Indeed, some of our universities have seen
the value of this course, and are gradually lifting the M.A. into
a sign of real distinction. One serious impediment now in the
way of this reform is the belated ignorance of those presidents
and trustees of colleges who insist on a Ph.D. after the name
of a candidate to their faculties, and so attach to the degree a
factitious commercial value . They have been educated into
this error and must in turn be educated out of it.

Affiliation with the classics instead of mediaevalism and the
honoring of an assimilative degree beside the German doctorate are not impractical counsels of perfection; they are directly
in the way of our modern language departments, they are
comparatively easy to take, and they are already much talked
of. In particular the choice lies before the department of English: it may suffer the tyranny of the pedant, and so go the
path from which the classics are so wearily retracing their
steps; or it may take warning and turn toward the scholarship
if ideas. In this way it can preserve itself from the wiles of the
dilettante and maintain its honorable position in the academic
world; and in this way, too, it can be an indirect but incalculable aid to literature, for our literature today needs above everything else to add to its cleverness the discipline of ideas and
the reverence for long tradition.

1   This article was published anonymously in *The Nation* (May 11, 1911) and the
    Evening Post (May 13, 1911). It is a good example of More's journalism. One
    wishes that More had worked it up as one of the *Shelburne Essays.*
2   "Philosophy, how poor and naked your are!"
3   Paul Shorey (1857–1934). See his "The Case for the Classics," *School Review,*
    November, 1910; and "The Assault on Humanism," *Atlantic Monthly,* July,
    1917.
4   Probably Benjamin Jowett (1817–1893), Master of Balliol from 1870 to 1893.

The Teaching
of the Classics[1]

A good deal has been written of recent years about the failure of our classical teachers to maintain their place in the educational field, and to any one familiar with the situation from within it is clear that these gentlemen have not only been brought down from their high pretensions but have been thrown into a state of sullen self-defense or apology, not to say panic bewilderment. Some of this criticism, we will admit, has been unjust. The college teacher of Greek or Latin can plead that his pupils come to him so ill-furnished that most of his strength must go to doing the work properly belonging to the preparatory school. And he can fairly boast that the classics, even as they are taught, still remain the best discipline offered by our colleges, training men to think clearly and to express themselves in orderly fashion as no other study has succeeded in doing. But it is also true that they are slowly losing this distinction, while they have failed to reach out into the higher sphere of ideas. It is a fact, I believe, that in all these years no one book of serious human interest has been produced by a classical scholar of this country. When you stop to think of it, and when you count the number of piddling text-books turned out annually, this is an utterly ruinous accusation. And the young men are not unaware of this disgraceful failure. I observe that at Harvard this year only a single student has come up for the doctor's degree in classics, and that his work is purely linguistic. *Quousque tandem?*[2]

In this murky state of the educational atmosphere Prof. Irving Babbitt's "Literature and the American College" (Houghton, Mifflin & Co.)[3] comes like a stroke of clear lightning. If our classical instructors have been in any doubt as to the growing sense of rebellion among thoughtful men against their ostrich-like attitude, they may get the needed enlightenment from these pages. For cutting satire nothing equal to this arraignment has been produced since Lowell's day. The book was not written by a member of the classical faculty and its survey is by no means confined to the classics, but it deals with them as the *fons et origo*. And it not only sets forth the evil of the present system of instruction, but points the way constructively to a wholesome reform. Starting with a definition of humanism as a disciplined balance of all the faculties and a state of equipoise between religious absorption in the one and naturalistic surrender to the many, Professor Babbitt then contrasts with that ideal Bacon's scientific humanitarianism and Rousseau's sentimental humanitarianism, and shows how these between them have gradually taken possession of the field of education.

Now the value of the classics lies first of all in the fact that more than any other study they are able to create that desired equipoise of mind between the one and the many. But to attain that result they need for our present life to be presented in a new manner, and to this exigency the keepers of the classical tradition have hitherto shown themselves blind. The purely linguistic and archaelogical ransacking of antiquity should always, of course, in any rational system of education, be kept in the background, necessary as a preparation but dangerous as a goal. As Quintilian said long ago: "These studies do no harm to those who pass through them, but to those who stick to them." Formerly there was less danger in such pendantry than now because always there was present the feeling that the wisdom of the world was bound up in these ancient books, and in a thousand different ways there was a continual and unconscious application of ideas to the criticism of life. Izaak Walton, in his account of Sir Henry Wotton as Provost of Eton, gives a beautiful example of this influence:

He was a constant cherisher of all those youths in that school, in whom he found either a constant diligence or a genius that prompted them to learning; for whose encouragement he was (besides many other things of necessity and beauty) at the charge of setting up in it two rows of pillars, on which he caused to be choicely drawn the pictures of divers of the most famous Greek and Latin historians, poets, and orators; persuading them not to neglect rhetoric because Almighty God has left mankind affections to be wrought upon. And he would often say that none despised eloquence but such dull souls as were not capable of it. He would also often make choice of some observations out of those historians and poets; and would never leave the school without dropping some choice Greek or Latin apothegm or sentence, that might be worthy of room in the memory of a growing scholar.

That is not the manner of the present-day college president, nor is it primarily the fault of our teachers that this power of the classics as the unique repository of human wisdom has past away. A hundred years ago Freneau, our first poet, saw the change that was coming:

> This age may decay, and another may rise,
> Before it is fully revealed to our eyes,
> That Latin and Hebrew, Chaldaic and Greek,
> To the shades of oblivion must certainly sneak;
> Too much of our time is employed on such trash
> When we ought to be taught to accumulate cash.

That other age has arrived, and some may think we are drilled even too strenuously in practical wisdom—whether we succeed or not in accumulating cash. But apart from any such common lowering of ideals, which may well be disputed, it has grown increasingly clear with time that wisdom and virtue did not cease with the writing of Greek and Latin, that the world moves from stage to stage, always with its new problems and its fresh solutions, and that by too much reverence for the past we may become blind to the present. Great literatures of our own age press upon us with their various interpretations of man's destiny, and in a certain sense we have all become students of history, not out of docile respect for what has been done and said, but as concerned with the unending process of change and development in which we are ourselves involved.

For such a shifting in the educational center of gravity our classical faculties are in no wise, or to a small degree, responsible. But they are censurable for their failure to adapt themselves to the change. They have been thrust from their preeminence as wardens of the sacred and stationary truth; instead of laying hold upon the new aspect of truth, they have clung desperately and almost despicably to their linguistic gerund-grinding and their archeological pothunting—infinitely skilled

> . . . To chase
> A panting syllable through time and space.

And how magnificent is the field neglected! For if it was true in the old days that every road led to Rome, it is still the fact today that almost every path of history leads to Rome, and from Rome to Athens. There began our literature and our arts; in those two cities grew up that body of religious and philosophic ideas that were transmuted into Christianity and moulded the new world; jurisprudence and the science of government are rooted in the same soil. It was but the other day I was talking with a distinguished sociologist who has no training in the classical languages and certainly no reason to be prejudiced in their favor. He had been expounding various advanced notions of sociology and predicting what was to be, when he stopped and remarked, with an odd lowering of the voice, "But do you know, all these ideas were discussed by Aristotle long ago!" There lie the sources. We have combined and added and recombined, but the beginnings are all there, and their influence in unobserved ways is still working upon us with incalculable force. On the men of our classical departments more than on any others it is incumbent to be familiar with the development of the centuries and to impart it in their instruction, not wholly or chiefly, perhaps, by direct historical teaching, but by inference and allusion and unpremeditated comparison, and the inevitable outflowing of a mind stored with the learning of many ages. And such instruction might be not only attractive to large groups of students who are now repelled from their classes, but highly formative. Much of the flightiness of modern minds, much of the waste of our powers, is due to the fact that we look on too small a segment of the great circle of history; we misjudge human nature thereby and we lose sight of forces lying too deep for our hasty ken. To have the beginnings firmly fixed in memory, to have followed these forces through the long unfolding of human history, gives a gravity to judgment, an ability to discriminate between ephemeral change and organic growth, a steadiness of purpose against the shifting winds of opinion, a total wisdom, that are not likely to come to a man from any other source.

It is thus, by the breadth of our view, that while engaged in the changing phenomenal world of present, which Plato called the many, we may preserve the due humanistic balance. Nor would our inborn craving for the unchangeable pass un-satisfied. If much of Greek thought is valuable for what has grown out of it, there are achievements also in which they remain unsurpassed, seemingly unsurpassable, and to have trained the mind to an appreciation of these achievements is to hold forever after a touchstone to distinguish between the higher and the lower pleasures. No later writer of narrative verse has equaled Homer; no dramatist has ever surpassed Sophocles; no lyric poet ever sang more entrancingly than Sappho; no sculptor rivaled Phidias; no philosopher looked so deeply into the human soul as Plato. The work of these men is still a norm of taste, and the full and sane measure of artistic joy can be known only by those whose emotions have been trained to respond to these models. And who would ever guess this truth while sitting in the classical room of an American college?

If you ask why our classical teachers have failed to grasp their opportunities, many answers could be given. Perhaps the chief cause is their enormous ignorance. There are, no doubt, honorable exceptions, but as a body it is simply the truth that they have no solid reading outside of their prescribed field, and are hence incapacitated for the larger historical survey of their subject and for conveying ideas of life through their instruction. In some cases this is due to laziness and intellectual ineptitude. More generally it is the result of a system of study which consumes all their strength over vicious or worthless philological monographs out of Germany; no man of ordinary capacity, for instance, can master the whole literature of the so-called Homeric question—most of it foolish or dishonest—and have time to follow the track of Homer in modern times. The classical men in our larger universities, who give the tone of these studies for the country, have been brought up under the philological system, and they perpetuate their kind, not only by their influence, but by the selection of their successors. The gist of the whole matter is briefly this: We want men in our universities to continue the great work of linguistic and archeologic investigation—against these in themselves there can be no proper complaint; they are indeed the basis of all the rest —but we must also have, if the classics are to remain alive, men not strictly philologians, who have a large philosophic and literary training, and by their wider view of the growth of ideas, can teach the classics so as to relate them to the great currents of history.

---

[1] This article is taken from the *Independent* for August 6, 1908, and deserves to be read along with "Academic Leadership" and "Natural Aristocracy."

[2] "How long?" (From Cicero's "How long will you abuse our patience?")

[3] First published in 1908.

The Historic Sense[1]

Readers of the English reviews may have seen very favorable notices of a book, "The Great Days of Versailles," by G.F. Bradby.[2] It is, indeed, an entertaining work. Here you may follow the daily life of Louis XIV. and his court to the minutest details—what they ate and wore, how they talked and quarrelled and loved—a strangely vivid picture. Only one aspect of that existence is omitted: there is scarcely a word to indicate why those days should be called "great." The monotony of court life is set forth in full, but nothing is added to explain how this monotony was only the last rigid stage of the ideal of uniformity, or rather conformity, which had produced the literature of the grand siècle. Something is said about the production of Racine's "Esther" at Saint-Cyr, but chiefly to show the vexations the play brought upon Madame de Maintenon. Nor does religion fare better. Here you shall read of the trick by which the sham devotion of the great ladies was exposed to Louis; Madame Guyon also is mentioned, and Fenelon's connection with the Quietists, but for petty reasons only. Louis's own submission to the Church is related, but there is nothing to indicate the deep religious current that ran through the age side by side with its worldliness, sparing in its course not even Versailles.

However, we have no quarrel with Mr. Bradby's book, which is excellent in its kind. It concerns us here only as rather an extreme example of what is growing more and more evident in recent literature—the absence of the historic sense. It used to be the boast of the nineteenth century that it was the creator of science and of the historic sense; and in a way the boast was justified. Certainly, no previous century had undertaken to worm itself into the secrets of the past as did the century of Renan and Taine and Sainte-Beuve. From the great doctrine of relativity and of development inculcated by Germany from Kant to Hegel, came the notion that an era of the past is something distinct in spirit, something to be comprehended by getting outside of present associations. To this end the study of details was to be carried to indefinite lengths, for gradually, through the accumulation of minute point after point, the picture of a past environment was to be produced, and from this knowledge of surroundings we were to infer the nature of the soul of the period. The historic sense, as then understood, was thus an offshoot of scepticism and science, of *skepsis* in the double meaning of that ancient word. As scholars lost faith in the immutable and universal principles of human nature, they became more interested in tracing the path of what is changeable and locally determined. As the past lost in authority it seemed to grow more valuable to us as a field upon which we could exercise our unconcerned love of abstract truth. Those who have read Buckle will remember how the methods of science were adapted to this pursuit. Or, better yet, there is Taine's attempt to analyze the products of English literature as if they were so many chemical compounds.

It is a question whether there was not a certain admixture of self-deception in all this brilliant resuscitation of the past, whether the historic spirit of the nineteenth century ever escaped quite so entirely from the clinging fallacy of the present as it supposed. It is at least significant that those who were loudest in proclaiming the new scientific and sceptical method are just those who are most rapidly losing credit today. Buckle, despite his erudition and eloquence, is no longer taken quite seriously; Taine is notoriously an unsure guide, and the "History of English Literature," written confessedly as an exemplification of his theory, is a continued distortion of the reality. One may doubt whether their vividness in reconstructing

what they called the past was not really due to the completeness of their implication in the spirit of the present: the picture
at least was intensely alive. It would be odd if in the long run
the earlier writers who were concerned with what they regarded as the unchanging elements of human nature should
prove to have been truer in their grasp of the past than these
disciples of scientific relativity.

On the whole, it is safer to admit a moment in the nineteenth century, when the older notion of continuity and authority combined with the newer theory of development and
relativity to create a genuine historic sense. A perfect example
of this may be seen in the *Port-Royal* of Sainte-Beuve, where
a writer essentially sceptical reproduces a society dominated
by religion; in English we have the greater historical novels
culminating in *Henry Esmond*. What cannot be ignored is the
fact that for many years the historic sense, that is, the power
of calling forth any true illusion of the past, has been surely
waning. The abuse of the documentary method of study may
have something to do with this, by habituating the mind to
dulness, but the real cause lies deeper. The means has destroyed the end, and those who try to be most entertaining are
likely to be least historical. The effort to accumulate picturesque details has blinded us to the purpose for which these
details were first desired. Of this Mr. Bradby's book affords a
striking example. At first the attention of the reader is deeply
engaged; he expects to be led into the very spirit of the age.
Presently he is chagrined to discover that the picturesque
anecdotes and descriptions lead nowhere. Because the inspiration of that age was different from ours, it is simply non-exist-
ent to the author; he has no standard by which to measure the
relation between the uniformity and restraint of manners on
the one hand, and on the other the discipline of mind that
showed itself in so many works of genius. And missing this
interest in the higher things of humanity which make of that
age a lesson and authority, he falls into the most vicious fallacy
of the present. Because we with our habits and conveniences
should be bored and shocked by the physical conditions of that

life, he represents the great days of Versailles as a time of almost unmitigated boredom.

1   Like the essay immediately preceding, this essay is another example of More's careful journalism and an illustration of what he thought an editor's responsibility was to his readers. It was published anonymously in both the *Evening Post* (January 19, 1907) and *The Nation* (January 24, 1907) and is here reprinted for the first time.
2   Godfrey Fox Bradby, *The Great Days of Versailles; Studies from Court Life in the Later Years of Louis XIV*. New York and London, 1906.

A New Intrusion of Pedantry[1]

It needs a strong hand now and then to smite those Philistines of the schools whom we call pedants, and such a hand Mr. Trevelyan, the eminent biographer and historian, has raised in defence of the finer aspects of his art. In an inaugural address, delivered just a year ago at Cambridge University, Professor Bury asserted roundly that history is a science, not an art, and that the imagination and the emotions have no concern in its writing. If he relented at all in this austere rejection of the graces, it was only in favor of "generations very remote":

> The gathering of materials, he declares, bearing upon minute local events, the collation of MSS. and the registry of their small variations, the patient drudgery in archives of states and municipalities, all the microscopic research that is carried on by armies of toiling students—it may seem like the bearing of mortar and bricks to the site of a building which has hardly been begun, of whose plan the laborers know but little. This work, the hewing of wood and the drawing of water, has to be done in faith—in the faith that a complete assemblage of the smallest facts of human history will tell in the end. The labor is performed for posterity.

Against this promulgation of the new school, Mr. Trevelyan has protested vigorously in the *Independent Review*, showing with admirable persuasiveness that the labor of sifting evidence and establishing facts is only the beginning of the student's task, and that no generation can safely forego the real objects of history—which are, as he thinks, to teach political wisdom, to restore our heritage in the ideals of the past and the lives of the noble dead, and to awaken a feeling for the poetry of time.

We could wish that some champion of the finer scholarship, as Mr. Trevelyan sees it, might arise in this country and smite hip and thigh the pedants who are fast bringing the study of history into the same disrepute among men of the world as that into which the classical languages have long since fallen at the hands of our learned philologians. The root of the disease lies in a misapprehension of the term science—in a sort of hypnotic spell which this word has cast over the minds of all who practise in the profession of knowledge and wisdom.

To suppose there can be a science of history in any sense corresponding to the science of material phenomena, is merely to bow down before the many-tongued idols of the marketplace. Truth is the aim of the historian, as it is of the scientist—as it is of the poet even; but it has not yet appeared that the only road to historic truth is by the "town-pump" method of instruction, as the cynical have denominated the pedantry of our schools. Unless history recreates the life of a past age, with all the passions and aspirations of that bygone world at play, it is not easy to perceive what profit arises from its pursuit. Accurate sifting of documents and weighing of evidence is necessary, but to stop there, as Professor Bury demands and as too many of our college men do in practice, is to harrow the soil without planting the seed; more than that, it is to waive the one instrument at our service for controlling the traditions and documents that descend to us. Human passion was the source and formal cause of that life, and only by passion can its meaning be brought back to us of the present. "Men act from passion," Hazlitt wrote, "and we can only judge of passion from sympathy. Persons of the dry and husky class above spoken of often seem to think even nature itself an interloper on their flimsy theories." And again: "Passion, in short, is the essence, the chief ingredient in moral truth, and the warmth of passion is sure to kindle the light of imagination on the objects around it."

There may seem something startling in this setting up of passion as the discoverer of historic truth; and yet, if the matter be examined into, it will be found that the historian whose works endure and whose portrayal of a certain period has gained the common approval of readers, has almost invariably written, not coldly and pedantically, but with strong forejudgment. His absorbing feeling kindles the imagination; by it he is able to comprehend the other human impulses at work as no cold registrar of documents can conceive them; and in reading his works it is perfectly easy to bear in mind that "personal equation" which is easily discounted since it is unconcealed. In this way, Carlyle discovered and gave to the world the character of Cromwell—by passion. In this way, to name no other instance, Tacitus presented a picture of the Roman Empire, whose fundamental truth no mere maker of themes can shake, and whose exaggerations the reader can readily account for; he has made the age forever alive and forever a lesson to the world.

Now, it is needless to say that passion in the writer of history does not mean any deliberate coloring of the truth, and it is equally needless to say that passion has no place at all in the pursuit of science. The error of Professor Bury and of the growing school he represents is the same error that vitiates so much that comes from pulpit and desk—the failure to perceive distinctions. True science has her own glory, from which no caviller may detract. This science falsely so called is no better than a parody and a stale imitation. Even if historic truth were to be found within the limitations set by Professor Bury, where were the profit? It still holds good of such pedantry—

> That truth itself is in her head as dull
> And useless as a candle in a skull.

The peril of allowing restrictions of this sort to creep into any field of university work is too serious to be ignored by those who have the really higher education at heart.

---

[1]   This essay was an anonymous editorial in both the *Evening Post* (December 19, 1903) and *The Nation* (December 24, 1903).

PART IV

Politics and Society

Justice [1]

(Justitia quid est? Animus quodammodo se habens.— SENECA.)[2]

It is an odd but undeniable state of things that a writer should feel a certain need of apology when he asks his readers to consider with him such a topic as that which stands at the head of this essay. For, after all, no other subject of debate, I suppose, is so perennially interesting and fruitful as the definition of the abstract virtues. That at least was the opinion of Socrates long ago, when he told his friends of the market place that he should like nothing better than to pass his whole life long in this kind of conversation; and any one who reads the newspapers today ought to know that, despite our apparent disdain of such themes, we really have the same insatiable curiosity towards them. What else is all our ocean of print about the present war[3] but an effort to fix the responsibility for its origin where it justly belongs? And what else is our discussion of the national traits of the various combatants, our talk of militarism, liberty, culture, humanitarianism, efficiency, and the like, but an endeavour to arrive at a clear definition of that virtue of justice upon which civilization itself is thought to hang?

Now, in a way, justice is easily defined: It is the act of right distribution, the giving to each man his due. Nobody will question this definition; but obviously, also, it carries us nowhere until we have further defined what is *right* and *due,* and have discovered some criterion by which we may know that a par-

ticular act in the conduct of life falls within our general definition.

The impulse of the modern man will be to look for an objective standard of justice in the law and operation of nature in
the animate world; and, immediately or inferentially, he will
find there what he seeks. He will observe first of all a great
variety of creatures and species existing side by side. He will
next be impressed by the fact that they differ one from another
in their similarity or dissimilarity to himself, and in their power
of satisfying his own sense of fitness and value. He will see that
among these creatures and species a struggle for existence,
sometimes open and sometimes disguised, now violent and
now gentle, is going on, and apparently has been going on for
an immeasurable space of time; and he will instinctively give
a kind of approbation when that creature or species prevails
to which he attributes the greater measure of fitness or value,
and which he calls the higher, as being in some way nearer to
himself. In general it will seem to him that in the course of
nature the stronger, which prevail over the weaker, are also,
as he judges, the higher. This common process of survival he
will call evolution, and its law will appear to him to be formulated in the axiom: Might makes right. To both of the meanings
implied in these words, viz., that might *is* right, as being the
higher in the order of nature, and that might *has* the right to
develop at the expense of the weaker, his reason will assent,
and, in its first motion at least, will assent without reservation.

But there is another aspect of evolution which will be forced
on the observer's attention. This process of subduing or elimi-
nating the weaker creature or species is often accompanied
with suffering. It cannot be pleasant for the less vigorous animal, when food is scarce, that the sturdier should gobble up
whatever is in sight, and leave him to starve. Nor do we suppose that it is altogether sport for the little fish to be chased by
the big fish. Sometimes the law of might acts by what has the
appearance of deliberate torture. Any one who has studied the
habits of pigeons in a dovecot will have seen a typical example
of Nature's way of dealing with weakness. Let one of the flock

suffer an injury or fall ill, and he is forthwith made the victim of downright persecution. Instead of pity, his comrades are filled with a kind of rage, striking him with beak and wing and driving him away to die in solitude.

Now our reason may tell us that all this is a necessary factor of evolution, and must occur if the higher creatures are to prevail over the lower. But besides reason we have feelings, and, however we may admire the widespread benevolence of Nature, from at least part of her operations our instinctive sympathy with suffering is bound to withhold its assent; we are bound to regard them as painful, and they may even seem malicious. Seeing these things, so impassionate an observer as Charles Darwin could be forced to exclaim: "What a book a Devil's-Chaplain might write on the clumsy, wasteful, blundering, low, and horribly cruel works of Nature." If, in judging the procedure of evolution, reason says that might makes right, feeling will often reply that weakness makes right, in the sense of having right, even when not being right.

Our attitude towards Nature is thus complex. Her work in a way, as Walpole used to say of the life of man, is a comedy to him who thinks, and a tragedy to him who feels. When the difference between two competitors is great, our reason predominates, and we feel little sympathy for the lower; our feeling may even side with reason against the sufferer. Certain creatures, whether because they are remote from us in the scale of being or because they are elusive enemies of our comfort, so affect us with disgust that we are quite ready to acquiesce in their torture. There is a joy for most men in destroying vermin and seeing it writhe in agony. No good American would feel compunction for the pangs of the brown-tailed or the gypsy moth, if some entomologist should discover and let loose a parasite to prey on the vitals of those pests. But when suffering comes to creatures higher up and nearer to us, we cry out that Nature is malign; and when our own welfare demands the death or discomfort of such creatures, we are likely to become apologetic, if not remorseful. There is "complicity in the shambles," as Emerson says, and so unbalanced men argue

that meat is baleful, and run to vegetarianism and other ex-
pedients to escape the inevitable law of evolution. Fanatics in
India have carried this repulsion so far as to make it a point of
religion to strain all the water they drink, lest some living
organism should inadvertently be swallowed, and to sweep the
ground before them lest some insect should be trodden under
foot. With them sympathy altogether outruns reason.

We see, therefore, that into our judgment of Nature two
elements enter, and that our sense of justice demands the
satisfaction both of our reason and of our feelings. And we see
also that there is nothing in the actual procedure of Nature
which would indicate any regard on her part for our judgment.
When we consider the persistent preservation of many low
forms of life whose welfare means for mankind only disease
and misery, we are almost driven to doubt whether the end of
evolution is even such as to satisfy our reason; and, without any
doubt at all, the method of evolution is often repugnant to our
most instinctive feelings. The fact is: the very idea of justice or
injustice has no real application to Nature. She proceeds by a
law and for a purpose of her own, and to judge her by our
human standard, as we inevitably do if we judge her at all, is
a pure fallacy. Our approval will not influence her a whit; not
all our clamours will move her to relent. She will continue to
warm us at the fires of life to-day, and to-morrow will ravage
our cities with earthquake and conflagration. She moves on her
way, impassionate and unconcerned, with sublime indifference to our creeds—the great mother at whose breasts we
have clung. And we, if we are wise, will curb our resentment
equally with our commendation; knowing that "ill is our anger
with things, since it concerns them not at all,"—

Τοῖς πράγμασιν γὰρ οὐχὶ θυμοῦσθαι χρεών·
μέλει γὰρ αὐτοῖς οὐδέν.

But there is another lesson to be learned from the indifference of Nature besides the need of regarding her works with
corresponding detachment. The very impertinence of apply-

ing our moral standards there where they are so openly disregarded is a proof that our sense of justice is not derived from watching her calm method of dealing with her own, but springs from something within our breasts that is not subject to her sway,—from a law, that is, that transcends the material law of evolution, being, if we use words strictly, not natural at all, but supernatural. Huxley was right and knew of what he spoke when he declared that our moral ideas have no relation to the doctrine of evolution.

Nevertheless, though we are debarred from the hope of finding in Nature an objective standard by which we can regulate our conduct, the manner in which we inevitably apply our idea of justice to the animate world is a clear indication of the character and composition of that idea. By analyzing the demands laid by us upon Nature we can see more plainly than by mere introspection what the condition of justice in the soul itself must be—rather, perhaps, the mind unaccustomed to the painful labour of self-study can here see itself magnified, so to speak, and projected upon a screen. Our idea of justice would be fulfilled if we saw that Nature satisfied two different faculties, or kinds of activity, of the soul—the reason, which demands that what is the stronger and more like itself should prevail, and the feelings, which demand that the higher should prevail with no suffering, but with the happy acquiescence, of the lower. And so we infer that the soul itself would be in this ideal state if the relation of its own members satisfied these demands. We reach, therefore, a clear definition of justice: it is that government and harmonious balance of the soul which arises when reason prevails over the feelings and desires, and when this dominance of the reason is attended with inner joy and consenting peace; it is the right distribution of power and honour to the denizens within the breast of the individual man.

The definition is not new, but was known of old to philosophers and poets who held it sufficient to look within themselves for moral guidance, with no thought of seeking in the inhumanities of Nature for corroboration of their faith. You will find such a portrait of the just man drawn at full length by Plutarch in his life of Aristides, whose righteous decisions swerved "neither for good will nor for friendship, neither for wrath nor for hatred," and upon whom we are told that all the spectators at a play once turned their eyes on hearing the poet's praise of a hero:

> For not to seem but to be just he seeks,
> And from deep furrows in the mind to reap
> Harvest of ripe and noble counselling.

And Shakespeare draws the same portrait from a slightly different angle:

> For thou hast been
> As one, in suffering all, that suffers nothing;
> A man that fortune's buffets and rewards
> Hast ta'en with equal thanks; and blest are those
> Whose blood and judgment are so well commingled
> That they are not a pipe for fortune's finger
> To sound what stop she please.

These have been the commonplaces of self-knowledge, and have needed no confimation from without; but we are children of another age, and must see wisdom with our eyes and learn truth through our ears. And so we may profit by carrying the analogy of evolution a little further.

What we call the injustice of evolution is due to the fact that the struggle in Nature is always between two distinct and different organisms, and that therefore the prevalence of the one is likely to be at the expense of the other. Hence we should infer, as indeed we know from quite other lines of argument, that, if the idea of justice can be realized in the soul, this is because the faculties of the soul are not separate entities but merely different members of one and the same entity. And so, looking into our experience, we find the matter to be. We find, that is, that as the attainment of justice means the subordination of one part of the soul to another, it is accompanied with the manifest satisfaction of the reason, and at the same time not infrequently with mortification of the feelings. We can have the approval of conscience only by controlling and, on occasion, denying a stream of desires which spring up in the breast and clamour for free course; and this act of control, when it is exercised in the form of denial, is necessarily attended with some degree of pain. If that were all, the analogy between nature and the soul would be complete—but with contrary results. For, whereas nature appears on the whole to go her own way serenely, sacrificing the lower of her creatures to the higher with no care for the pain she may inflict, or, rather, scattering pleasure and pain with impartial hand, in man the consequence would be a repudiation of justice altogether, and the surrender to the desires of his heart, with no thought of moral progress. It is absurd to suppose that any man in his senses would sacrifice his pleasures and voluntarily inflict pain upon himself. Humanity would not place itself in the position of a Brutus, who, having striven all his life to act justly, and having found that fortune took no account of his principles, was ready to leave it all with the bitter cry: "O miserable virtue! thou art but a word, and I have been following thee as a real thing!" It is no answer to say that, even in the balance of pleasure and pain, justice in the end is profitable. If the truth is so, as it may well be in the sum of time, that consummation seems so far away, and often takes so little account of the individual, as to afford but a feeble counterweight to the urgency of many immediate desires. Were there nothing beyond this, justice would be admired perhaps, but scarcely practiced. Nor is it sufficient to hold that the desires will be checked by the stronger desire to enjoy the good opinion of one's fellows. There is the old fable, which has troubled the moralists for thousands of years, of Gyges, who by means of a magic ring could make himself invisible, and so fulfil all the lusts of the flesh while retaining the reputation of virtue. In a lesser degree that power is within the reach of every man.

No, we have another motive to justice besides the calculation of pleasures or the force of public opinion, a law of reward and punishment that does not follow afar off on limping feet, but is ever at the side of the man when he acts, rather is within him, is his very self. The just man may be, and often is, torn by the conflict between the knowledge that he is satisfying the demands of his reason and the feeling of pain that arises from the suppression of certain desires, but the soul of the just man is nevertheless one soul, not two souls, however it may be divided against itself; and besides the feelings of pleasure and pain that trouble one of its members, he has another feeling, greater and more intimate, that belongs to his soul as a unit. This is the feeling of happiness, which is not the same as pleasure, and may exist in the absence of pleasure, and despite the presence of pain; and opposed to it is the feeling of misery, which is not the same as pain, and may exist in the absence of pain, and despite the presence of pleasure. It is not easy to explain these things, it may be impossible to analyse them satisfactorily; but we know that they are so. History is replete with illustrations of this strange fact, and he who weighs his own experience honestly will find it there also, that a man conscious of doing what he believes is right, may be lifted up into a supreme happiness, against which the infliction of pain, though it be torture to the death, is as nothing. And so a man may enjoy all the pleasures that this world can give, yet suffer a misery for which the only relief is madness. Philosophy and history together have given a peculiar fame to the letter sent by Tiberius to the Roman Senate from the luxuries of Capreæ: "May the gods and goddesses bring me to perish more miserably than I daily feel myself to be perishing, if I know what to write you, Senators, or how to write, or what indeed not to write at this time." It is not only the mind of the tyrant which, if opened, would be found lacerated within by the wounds of passion and evil desires, as the body of a slave is lacerated by the scourge; every unjust man shall know that the misery of the whole soul is something different, not in degree but in kind, from the pain of thwarted desires. A great English artist who painted the portrait of one of the older generation of our railway financiers, whose name has become also a synonym for the reckless abuse of power, is said to have observed that the face of his sitter was the most miserable he had ever seen. Only the heart of the unjust man knoweth its own bitterness. And, in like manner, every just man shall know that happiness is not a balance of pleasure against pain, but a feeling different in kind from pleasure. Happiness is a state of the whole soul, embracing both the faculties of reason, on the one hand, and of the desires, with the feelings of pleasure and pain, on the other hand; or, one might say, it is the state of some superior element of the soul, which finds its good in the harmonious action of those faculties. And it is because we discover no such higher unity in the field of Nature, where she can make compensation for the suffering of evolution, that we are debarred from applying the canon of justice and injustice to her procedure.

And not only is happiness the reward of that deep spiritual health which we call justice, but it is the warrant and test of that condition as well. We may err in our judgment of what is right at any moment, and err sadly in the choice of those desires which we suppress and those to which we give free rein, and our errors may be clear at the time to those who are more enlightened than we are; we have no guide to practical wisdom in this world, save the oracles of experience that direct us by the flickering signals of pleasure and pain. But we have a sure monitor of the will to act righteously in the present feeling of happiness or misery, and we have a hope—a divine illusion it may be, for it has never among men been verified by experience—that in some way and at some time happiness and pleasure shall be completely reconciled by Nature, who, by mysterious deviations beyond our mortal ken, is herself also a servant of the law of justice. And so, if we were right in defining justice as the inner state of the soul when, under the command of the will to righteousness, reason guides and the desires obey, we can express the same truth in this brief equation of experience: *We seek justice for the sake of happiness, and we are just when we are happy;* or, more briefly still: *Justice is happiness, happiness is justice.*

But man is a political animal. His life is closely knit with that of his fellows, and it is not enough to trace the meaning of justice to a state of the isolated soul; we must consider how this virtue bears on the conduct of a man among men, in society. Now, we might be content to say that a man is just in his conduct when, having attained to equilibrium of his own faculties, he acts in such a way as ought to produce in others the same condition; and this indeed is the sum of the law in the unrestrained dealing of a man with his neighbour. But society is something more than the spontaneous association of free units; it is an organization with traditions and government, necessary to it for the reason that it is made up of individuals who, not being infallibly just and wise, must be guided and constrained by a conventional code of relations. Hence there is a social justice of the community which complements, or even supplants, the conscience of the individual, as there is in the same sense a social injustice. Manifestly the problem here is far more complicated than when it is isolated in the individual soul.

Abstractly, no doubt, the definition of this social justice is simple and ready at hand. Society is composed of men who vary in the degree of individual justice to which they have attained, some being by disposition and training more self-governed, more rational, than others. By an inevitable analogy, therefore, we extend to society the idea of justice learned from our personal experience, precisely as we extended it to Nature. We cannot, in fact, do otherwise, since this is the only idea of justice possible to us. We think that society would be justly organized if its members were related to one another in the same manner as the faculties within the breast of the just man. The application of the analogy to nature showed that progress was obtained there not by justice at all, but by the operation of a law which in our human arrogance we often condemned as unjust. What shall we find in society?

Here, first of all, we come into conflict with two opposite theories of social justice which are as old almost as history, and which will doubtless go on flourishing as long as the human mind retains its tendency to gravitate to the indolent simplicity of extremes. One of these theories passes now under the name of Nietzsche, who sums it up in the famous maxim: *unusquisque tantum juris habet quantum potentia valet.*[4] If we are impelled by present circumstances to abhor such a conception of social justice, we should at least remember that it is no startling creation of a logic-ridden madman, but was promulgated in all its essentials by various sophists and politicians several hundred years before the Christian era, if it does not go back to brother Cain himself. Nietzsche, however, derives his principle avowedly from the apparent procedure of evolution. He approves of that procedure without reservation and converts the law of might into a criterion of social justice because he judges the acts of Nature by the reason alone, regarding pity as the last temptation of the sage. His theory is falsified by a double error: it supposes that mankind will be willing to base its conduct on an idea of justice derived from natural evolution, and in despite of that inner consciousness which demands the satisfaction of both the reason and the feelings; and it assumes that social progress guided by strength and reason alone, whether possible or not, would be towards the higher, because happier, life. And even thus, I am taking Nietzsche on his rational, or philosophic, side. In practice, as men are made, Nietzscheism would not result in the control of reason, but would give loose rein to a particular group of desires, the *libido dominandi.*[5] There is this real inconsistency in the system, but for purposes of illustration I am justified in isolating one aspect of it. Nietzsche's "will to power" does in theory demand the prevalence of those individuals whose survival in evolution meets with the approval of reason, however in effect it might mean the predominance of the inferior type.

The other theory springs from the same tendency of the mind to sink to extremes, suffering in this case the attraction of the feelings. It has various names, humanitarianism, socialism, equalitarianism,—masquerading in as many a lovely *ism,* or *isme,* or *ismus* as any other international mania, and sometimes arrogating to itself the more plausible title of democracy.

Neither is this theory essentially new, whatever superficial development it may have taken on in recent times. When Solon was chosen to reform the Athenian Constitution, a current saying of his, that "equality breeds no war," flattered the turbulent populace into acquiesence because they took the word "equality" in its absolute sense. Whereas in reality Solon was thinking of fair proportion, and on this principle reduced the oppression of the rich, while refusing to the poor an equalitarian Constitution. He saw, as we must see to-day, that the ideal of absolute equality is not only impossible in practice, but is contrary to our sense of justice. It is false and one-sided, being based on the exclusive appeal of the feelings, just as Neitzscheism is, theoretically, based on the claim of the reason. We think there is a higher and a lower in the scale of nature, we are conscious of reason and feeling in our own souls, we observe a similar distribution of characters in society. It would be pleasant, no doubt, to feel that every man had all his desires gratified, but reason, which is the faculty of seeing distinctions, binds us to believe that the State cannot progress in the orderly manner of evolution unless there, as in Nature, a certain advantage of honour accrues to those individuals who are themselves governed by reason, with the privilege of imposing their will upon those who, from the rational point of view, are inferior to them.

Social justice, then, is neither Nietzschean nor equalitarian. It is such a distribution of power and privilege, and of property as the symbol and instrument of these, as at once will satisfy the distinctions of reason among the superior, and will not outrage the feelings of the inferior. And if no precise rule can be given for striking this balance in law and institution, any more than an absolute code of morals can be formulated for the conduct of the individual, yet we have the same criterion for determining practically our progress towards this ideal as towards the ideal of individual justice. For there is a "pursuit of happiness" which is the right of every society, and which differs totally in principle from the license of pleasure—a feeling, which, by permeating society, may in a measure transcend and reconcile the envious divisions of discontent. Social justice and personal justice are both measured by happiness.

Obviously the problem is rendered difficult in the State by various complications, and obviously it can never be perfectly solved there, as, within the limits of human frailty, it can be solved in the inner life of the individual. For society (and in this complication lies the sum of the whole matter) shares both the character of the individual soul, as being composed of souls, and the character of nature, as being fundamentally not a unit but a collection of units. The constitution of a just society, therefore, will inevitably have this double aspect: it will correspond to what is justice in the individual soul, and at the same time it will disturb us by admitting elements of that seeming oppression which we are wont to call injustice in the procedure of evolution, but which is really the fatal inhuman law of things. In other words, in aiming at a just State we must always, while men are men, act in such a way as will seem unjust to those who, judging for themselves, judge by the feelings alone. The duty of the legislator, under these circumstances, will be to enact laws which shall conform so far as possible with the idea of rational proportion, distributing the advantages of power and property in accordance with the claims of superiority indeed, but not by the demands of an arrogant egotism; and measuring the probabilities of superiority by the most practical means at his disposal.

And there is another function of equal importance with that of the legislator. It shall be the duty of the teacher and moralist to impart to men the knowledge and to instil into them the feeling that their own true happiness as individuals depends neither on the unpitying exercise of strength nor on the envious striving after equality, but is bound up with that social happiness which can exist only when each division of society, such as male and female, and each member of society, has a distinct place and responsibility, and is recognized and rewarded accordingly. There is in every breast a spark of reason and a gleam of that self-knowledge which is happiness. On this the moralist must depend for confirmation of his teaching. There were indeed no society at all, unless a voice within each of us, in all but those quite brutalized by the lust of pleasure, responded to the law that men must serve as well as command.

Of both lawgiver and teacher the work is one of mediation, as social justice is itself always a shifting compromise. But the first rule for both, as the first and hardest lesson for each right-minded man in these days, is to discipline the heart to accept with equanimity the fatal fact that social justice must include a considerable amount of that disposition of Nature in dealing with her own which we, judging by the standard of the individual soul, are so ready to call injustice. The first step towards the equipoise of a soul just within itself is to recognize the necessity of a measure of injustice in the relation of man with man and with the world. We must learn from the god of realities how "ill is our anger with things, since it concerns them not at all."

[1]   This essay, another included in the Ninth Series of *Shelburne Essays*, was first published in the July, 1915, issue of the *Unpopular Review*. Sixteen years later it was translated into Swedish and published in *Nya Dagligt Allehanda*, Stockholm, November 8, 1931.

[2]   "What is justice? A mind holding itself in a certain manner."

[3]   The First World War.

[4]   "One has as much justice as he has power."

[5]   "The lust to rule."

Property and Law[1]

There has been, as every cne knows, a long strike in the mines of Colorado, with violence on both sides and bitter recriminations. On the 27th of April, 1914, there was a meeting of some two thousand persons in Carnegie Hall, of New York, before whom Morris Hillquit made this savage statement:

> The investment of the Rockefellers in the coal fields of Colorado is largely for the hiring of criminals and thugs to shoot the strikers, and the pious son of America's money king knows and sanctions the object. When it was alleged of ex-Lieutenant Becker [the convicted police officer of New York] that he had hired four gunmen to kill one gambler, he was indicted on the charge of murder in the first degree. Why not indict the man who has admittedly hired whole bands of gunmen to kill scores of workers?

In sympathy with this idea that in hiring men to protect his property a mine owner is in the same class with a sordid murderer, it will be recalled that a number of men and women paraded before the office of Mr. John D. Rockefeller, Jr., wearing bands of crêpe. On April 28 Mr. Rockefeller issued an official reply, of which the gist was contained in the following paragraph:

> Are the labor unions, representing a small minority of the workers of the country, to be sustained in their disregard of the inalienable right of every American citizen to work without interference, whether he be a union or a non-union man?

Surely the vast majority of American citizens will, without fear or favor, stand for evenhanded justice under the Constitution, and equal rights for every citizen.

To this appeal the United Mine Workers responded the next day:

Of course the right to work is inherent. If, however, the miners exercise their rights as guaranteed by the Constitution and the laws of our country to have a collective voice in establishing the conditions under which they shall work or shall not work, it ought not and cannot be denied by Mr. Rockefeller.

In the same issue in which this response was published, the New York *Sun* printed a brief and pungent editorial, to this effect:

Whatever the demagogues prate, an elementary and indispensable and indefeasible right is at stake in Colorado. In defending that right to labor, in refusing to yield to timorous counsels from Washington, Mr. Rockefeller has shown civic courage and a just sense of the equal claim of all to liberty and protection.

Now in regard to the truth of the charges of violence and other misconduct urged alternately by the strikers and the owners and by their sympathizers, one may be unable to decide on the evidence; nor is that the question here considered. The remarkable point is that not a single word was uttered on either side for property itself, as at least a substantial element of civilization. Such a silence was no doubt natural on the part of the strikers; but what of the owners? One suspects that Mr. Rockefeller, away from the Sunday school, and in his private office, thinks a good deal about the privileges of property, and one knows that the *Sun* is interested in those privileges. Yet for these neither Mr. Rockefeller nor the *Sun* would appear to have the slightest concern; they are only voluble in behalf of the independent labouring man and on the indefeasible rights of labour! Is this self-deception, or hypocrisy, or merely the policy of men who understand the feelings of a democratic populace, and desire to present their case in the most plausible light? A hundred years ago, in England or America at least, their present attitude would have been impossible; they would have appealed boldly to the public, their public, on the basis of sheer property rights. Twenty years ago such a position as they now assume could scarcely have been anything but ignoble hypocrisy. To-day their motives cannot be classified in any such simple fashion. It is not improbable that, along with the transparent motive of policy, they are a little troubled to know whether their instinctive feelings as property owners are not in some way unethical. At least we can say with entire confidence that such, under such circumstances, would be the complex state of mind of a considerable, certainly also a growing, body of men.

Now what is the meaning of all this? What is the origin of this state of mind which is so manifestly illogical and self-contradictory?

We shall perhaps discover the first plain enunciation of such a growing view of property in the writings of that master of truth and sophistry, Jean-Jacques Rousseau, especially in the *Discours sur l'origine de l'inégalité* and the *Contrat social*. According to the theory there developed, the most blessed stage of human existence was that exemplified by our North American Indians, who, as Rousseau pictured them from certain travellers' fairy tales, had risen to the beginning of social life, but possessed no property beyond the most rudimentary sort—none at all in our sense of the word. Happy indeed was such a state, if innocence is happiness: for, as the all-knowing Locke had observed, there can be no wrong-doing where there is no property. "It was," adds Rousseau sententiously, "the discovery of iron and grain that civilized men, and ruined the human race." Two consequences followed the creation of property: civilization and injustice. There is, Rousseau admits, a natural inequality of faculties among men, but this is of little moment until fixed and reinforced by extrinsic advantages. An unnatural inequality, or injustice, arises as soon as those who are the stronger by nature acquire increase of strength by the aid of superior possessions. And this injustice is fixed by a clever ruse. The few whose natural strength has been enhanced by property, seeing that they should still be at the mercy of the united mass of the poor and weak, delude the mass into binding themselves by passing laws in defence of property. Law is thus the support at once of civilization and of injustice.

The syllogism is rigid, and the inevitable conclusion would be: abolish law, and let mankind return to the happier condition of barbarism. But such a conclusion forces us to reconsider our premises, and we immediately see that the argument rests on two assumptions, one true and the other false. It is a fact that property has been the basis of civilization, and that with property there has come a change from natural inequality to what is assumed to be unnatural injustice. But it is not a fact that barbarism is in general a state of innocence and happiness. Rousseau himself really knew this, and he felt also, when his words began to be taken seriously by men of affairs, that he should be merely stultifying himself if he called on them to abolish what he recognized as the basis of civilized society: under no glamour of a remote paradise would men go to work deliberately to destroy civilization, whatever might be the evils it embraced.

Hence Rousseau proceeds to develop a theory of the State which shall retain the civilization created by property, while avoiding the injustice inherent in it. To this end he would make *tabula rasa* of the existing forms of authority in government, and in their place introduce, as sole sovereign, a power which he describes as the *volonté générale*. By this he does not precisely mean socialism: for still regarding private ownership as the basis of civilization, he cannot admit collective ownership. His notion is that a government by means of the "general will," while acknowledging the need of private ownership, would do away with injustice, because, in such a State, "the sovereign, being formed only of the individuals which compose it, neither has nor can have any interest contrary to theirs." This may be a true proposition metaphysically, if, in the manner of the medieval realists, we regard the general idea of humanity as an active entity, and individual men as mere accidents. But what does the "general will," when stripped of its metaphysical disguises, mean for Rousseau? Nothing but the unrestricted desire of the majority at any given moment. Now we, who are the inheritors of the French Revolution and the humble audience of socialistic oratory, have seen the operation of a government, or at least have heard the demands of much applauded demagogues, close enough to the spirit of Rousseau's philosophy, to know what the immediate and unrestricted will of the majority means in practice. Whether it means justice to you or not, may depend on your particular sympathies and interests; it manifestly does not mean a careful regard for the rights of property.

Rousseau's scheme, in fact, involves a self-contradiction: by a juggling of words it supposes that the innocence of man in a state of nature, itself an assumption contrary to fact, can somehow be made to continue in a society which has built itself up on what he regards as the cause of injustice. In simple truth, property may rightly be called the cause of civilization, but, strictly speaking, it is only the occasion of injustice: injustice is inherent in the imperfection of man, and the development of the means of living merely brings into greater prominence what is an unavoidable feature of existence, not for man only but for the whole range of creation, in this puzzling world of ours. Rousseau, by inflaming the passions of men against the wrongs of society which by his own hypothesis are inevitable, was, and still is, the father of frightful confusions and catastrophes; but he performed a real service to philosophy by stating so sharply the bare truth that *property is the basis of civilization.*

The socialistic theories of communal ownership give the argument, I admit, a new turn. Socialism rests on two assumptions. First, that community of ownership will, for practical purposes, eliminate the greed and injustice of civilized life.

This I deny, believing it to be demonstrably false in view of the present nature of most men, and, I might add, in view of the notorious quarrelsomeness of the socialists among themselves. Secondly, that under community of control the material productivity of society will not be seriously diminished. This question I leave to the economists, though here too it would appear to follow demonstrably from the nature of man that the capacity to manage and the readiness to be managed are necessary to efficient production. Certainly, there has been a convincing uniformity in the way in which wealth and civilization have always gone together, and in the fact that wealth has accumulated only when private property was secure. So far as experience or any intelligent outlook goes, there is no sufficient motive for the creation of property but personal ownership, at least in a share of joint property. The burden of proof is entirely on those who assert the sufficiency of communal property; their theory has never been proved, but in innumerable experiments has always failed. And, in fact, the real strength of socialism, the force that some think is driving us along the edge of revolution, is in no sense a reasoned conviction that public ownership is better than private ownership, but rather a profound emotional protest against the inequalities of ownership. The serious question is not in regard to the importance of property, but in regard to the justice of its present distribution. Despite all the chatter about the economic interpretation of history, we are to-day driven along by a sentiment, and by no consideration of economics.

Not even a Rousseau could cover up the fact of the initial inequality of men by the decree of that great Ruler, or Law, call it what you will, which makes one vessel for dishonour and another for honour. That is the so-called injustice of Nature. And it is equally a fact that property means the magnifying of that natural injustice into that which you may deplore as unnatural injustice, but which is a fatal necessity, nevertheless. This is the truth, hideous if you choose to make it so to yourself, not without its benevolent aspect to those, whether the favorites of fortune or not, who are themselves true—ineluctable at least. Unless we are willing to pronounce civilization a grand mistake, as, indeed, religious enthusiasts have ever been prone to do (and humanitarianism is more a perverted religion than a false economics), unless our material progress is all a grand mistake, we must admit, sadly or cheerfully, that any attempt by government or institution to ignore that inequality, may stop the wheels of progress or throw the world back into temporary barbarism, but will surely not be the cause of wider and greater happiness. It is not heartlessness, therefore, to reject the sentiment of the humanitarian, and to avow that the security of property is the first and all-essential duty of a civilized community. And we may assert this truth more bluntly, or, if you please, more paradoxically. Although, probably, the rude government of barbarous chiefs, when life was precarious and property unimportant, may have dealt principally with wrongs to person, yet the main care of advancing civilization has been for property. After all, life is a very primitive thing. Nearly all that makes it more significant to us than to the beast is associated with our possessions—with property, all the way from the food we share with the beasts, to the most refined products of the human imagination. To the civilized man *the rights of property are more important than the right to life.*

In our private dealings with men, we may, if we choose, ignore these claims of civilization with no harm resulting to society; but it is different when we undertake to lay down general rules of practice. In allowing our emotions and our sense of abstract right to oversway us in our attitude towards politics and government, we forget that it is not ours to determine the fundamental relation of things, or to define justice, but to make rules of action in accordance with the decrees, immutable so far as we can see, of a superior power. We are, essentially, not legislators but judges.

And what then, you ask, of human laws? In sober sooth it is not we who create laws; we are rather finders and interpreters of laws registered in a court beyond our control, and our decrees are merely the application of our knowledge, or ignorance, of the law to particular conditions. When our decrees are counter to the law of fact, they become at best dead letters, and at worst, agents of trouble and destruction. The office of the legislator in general is not unlike that of the jurisconsults of the Roman Empire, upon whom was bestowed the right of giving binding responses to a judge when he was not clear in a question of equity or interpretation, and who thus helped to mould the law into the form in which it was finally codified and handed down to the modern world. And in a more special sense, the spirit that guided the trend of their opinions is worthy of scrutiny to-day, as its influence is still vastly stronger than is commonly understood. The expansion of Roman affairs had already begun to force the courts to substitute in general practice the *jus gentium*, or principles of law which seemed to be in effect among all peoples, for the old *jus civile*, or custom which prevailed among Roman citizens when these were a small and comparatively homogeneous body. The responses of the jurisconsults inevitably followed and emphasized this tendency, and, under the influence of late Greek philosophy, went even further in generalization. On the conception of a *jus gentium* these Stoic legalists superimposed the conception of a *jus naturale*, or law implanted by Nature in the heart of man, to which custom and statute should, so far as possible, be made to conform. It is not too much to say that this is one of the profoundest conceptions of the human mind; but it was as dangerous as it was profound. It brought into legislation the idea conveyed by the word *nature*, which is, perhaps, the most treacherous that ever slipped from the tongue of man. The ambiguity came from the philosophers themselves, especially from the Stoics, who used the word at one time to signify the forces and material of the world as they actually are, and at another time to signify the world as it ought to be. There might be no great harm in this ambiguity, were it not for the resulting confusion in ideas and practice. When we repeat the Stoic command to *Follow nature*, we really mean, as the Stoic meant, to follow our ideal of nature. We do not mean that a man should imitate the conduct of a tiger, which is yet entirely natural, nor of men as we see them daily acting, but that he should imitate his ideal of what a man should be. The command is unmeaning enough, and has force only because it seems to render the ideal concrete by confounding it with the actual. And there is its peril. We are prone to laziness and self-flattery, and so we are constantly justifying ourselves in imitating the baser actions of men, under cover of the command to follow human nature. Is not nature what all men are doing? It would, in fact, be easy to show that in the sphere of private morals this command has resulted in a curious mixture of good and evil, by clothing custom in the garb of the ideal.

But the peril for law, as law is what we propose for other men in the mass rather than for ourselves, is of the contrary sort. Law is not a code of ideal virtues nor a guide to individual perfection, but a rule for regulating the relations of society for practical purposes. Just so soon as, in any large measure, it fails to recognize the actuality of human nature, or pronounces in conformity with an ideal of human nature, it becomes inoperative or mischievous. If law supposed that all men were honest, what would be the consequence? Or, if law demanded that all men should be kind-hearted, what would be the consequence? These are absurd extremes, but an error of really the same character has obtained a kind of philosophical excuse through the treachery of such a phrase as *jus naturale.* The experience and hard-headedness of the earlier jurisconsults saved the Roman law from falling a prey to an undue idealism, although it is a fact that in Byzantine times there was introduced a certain degree of humanitarianism corresponding with the decay of civilization.

But for reasons which lie deeply imbedded in the sources of our modern life, we are in great and continual peril of a humanitarianism springing from a mistaken conception of the *jus naturale.* The whole impetus of Rousseau's revolutionary philosophy is really derived from his reassumption and eloquent expansion of that conception. We are bound, in any clear-sighted view of the larger exigencies of the relations of man with man, to fortify ourselves against such a perversion of the institutions of government as would adapt them to the nature of man as he ought to be, instead of the nature of man as he actually is, and would relax the rigour of law, in pity for the degree of injustice inherent in earthly life. If our laws, as we call them, being indeed but attempts to copy a code we have not made and cannot repeal, are to work for progress rather than for retrogression, they must recognize property as the basis of civilization, and must admit the consequent inequality of conditions among men. They will have little or no regard for labour in itself or for the labourer in himself, but they will provide rigidly that labour shall receive the recompense it has bargained for, and that the labourer, as every other man, shall be secure in the possession of what he has received. We may try to teach him to produce more and to bargain better, but in face of all appeals of sentiment and all reasonings of abstract justice, society must learn again to-day that it cannot legislate contrary to the decrees of Fate. In this way, looking at the larger good of society, we may say that the dollar is more than the man, and that *the rights of property are more important than the right to life.*

So directly is the maintenance of civilization and peace and all our welfare dependent on this truth, that it is safer, in the utterance of law, to err on the side of natural inequality than on the side of ideal justice. We can go a little way, very slowly, in the endeavour to equalize conditions by the regulation of property, but the elements of danger are always near at hand and insidious; and undoubtedly any legislation which deliberately releases labour from the obligations of contract, and permits it to make war on property with impunity, must be regarded as running counter to the first demands of society. It is an ugly fact, as the world has always seen, that, under cover of the natural inequality of property, evil and greedy men will act in a way that can only be characterized as legal robbery. It is strictly within the province of the State to prevent such action so far as it safely can. Yet even here, in view of the magnitude of the interests involved, *it is better that legal robbery should exist along with the maintenance of law, than that legal robbery should be suppressed at the expense of law.*

No doubt there is a certain cruelty in such a principle, as there is a factor of cruelty in life itself. But it does not, in any proper sense of the word, involve the so-called economic interpretation of history. On the contrary, this principle recognizes, far more completely than does any humanitarian creed, that there is a large portion of human activity lying quite outside of the domain of physical constraint and legislation, and it is supremely jealous that the arms of government should not extend beyond their true province. All our religious feelings, our aspiring hopes, our personal morality, our conscience, our intellectual pursuits, all these things, and all they mean, lie beyond the law—all our individual life, as distinguished from the material relations of man with man, reaches far beyond the law's proper comprehension.

Our most precious heritage of liberty depends on the safeguarding of that realm of the individual against the encroachments of a legal equalitarianism. For there is nothing surer than that liberty of the spirit, if I may use that dubious word, is bound up with the inequality of men in their natural relations; and every movement in history to deny the inequalities of nature has been attended, with an effort to crush the liberty of distinction in the ideal sphere.

As the rights of property do not involve the economic interpretation of history, so neither do they result in materialism. The very contrary. For in this matter, as in all other questions of human conduct and natural forces, you may to a certain degree control a fact, but if you deny a fact it will control you. This is the plain paradox of life, and its application is everywhere. Just so sure as you see a feministic movement undertaking to deny the peculiar characteristics and limitations of the female sex, you will see this sex element overriding all bounds —you will, to take an obvious illustration, see women dressing in a manner to exaggerate their relative physical disability and their appeal to the other sex. I do not say that the feministic denial of facts is the only cause that may bring about this exaggeration; but it is indisputably one such cause. So, in a more general way, the denial of the body, or the romantic idealization of love, will end by producing a state of morbid eroticism, as history abundantly testifies. And, in another direction, the encouraging of a false sentimentality in the idea of marriage, and the slurring over of its importance as a social institution and as the basis of the family, is one of the sure ways of degrading that natural relation into something we do not like to consider.

Again, if you hear a man talking overmuch of brotherly love and that sort of thing—I do not mean the hypocrite, but the sincere humanitarian whom you and I have met and had dealings with and could name—if you hear such a man talking overmuch of serving his fellows, you are pretty sure that here is a man who will be slippery or dishonourable in his personal transactions. I do not say that there are no exceptions; but the "reformer" is a type well known. And societies are much like individual men. As soon as a nation begins to deny officially the inherent combativeness of human nature, it is in a fair way to be hurried into war. We have seen a group of obstinate humanitarians in Washington, by denying the facts of the Mexican situation, drag this country at Vera Cruz into the hypocritical but fortunately short-lived pretence of waging a "war for service." What is the cause of the evils, physical and moral, that have perplexed our Southern States since the era of Reconstruction? Certainly in large measure the humanitarian ideas of justice and equality which were in flagrant disregard of the facts of a particular stage of civilization, and made a cover for every kind of rascality and stupidity. We are seeing something of the same sort beginning to happen in Turkey and Persia and China, and are like to see it in many other places. Again, of course, I do not say that humanitarian denial of the facts is the only cause of war and national dissolution—would to heaven it were!—but it is just as certainly one such cause, or contributing cause, as it is certain that we shall hurt our fingers if we grasp a burning coal under the notion that it is not hot.[2]

And the same paradox holds true of property. You may to a certain extent control it and make it subservient to the ideal nature of man; but the moment you deny its rights, or undertake to legislate in defiance of them, you may for a time unsettle the very foundations of society, you will certainly in the end render property your despot instead of your servant, and so produce a materialized and debased civilization. Let me illustrate what I mean by a single example of the practical working of humanitarianism. I quote from a striking article on *The Law's Delays*, by Professor Tyrrell Williams:

> The apotheosis of debtors in America began about a hundred years ago, and has continued to the present time. In its origin the movement was humanitarian and praiseworthy. Imprisonment for debt was a reality in those days. But has not the movement gone too far, and become ridiculous? The traditional debtor is a hardworking farmer or mechanic struggling to keep the wolf from the door. Is that a true picture of the twentieth-century debtor, who glories in delay of justice? Most certainly not. The typical debtor of the twentieth century is a corporation organized along the lines that were so popular in New Jersey before Woodrow Wilson was elected Governor. The transportation and other public-service corporations are the champion debtors of America. They have been very clever. They have capitalized the ordinary American's sentimental affection for debtors. These corporate debtors are the chief beneficiaries of delay of justice in America, and they know it. That is why directly and indirectly they oppose all serious efforts to reform judicial procedure, and why they employ attorneys who are experts at "filling the record full of error."

This is but a single instance of a false sentiment opening the door to the prowling thieves of the highway. More generally, it is in accordance with the law of human nature that the sure way to foster the spirit of materialism is to unsettle the material basis of social life. Manifestly, the mind will be free to enlarge itself in immaterial interests only when that material basis is secure, and without a certain degree of such security a man must be anxious over material things and preponderantly concerned with them. And, manifestly, if this security is dependent on the rights of property, and these rights are denied or belittled in the name of some impossible ideal, it follows that the demands of intellectual leisure will be regarded as abnormal and anti-social, and that he who turns to the still and quiet life will be despised as a drone, if not hated as an enemy of the serious part of the community. There is something at once comical and vicious in the spectacle of those men of property who take advantage of their leisure to dream out vast benevolent schemes which would render their own self-satisfied career impossible.

No doubt the ideal society would be that in which every man should be filled with noble aspirations, and should have the opportunity to pursue them. But I am not here concerned with such Utopian visions, nor, as I have said, am I arguing with those who are honestly persuaded that a socialistic régime is, in our day, or any day, economically or psychologically feasible. My desire is rather to confirm in the dictates of their own reason those who believe that the private ownership of property, including its production and distribution, is, with very limited reservations, essential to the material stability and progress of society. We who have this conviction need very much to-day to strengthen ourselves against the insidious charms of a misapplied idealism; we need to remind ourselves that laws which would render capital insecure and, by a heavy income tax or other discrimination in favour of labour, would deprive property of its power of easy self-perpetuation, though they speak loudly in the name of humanity, will in the end be subversive of those conditions under which alone any true value of human life can be realized.

This, I take it, is the reason that the Church and the University as institutions have almost invariably stood as strongly reactionary against any innovations which threaten the intrenched rights of property. It is not at bottom the greed of possession that moves them—though this motive also may have entered into the attitude of their governors, as into all the theories and practices of men—nor are we justified in casting into their teeth the reproach that they who profess to stand for spiritual things are in their corporate capacity the most tenacious upholders of worldly privilege. They are guided by an instinctive feeling that in this mixed and mortal state of our existence, the safety and usefulness of the institutions they control are finally bound up with the inviolability of property which has been devoted to unworldly pursuits, and removed from the control of popular passions and hasty legislation. They are the jealous guardians of that respite from material labour which they hold in fee for those who are by character destined more specifically to be the creators and transmitters of the world's intellectual and spiritual heritage. Nor does the need of privilege end with institutions. One shudders to think of the bleak pall of anxiety and the rage of internecine materialism that would fall upon society were the laws so altered as to transfer the predominant rights from property acquired to the labour by which it is produced. For *if property is secure, it may be the means to an end, whereas if it is insecure it will be the end itself.*

---

1   This essay has probably angered more people who have read More than any other, since it flies in the face of the popular views about human rights predominant in this century. More first read it before the Phi Beta Kappa society of Princeton on March 22, 1915, after which he published it in the *Unpopular Review* for April of the same year. Like "Justice," it was included thereafter in the Ninth Series.

2   Again, I must call attention to the fact that most of this book was written before the present war. These illustrations sound strangely antiquated today; but the principle involved has not been altered. [More's note]

Rousseau[1]

We are perhaps hearing too much of Rousseau these days, and he threatens to become a kind of fetich of criticism. To the French he is, more than any other one man, the author of the Revolution with all the subsequent good or evil implied in that movement. And now the Germans have discovered in him the father of their romanticism. "In reality his influence is accomplished on German soil," says Paul Hensel in the latest monograph on the subject; "here Rousseau was not the basis of a guillotine, but of a new culture. . . . Kant and Herder, Goethe and Schiller are not to be conceived without Rousseau, and through them is formed the new science, the new philosophy, the new poetry of German idealism."[2] One has an impulse to avoid a theme that has grown cheap from too much writing of this sort; but how escape the writer who gathered up in himself the floating ideas of his age, and, by simplifying them to a portable creed and infusing into them the carrying power of his own great personality, made them the chief formative influence down to our own times?

Only by keeping in view this new emotional element can we understand how the intellectual life of to-day has its source in Rousseau more than in any other single man, for the ideas themselves—liberty and progress and natural religion and innate goodness—were in no wise original with him. If, indeed, disregarding the complexities of a civilisation and obscurer influences, we undertake to analyse the revolution of the eighteenth century, we shall find that the guiding principles and the original dynamic impulse of the age came from England, that the translation of these into a homogeneous social law was the work of France, and that their conversion into a metaphysical formula was finally accomplished by Germany. Certainly, the starting place of this movement, the caldron, so to speak, in which this great fermentation began, was the turbulent England of the seventeenth century. There, the notion of liberty took practical form in the acts of the Rebellion and the Revolution and in the writings of such republicans as Algernon Sidney.[3] Is it not almost, if not quite, the accent of Rousseau's *Contrat Social* we hear in Sidney's brave reply to Hobbes and Filmer: "If men are naturally free, such as have wisdom and understanding will always frame good governments; but if they are born under the necessity of a perpetual slavery, no wisdom can be of use to them"? Certainly, too, the most fecund idea taken over by the nineteenth century from its predecessor, the conception of indefinite moral progress based on the accumulating knowledge of physical laws, had been proclaimed by Bacon with the grandiose fervour of a Hebrew prophet. And the accompanying change of religion from a belief in superrational revelation to a rational deism was also formulated in England. It was Lord Herbert of Cherbury who, as far back as 1624 in his *De Veritate*, gave the first clear exposition of religion as the product of a purely natural instinct. Later he resolved this religious instinct into five theses which became the "charter of the deists," and which may be found simplified and summed up in the three articles of Chubb's *True Gospel*.[4] There is, if we may believe that inspired tallow-chandler of Salisbury, no demand in the Gospel for subscribing to a supernatural scheme of salvation, nor is the new birth anything more than a "figure of speech." On the contrary, "the Gospel of Christ is a plain, simple, uniform thing," as thus:

> *First*, he [Christ] requires and recommends [note the curiously unreligious word] a conformity of mind and life to that eternal and unalterable rule of action which is founded in the

reason of things, and makes or declares that compliance to be
the only, and the sole ground of divine acceptance, and the
only, and the sure way to life eternal. *Secondly,* if men have
lived in a violation of this righteous law, by which they have
rendered themselves displeasing to God, and worthy of his just
resentment; then Christ requires and recommends repentance
and reformation of their evil ways as the only, and the sure
grounds of the divine mercy and forgiveness. And *Thirdly,*
Christ assures us that God has appointed a time in which he will
judge the world in righteousness, and that he will then approve
or condemn, reward or punish every man according to his
works.[5]

It is worth while to quote this remarkably lucid summary of
deism, unobscured as it is by the glamour of the imagination
thrown over the creed by Shaftesbury and his school, if only
to show how closely Rousseau, who was well-read in these
authors, adhered to his sources. Here, in a paragraph, is the
whole skeleton of the *Profession de foi.* And here in few words
is, without the surrender of a religious semblance altogether,
the last and inevitable stage of that Pelagianism against which
St. Augustine had for the time inveighed so successfully and
under which the Port-Royal of Pascal was at last beaten down.

It is by no means easy to trace the evolution of our secular
belief in the essential goodness of human nature. It was implicit, no doubt, in the first contention of Pelagianism that
salvation is primarily the work of man, but it has become the
driving force of society only since the notion of a needed reconciliation with God has been quite eliminated. Nor was it a
product of the Renaissance in so far as that movement implied
a return to the past. Total depravity may have been Christian
and mediæval; but total goodness can find no authority in the
classical writers of Greece and Rome, and is, in fact, the mark
of modern humanitarianism as distinguished from Renaissance
humanism. It should seem to be rather a secularisation of mediæval theology, if such a term is not self-contradictory. Grant the
longing for personal justification and supreme bliss which passed
from the Middle Ages into the freer emotional life of the Renais-

sance, take away the supernatural scheme of redemption, and
the Pelagian confidence in man's ability to satisfy God might
easily pass into a belief that human nature, being essentially
right, has within itself the power to expand indefinitely, without any act of renunciation, toward some far-off, vaguely-
glimpsed, "divine event."

The ideas of progress and innate goodness are thus compan-
ions; they sprang up side by side with humanism, but they are
not a product of the classical revival in the sense that humanism was such a revival, and in the end they killed humanism.
Nothing is more curious throughout the seventeenth and the
first half of the eighteenth century than the way in which the
contradictory notions of essential evil and essential goodness
alternate with each other, sometimes in the same writer. The
neo-classicists as a rule, the great human moralists of France,
have no doubt of the inherent selfishness and depravity of the
human heart; and a pure sceptic like Bayle,[6] at a time when
deism was in full vein, can still be absolutely convinced that
"man is incomparably more drawn to evil than to good." The
English deists on the other hand were necessarily driven to
believe in man's native soundness; for what indeed is the excuse for natural religion if nature is estranged from the supreme good? Yet even here there are strange compromises
and inconsistencies. A Bolingbroke might preach philosoph-
ically that this is the best of worlds, but as a politician and
somewhat deeply versed man of the world he treated mankind
with a perfectly cynical distrust. Nowhere does this contrast
glare more impudently than in Pope, who learnt his satire
from Dryden and the neo-classicists and his optimism from
Bolingbroke and the deists; and Pope, it must be remembered,
was accepted seriously as a moral teacher not only in England
but in France and Germany as well. Nothing is more bewildering than to read Pope's general justification of human passions
and instincts in his *Essay on Man* and then in the same poem
to find his scathing denunciation of these passions in a Bacon
or a Gripus (his friend Mr. Wortley Montagu). On one page we
find this pleasant optimism:

> The surest virtues thus from passions shoot,
> Wild Nature's vigour working at the root;

but turn the leaf and all is changed:

> As man, perhaps, the moment of his breath,
> Receives the lurking principle of death;
> The young disease, that must subdue at length,
> Grows with his broth and strengthens with his
>   strength;
> So, cast and mingled with his very frame,
> The mind's disease, its ruling passion came.

Pope might try to carry this double-faced attitude off under the effrontery of assuming an enormous paradox in the nature of things, but it was in truth a real inconsistency due to the confusion of two diverse tendencies of thought. Did not Voltaire also, the spokesman of the age, pass his life ridiculing the pretensions of mankind to virtue and at the same time advocating the liberation of mankind from the restraints that would keep vice within bounds? It required more than one century to root out the ancient conviction that the heart of man is naturally disposed to evil.

Meanwhile, it is clear that these dominating ideas of the age, whether they received their vital force from England or France or elsewhere, all imply a denial of that sense of dualism which hitherto had lain at the base of religion and philosophy, and that lacking this sense they seem always to be shirking certain of the more troublesome problems of life. The artificiality of that literature has become a proverb. This is not to say that the eighteenth century did not have its own theories of dualism. There was in Germany, for instance, that amusing doctrine of the *harmonia præstabilita*, spun by a discursive wit who imposed on the world as a profound philosopher. "The soul," says Leibnitz, "follows its proper laws, and the body likewise follows those which are proper to it, and they meet in virtue of the preëstablished harmony which exists between all

substances, as representations of one and the same universe."
According to which system, "bodies act as if there were no
souls, and souls act as if there were no bodies, and yet both act
as though the one influenced the other," etc. But these vagaries of a mechanical parallelism are, so to speak, a by-product
of the age, developed from the metaphysics of Descartes, aside
from the naturalistic influences of England. The dominating
line of thought runs from Newton and Locke,[7] who formulated
the laws of nature in the physical world and in the human
intellect, through the French *philosophes*, to Condillac, who
banishes dualism so far as to derive the whole man, including
Locke's reflective faculty, the moral sense, and consciousness,
from the effect of physical impact.

One thing was wanting to all these theories—to the dead
parallelism of Leibnitz, to the moral rationalism of Toland and
Chubb, to Shaftesbury's florid deism of the imagination, to the
cynical or boisterous philosophy of Voltaire and Diderot—they
all excluded the sense of that deep cleft within the human soul
itself, which springs from the bitter consciousness of evil. This,
in a way, Rousseau supplied, and through him what was a
theme of speculation for the few was vivified into a new gospel.

How thoroughly Rousseau was a child of his age is proved by
the continual recurrence of English names in his works. Intellectually, he has little that is original; his deism, his passion for
liberty, his doctrine of instinctive goodness, are all avowedly
from over the sea, and even his minor ideas can, for the most
part, be traced to various predecessors. It was because he made
all these subservient to a passionate proclamation of a dualism
between the individual and society, between nature and art,
that he became so powerfully provocative of change. In a way,
even this dogma—for it is as arbitrary a dogma as any set up
by St. Augustine—was not his own. It may be found implicit in
English deism, in the discrepancy between Pope's praise of the
savage, to whom "full instinct is the unerring guide," and his
satire of a malignant society; it underlies the *Night Thoughts*
of Young:

> . . . These tutelary shades
> Are man's asylum from the tainted throng;

it could even, in a later day, temper the rigid orthodoxy of
Cowper:

> God made the country, and man made the town.

In his *Fable of the Bees* Mandeville had given it an odd twist
by vindicating the old notion of inherent evil and making the
progress of society depend on this corruption of the individual.
But these were unfruitful hints and thoughtless inconsistencies; they became a social force through the temperament of
one man who, as Madame de Staël said, discovered perhaps
nothing, but set everything ablaze.

From lonely brooding on his own divided self, Rousseau was
led to erect the dualism implicit in the philosophy of his day
into a formula with all the popular persuasiveness of a religion.
The Pelagian doctrine of man's potential goodness united with
his intense egotism to create the idea of the individual, conceived in himself and unmodified by others, as a pure uncon-
taminated product of nature. He, Rousseau, was, he felt, by his
instincts good, yet he was painfully aware of his actual lapses
into turpitude and shame; he could only shift the responsibility
of this corruption upon outside influences. Here was no room
for the Augustinian idealisation of the good in man as an infinite God set over against the finite and hence erring natural
man, nor for the conception of man as bearing within himself
infinitely diverse promptings toward good and evil; on the
contrary, he was driven to the idealisation of his own personality, and of every personality in so far as he projected himself
into another, as good, and of other personalities, in so far as
they are hostile to him and limit or pervert his native proclivities, as evil. Hence the dualism of the individual regarded in
the state of nature and in the state of society, of the one and
the many without the old accompaniment of the infinite and
the finite. And evil to Rousseau was not a thing of jest and

satire, but, by the whole weight of his emotional being, a power to be feared and spurned. As embodied in society it looms up in his writings like some living and malign monster, lying in wait to corrupt and destroy the unwary individual. It is the Devil of the mediæval monks reborn in the height of the boastful age of reason to trouble the consciences of men, for who can say how long a time.

The first serious work of Rousseau was the prize essay, written at the age of thirty-eight, on the question proposed by the Academy of Dijon as to *Whether the Progress of Science and Art has Contributed to Corrupt or Purify Morals*. Either by the advice of Diderot or, more probably, by the natural bent of his mind, he there advocated the thesis, by no means so novel as he seems to have believed, that civilisation results in the perversion of society. It is at best a slight academic exercise, but it fell in with the mood of the day sufficiently to arouse discussion, and gave the author a position to defend. Five years later, in 1755, he published his *Discourse on Inequality*, in which this theory is found fully developed. Here we have the picture of primitive man, living in solitude, mating by chance, and following undisturbed his healthy animal instincts. The first law of nature is love of self, and in this paradise of primeval isolation there is nothing to distort that innocent impulse. When by chance man meets with man he is kept from wrongdoing by the feeling of sympathy and pity which is, after the instinct of self-preservation, the second law of nature. But— "The first man who, having enclosed some land, thought of saying 'this is mine,' and found people simple enough to believe him, was the real founder of civilised society. How many crimes, wars, murders, how many miseries and horrors would have been spared human nature had some one snatched away the stakes, or filled in the ditch, calling out to his neighbours: 'Beware of listening to this impostor'!"[8] With the acknowledgment of property comes the division of more and less out of which springs all the brood of ambitions, crimes, penalties. Sympathy is stifled in envy, and harmless *amour de soi-même* is converted into that social disease *amour-propre;* in a word, property means society. There is nothing fanciful in comparing this marvellous change from the individual in a state of natural innocence to the same individual as corrupted by society with the theological doctrine of the Fall. They are both an attempt to transfer the inexplicable dualism within the heart of man to some ancient mythological event; nor does Rousseau denounce the evil introduced by property with less unctuous and priestly fervour than was used by a Bossuet in laying bare the depths of total depravity. For the rest of his life he merely developed in various ways the thesis of his *Discourse on Inequality*. As he said himself at the end of his career, speaking of his own works:

> Following as best I could the thread of his meditations, I saw everywhere the development of his main principle, that nature has made man happy and good, but that society depraves him and renders him miserable. And particularly *Émile*, that book so much read, so little understood, and so ill appreciated, is nothing but a treatise on the original goodness of man, with the aim of showing how vice and error, strangers to his constitution, are introduced from without and imperceptibly work a change.

In reality *Émile* is something more than a treatise on original goodness; it is an elaborate plea for a form of education by which the individual may be rescued from the perverting influences of society and restored to his primitive state of innocence. It is thus in a manner to the *Discourse* what *Paradise Regained* is to *Paradise Lost.* The instincts implanted in the child by nature are right; therefore the aim of education is to place the child in such a position that these instincts may develop freely without any thwarting control from master or society. To this end he separates his typical child Émile from family and comrades, and gives him a home in the country with a guardian, whose duty is, not to instruct, but to preserve him from physical accidents, and to act as a kind of concealed Providence. Books during his early years are eschewed; all information is brought to the boy through the pleasure of observing natural processes and through play cunningly directed to manual training. Such a plan is, as Rousseau willingly acknowledged, impossible except for a favoured few, if not for all; but as an ideal toward which education might tend, it has exercised through the theories of Pestalozzi, Froebel, and other German pedagogues an enormous influence, and is still to-day the inspiration of most writers on education. In part the book is admirably wise; in its provision for training the body, in many other details, even, one gladly admits, in its opposition to an unreasoning system of compression, it was not only a wholesome reaction from the practice of the day, but is full of suggestions of permanent value. But there is a growing belief among a certain class that the fundamental thesis of the book has worked, and is still working, like a poison in the blood of society. To make instinct instead of experienced judgment the basis of education, impulse instead of control, unbridled liberty instead of obedience, nature instead of discipline, to foster the emotions as if the uniting bond of mankind were sentiment rather than reason, might seem of itself so monstrous a perversion of the truth as to awaken abhorrence in any considerate reader. And, indeed, these notions were slow in making their way against long-established traditions. Yet so honorable is the name of liberty, even when it is a mask for license, so flattering is the appeal to the individual's desire of unchecked autonomy, that Rousseau's "education of nature" has deeply modified, if it has not entirely transformed, the practice of our schools. It is seen at work in the vagaries of the elective system, in the advocating of manual training as an equivalent for books, in the unbounded enthusiasm for nature-study, in the encroachment of science on the character-discipline of the humanities, in the general substitution of persuasion for authority. To some observers certain traits of irresponsibility in the individual and certain symptoms of disintegration in society are the direct fruit of this teaching.

To find the source of the nature-cult raised by Rousseau to so predominant a place in imaginative literature it might seem sufficient to go back to English naturalism, and no doubt many pages of the *Nouvelle Héloïse* and of *Émile* were in this respect

inspired by Shaftesbury and Thomson and the other deists.
More particularly *The Wanderer* (1729) of Richard Savage and
that strange and neglected book, *The Life of John Buncle*
(published in 1756, five years before the *Nouvelle Héloïse*), are
filled with a Rousselian mixture of deistic enthusiasm and grandiose eloquence on the aspect of romantic mountain scenery.
But there is withal a new accent in Rousseau, which derives its
penetrating quality from his developed dualism of the individual and society, and which renders him the true father of
modern nature-writing. Man before the social Fall was a compound of harmless self-love and sentimental sympathy. Who-
ever seeks any spark of this innocence in an age when self-love
is changed to egotism and sympathy to envy must go out from
society and make his peace alone with Nature. There, by a
pathetic fallacy, the sympathy which he vainly demands of
men flows to him freely from the beauty and solitude of the
inanimate world; there he meets no contrary will to frustrate
his own, nothing to prevent him from personifying his emotions in some alter-ego that smiles at him benignly from field
and brook, echoes his loneliness, and weeps with his self-pity.

From this it is but a step to the religion of Nature. Everybody
is familiar with the scene in *Émile* where the Savoyard vicar
leads his young friend at sunrise to a hill rising above the fair
valley of the Po and looking off afar to the chain of the Alps,
and there in language of melting charm expounds his profession of faith. There is much that is discordant in the ideas of
that document. The retention of the old belief in a heaven and
hell has no justification in Rousseau's theory of man's essential
goodness, and in fact might without injury be removed from
his profession. The gist of his faith is a pure deism, a trustful
reliance on some beneficent God who is united with Nature by
a mutual sympathy corresponding to that which he himself
feels, and who is in fact no more than a magnified projection
of his own innocent personality into the infinite void—himself
and Nature, God and Nature. Beyond this is no need of dogma
or revelation or faith. Rousseau felt the instability of such a
religion, and recommended a compliance with the popular

forms of worship in whatever land a man might be, as a guide and stay, so to speak, to this vague emotionalism. It is a pretty theory, not without its advantages, and has warmed the fancy of more than one poet to noble utterance. But it has one insurmountable element of weakness. It depends for its strength, for its very vitality, on the more precise faith of those whose worship it adopts. So long as these believe energetically in the virtue of forms and creeds, your deist may prey upon their emotions; but a lasting church made up of deists is inconceivable. Rousseau's deism in fact came toward the end and not at the beginning of a movement; it flashed out into a grotesque worship of the *Être Suprême* at the Revolution, but it has had no permanent and fruitful results. Rousseau has, more than any other one man, given us our religion of today, but it is a religion of the State, and not of God.

That change from theology to sociology is announced in the most radical of his works. "There is then," he says, "a profession of faith purely civil of which it pertains to the sovereign [people] to fix the principles, not exactly as dogmas of religion, but as sentiments of sociability without which it is impossible to be a good citizen or a faithful subject." The determining principle of this creed is the sanctity of the *Social Contract* as he has developed it in his treatise of that name. Man, he declares in his opening sentence, with that precision and vehemence that have made his words the battle cry of revolution —"man is born free, and everywhere he is in chains." Property has introduced a harsh inequality among men, and established those conventions of society upon which rests the right of the stronger. There is but one way in which liberty can be restored: society itself must be transformed into a composite individual equivalent so far as possible to the isolated individual in the state of nature. That is the work of the Social Contract. His theories reduce themselves to this single proposition:

> The complete alienation of each associate with all his rights to the whole community; for, in the first place, each man giving himself entirely, the condition is equal for all; and, the condition

being equal for all, no one has any interest in rendering it
burdensome to the others [oh, most holy innocence!]. . . . Each
of us places his person and all his power in common under the
supreme direction of the general will, and we receive back each
member as an indivisible part of the whole.

It would not be fair to say that Rousseau himself was unaware
of the absurdity in supposing that all men, granted even that
the nature of humanity is essentially good, will thus surrender
their separate desires and ambitions to this phantom of the
common interest; he endeavours to obviate such criticism by
a shadowy distinction between the *volonté générale* and the
volonté de tous, and indeed, it must be remembered that always he has in mind an ideal rather than any facile and probable revolution. At bottom his proposal comes to this: by some
persuasion of a divine legislator (he has an eye on himself) or
some intervention of Providence that sense of sympathy,
which we found in the natural man along with a harmless
self-love, may miraculously take possession of mankind, now
corrupted by society into a conglomeration of warring egotisms, and transform that society itself into a quasi individual
with a single purpose and a single will; and so the antinomy of
the one and the many shall be finally solved. It is a vain utopia
or a prophecy of terrible despotism, as you will; but you cannot
doubt that this ideal of social sympathy has wrought enormously in the civilisation of the present day.

In part, Rousseau's influence was gained by his pure literary
talent. His was the faculty of creating phrases which remain in
the memory after all the inconsistencies and chimerical follies
of his writings have been forgotten, and which ring like trum-
pet calls to action. But beneath it all lies the dæmonic personality of the writer, the inexplicable force that imposed the
experience of this man Rousseau—vagabond as he was, a foe
of convention, betrayer of sacred trust, morbid self-analyst
ending with fixed hallucination of a conspiracy of society
against him—the magic glamour that imposed the private
emotions of this man upon the world. As the creed of Chris-

tianity came to the Middle Ages coloured by the intense self-absorption of St. Augustine's *Confessions,* so the new faith has flamed up from the *Confessions* of Rousseau. The Roman had set an example for the pride of the saints; our modern confessor proclaimed a similar pride for all the weak and downtrodden. In the audacity of his self-justification as of one who dares say I am that I am, in his boastful admission that it was always impossible for him to act contrary to his inclination, in his defiant cry against a Providence that caused him to be born among men yet made him of a different species from them, in all this itching to exhibit himself, he was the father of romanticism and of a morbid individualism that seeks to hide itself under the cloak of a collective ideal.

For in reality his double motive of self-love and sympathy was one thing, and not two. The full development of the notion of sympathy will be found in Adam Smith's *Theory of Moral Sentiments,* where either independently or through the influence of Rousseau's *Discourse* morality is based systematically on that sense. Both the Scot and the Frenchman would perhaps admit that, to a certain extent, sympathy, as the faculty of putting one's self in the place of another, is a phase of *amour-propre,* in so far as we are led thereby to convert the pain of others into fear for ourselves and the joy of others into hope for ourselves. But neither of them recognises the cognate truth that when the condition of others is conceived in a causal relation to ourselves this order is reversed. That is to say, if the pain or loss of another in any way contributes to our own advantage, we rejoice in it, even when the feeling of uneasiness remains more or less consciously present; and contrariwise with the joy or gain of another which effects our own disadvantage. Thus a son must harbour some satisfaction in the death of a father whereby he comes into an estate; while at the same time he may feel a sorrow derived both from the severance of long ties and from the uneasy foreboding of his own future fate as brought home to him by the present example. It is because of this ambiguous character of sympathy that it can never take the place of discipline and justice in regulating the affairs of men; as it is at best an extension of self-love, so it is always, when interests clash, in peril of unmasking as downright selfishness. A little honest observation of the actual working of Rousseauism in modern society would confirm this opinion only too cruelly.[9]

It will have been remarked that one leading idea of the eighteenth century finds no place in Rousseau's system; the idea of progress he even repudiated. Yet, by a paradox, the believers in progress have found in him weapons ready-forged to their hands; for that doctrine, it is clear, derives its strength from a trust in the essential and natural rightness of human instincts, which need only freedom to develop into right institutions. In practice, however, this faith in evolution has assumed seemingly diverse forms as it has attached itself to the principle of self-love or sympathy. On the one hand we have the unabashed acceptance of egotism as worked out in the philosophy of Nietzsche, and as shown in the unconscious acts of the dominant controllers of the material world. Nietzsche's theory is beautifully simple. Society as he sees it now existent is a conspiracy against the individual. The religious creeds, with their preaching of sympathy and renunciation, the curbing laws of the State, are merely an organised hypocrisy by which the few strong are held in subjection to the many weak. In time the Will to Power *(der Wille zur Macht)* will become conscious and assert itself; then the instincts of the strong will break from pusillanimous control, and we shall have an harmonious civilisation in which the few, following their unhampered desires, will rise on the labours of the submissive many, as now man makes use of a beast of burden. On the other side stands the whole group of theories known as Socialism. To Marx and his followers mankind is divided between the great mass of workers and the few capitalists who by the iron law of wages exploit them ruthlessly. Such a condition is the result of economic evolution; it will be cured when the workers, through the growth of class-consciousness, learn their sovereign power, and take full possession of the sources of production and wealth. Competition and all its consequent suffering will thus cease when the people are welded into a unit by sympathy. The workers are in the solidarity of their interests a kind of individual oppressed and corrupted by the privileged class who represent the traditional institutions of the State.

It might seem fanciful to derive systems so contrary in tendency from the same origin, yet both are alike in that they regard the evils of civilisation as caused by that dualism of the individual and society, which was imposed upon the world as a new religion by one who sought in this way to escape the burden of personal responsibility. Both look to relief in the solution of that antinomy through the application of natural science to human affairs and through the resulting free development of man's natural instincts, one in the direction of egotism, the other of sympathy. Nor is this difference of direction so real as may appear. It is like a bad jest to suppose that under the Nietzschean regime, when the liberated superman has thrown off all sense of responsibility and self-control, the masses would not be driven by unity of interests to combine for retaliation. To many it will seem an equally bad jest to pretend that a social sympathy based avowedly on class hatred would not, if relieved from the constraint of that opposition, fly into an anarchy of egotisms. One wonders curiously, or sadly sometimes, that the preachers who abdicate the fear of God for humanitarianism, and the teachers who surrender the higher discipline for subservience to individual choice, do not see, or, seeing, do not dread, the goal toward which they are facing.

---

1   This essay had been gotten up as one of the lectures on the Nathaniel Ropes Foundation for the Study of Comparative Literature at the University of Cincinnati, January, 1909, and from an article written for *The Nation* and the *Evening Post*, April 30 and May 2, 1908, respectively. The original title had been "Rousseau and Education." It owes much to the thinking of Irving Babbitt, as More admits in the essay. More included it in the Sixth Series of the *Shelburne Essays*, devoted to studies in religious dualism.

2   Paul Hensel, *Rousseau* (Leipzig, 1919), pp. 103–4.

[3]   Algernon Sidney (1622–1682). See his *Discourses on Government*, first printed in 1698 after his death and thereafter reprinted many times.

[4]   Thomas Chubb (1679–1747), *The True Gospel of Jesus Christ* (1739).

[5]   If Chubb won applause by depriving faith of its superrational elements, a greater contemporary, Toland, exerted all his powers to explode what he deemed the fallacy of the religious imagination. The very title of his chief work, *Christianity Not Mysterious: or, a Treatise Showing that there is nothing in the Gospel Contrary to Reason, nor Above it: and that no Christian Doctrine can be properly call'd a Mystery*, would seem to be a challenge to Sir Thomas Browne. This is not to say that in the poetry and philosophy inspired by deism there is no proper use of the imagination. That faculty, as the power which renders concrete and real, visible so to speak to the inner eye, the intellectual and spiritual life of man, varies in action as the life to which it administers varies. In the work of deistic writers it is closely akin to its use by the scientific mind, though it may be lacking in the positive utilitarian advantages of science. [More's note]

[6]   Pierre Bayle (1647–1706), whose best known work is the *Dictionnaire historique et critique*, the edition of 1730 being the most complete.

[7]   As early as 1694, La Fontaine had felt the power of the new English philosophy:

> . . . Les Anglais pensent profondément:
> Leur esprit, en cela, suit leur tempérament;
> Creusant tous les sujets et forts d'expériences,
> Ils étendent partout l'empire des sciences.

Buckle in his *History of Civilisation* has an eloquent chapter on the influence of England at this time upon France, and Joseph Texte has elaborated this thesis into a well-known volume, *Jean-Jacques Rousseau, et les origines du cosmopolitisme littéraire*. Neither of these writers, so far as I remember, brings out the curious fact that just when England was borrowing its literary form from France the trend in philosophy was in the opposite direction. From the time of Voltaire's *Lettres anglaises* (1733), Newton and Locke may be called the fathers *par excellence* of the new *philosophie*. I have dwelt solely on the English sources of Rousseau because there, I think, lies the dynamic derivation; this is not to deny that many of his ideas can be found in contemporary and preceding French authors. [More's note]

[8]   The translation of this famous passage is taken from *Jean-Jacques Rousseau*, by Jules Lemaître, translated by Jeanne Mairet. (New York: The McClure Co.) M. Lemaître's lectures have all the bitterness of a converted Rousselian. He displays extreme cleverness in deriving all Rousseau's theories from personal weaknesses and vanities, showing in this perhaps a little too much of the animosity of a renegade. As a critical work it is not significant, except in so far as it is a sign that some of the best-instructed minds of France are turning away from the romanticism of Rousseau in which they were schooled. [More's note]

[9]   The place of egotism and sympathy in Rousseau's system and the general distinction between humanism and humanitarianism have been discussed fully and incisively in Irving Babbitt's *Literature and the American College* (Boston: Houghton, Mifflin & Co., 1908). I take pleasure in recording my large indebtedness to that work.—Burke's remark is well-known: "We have had the great professor and founder of the philosophy of Vanity in England. . . . Benevolence to the whole species, and want of feeling for every individual with whom the professors come in contact, form the character of the new philosophy." The philosophy is no longer new, but its nature has not altered in this respect. [More's note]

The New Morality[1]

Some ten or twelve years ago a certain young woman, then fresh from the hands of an esteemed but erratic professor of English literature, wrote a novel the plot of which was roughly as follows. A college graduate suddenly finds himself the inheritor of a shoe factory in a New England town. Filled with the benevolent ideas absorbed in the academic contemplation of economics, he undertakes to introduce profit-sharing with his employees and otherwise to conduct his business for the benefit of the community. So far, good. But hard times follow, and his competitors by lowering wages and reducing labour are able to undersell him. Now there is in his control a considerable sum of money which a widow had entrusted to his father to invest for her, and the question arises whether he shall shut down his mills and inflict suffering upon his men, or shall divert this trust fund to his business and so try to tide over the period of stress. He yields to his sympathies and virtually embezzles the trust fund; but fails nevertheless, and with his own loss brings ruin upon the widow. The story was called *The Burden of Christopher*,[2] with the implication that the hero was a bearer of Christ in his misfortune, and the author indicates pretty clearly her sentiment that in surrendering his personal integrity for the expected good of his working people he was following the higher of two conflicting codes of ethics.

The book no doubt has gone its own way to the "limbo large and broad," where the heroes of ancient fiction wander with

Embrios and idiots, eremites and friars;

but it made a lasting impression on one reader at least as the first popular presentation to come under his notice of a theory which now confronts him wherever he turns his eyes. There has, in fact, been an astonishing divulgation in the past decade of what is called, with magnificent audacity, the New Morality.

Perhaps the most honoured teacher of this code is the mistress of Hull House, who by her devoted life and her services to the people of Chicago in various times of need has won the right to speak with a certain authority for the striving generation of the day. And in one of her books, the *Newer Ideals of Peace*, Miss Addams tells of an actual occurrence and infers a moral which points in the same direction as the novel of *Christopher*. A family of five children is left motherless. The father, a drunkard, disappears, and the household is left to the care of a feeble old grandmother. Thereupon work is found for the oldest boy, "a fine, manly little fellow" of twelve, who feels keenly "his obligation to care for the family." But after a time he becomes "listless and indifferent," and at sixteen turns to professional tramping. It was through such bitter lessons as these," observes Miss Addams, "we learned that good intentions and the charitable impulse do not always work for righteousness." As the story is told there is a plain implication that to find work for a boy under such circumstances is "cruel and disastrous" (her own comment), and that society, and not his own nature, was responsible for his relapse. One would suppose that scarcely an honest workman, or prosperous merchant, or successful professional man had ever taken up the burden of a family in youth or childhood. Doubtless hardships and waste often come from the exigencies of life, but there is not a single word in Miss Addams' account to indicate that she has felt the need of developing in the future citizen a sensitiveness to the peculiar duties that will confront him, or has reflected on the evil that might have been done the boy if he had been relieved of his natural obligations and supported by society. "Our democracy," as she says with approval, "is making inroads upon the family, the oldest of human institutions."

This is not an isolated case in Miss Addams' works, nor does it in any wise misrepresent her. In another book, *The Spirit of Youth and the City Streets*,[3] the thesis is maintained and reiterated, that crime is for the most part merely the result of repressing a wholesome "love for excitement" and "desire for adventure." In the year 1909 "there were arrested and brought into court [in Chicago] fifteen thousand young people under the age of twenty, who had failed to keep even the common law of the land. Most of these young people had broken the law in their blundering efforts to find adventure." The inference to be drawn here and throughout the book is that one need only relieve the youth of the land from the necessity of "assuming responsibility prematurely," affording them meanwhile abundant amusement, and the instincts of lawlessness and the pursuit of criminal pleasure will vanish, or almost vanish, of themselves—as if there were no Harry Thaws[4] and the sons of the rich were all virtuous.

But it must not be supposed that Hull House occupies a place of lonely isolation as the fountain of these ideas. From every self-authorized centre of civic virtue in which a type-writer is at work, the stream proceeds. The very presses groan, as we used to say when those machines were still in the mythological stage, at their labour of supplying the world with the new intellectual pabulum. At this moment there lies before the writer of this essay a pile of books, all recently published, which are devoted more or less specifically to the subject, and from all of which, if he had courage to go through them, he might cull abundant examples and quotations. He was, indeed, about to enter this "hollow cave, amid the thickest woods," when, an unvaliant knight, he heard the warning of the lady Una:

> Yea but (quoth she) the perill of this place
> I better wot then you, though now too late
> To wish you backe returne with foule disgrace,
> Yet wisedome warnes, whilest foot is in the gate,
> To stay the steppe, ere forced to retrate.

We have in fact to deal with the consummation of a long and deep-seated revolution, and there is no better way to understand the true character of the movement than by turning aside a moment to glance at its historical sources. This attempt to find some basis of conduct to take the place of the older conception of personal integrity, as we see it exemplified in the works of Miss Jane Addams and a host of other modern writers, is in fact only one aspect of the slow drift from medieval religion to humanitarianism. For a thousand years and well into the second thousand the ethical feeling of Christian Europe may be said to have taken its colour from the saying, "What shall it profit a man, if he shall gain the whole world, and lose his own soul?"—which in extreme cases was interpreted as if it read, If he *reform* the whole world; and on the other, kindred saying, "Sell all that thou hast and distribute unto the poor, and thou shall have treasure in heaven, and come, follow me"—in which the command of charity was held to be not so much for the benefit of the poor as for the liberation of the giver's own soul from the powers of this world. Such was the law, and its binding force was confirmed by the conception of a final day of wrath when the souls of men should stand before a merciless tribunal and be judged to everlasting joy or everlasting torment. The vivid reality of the fear that haunted men, at least in their moments of reflection, may be understood from the horrors of such a picture as Michael Angelo's *Last Judgment*, or from the meditations of one of the most genial of English cavaliers. In his little treatise on *Man in Darkness* —appropriate title—Henry Vaughan puts the frank question to himself:

> And what madness then is it, for the enjoying of one minute's pleasure for the satisfaction of our sensual corrupt appetite, to lie forever in a bed of burning brass, in the lake of eternal and unquenchable fire? "Suppose," saith the same writer [Drexelius], "that this whole globe of earth were nothing else but a huge mass or mountain of sand, and that a little wren came but once in every thousand years to fetch away but one grain of that huge heap; what an innumerable number of years would be

spent before that world of sand could be so fetched away! And yet, alas! when the damned have lain in that fiery lake so many years as all those would amount to, they are no nearer coming out than the first hour they entered in."

No doubt practice and precept were at variance then, as to a certain extent they are at all times, and there were many texts in the Bible which might be taken to mitigate the harsher commands; but such in its purest, highest form was the law, and in the more sensitive minds this conception of the soul naked before a judging God must have created a tremendous anxiety. Morality was obedience and integrity; it scorned the world for an ideal of inner righteousness; it created a sense of individual responsibility for every word and deed; and, say what we will there is something magnificent in this contempt for the reckoning of other men beside that eternal fame which

> . . . lives and speaks aloft by those pure eyes,
> And perfect witness of all-judging Jove.

But there was also in this law something repellent and even monstrous. Who has not shuddered with amazement at the inscription which Dante set over the portal of Hell: E 'L PRIMO AMORE? Was it Love that prepared those winding coils of torture to enclose for endless time the vast majority of mankind? Was it even justice to make the everlasting doom of a soul depend on its grasp of truth in these few years spent in a world of shadows and illusions? There is something repulsively irrational in the notion of an unchanging eternity suspended on the action in a moment of time—*ex hoc momento pendet æternitas.* It should seem to be unthinkable, if it had not actually been thought. As a matter of fact the rigour and crudity of this doctrine had been mitigated in the Middle Ages by the interposition between man and God of the very human institution of the Church, with its substitution of temporal penances and pardons and an interposed Purgatory in place of the terrible paradox of irrevocable judgment. It remained for the Reformation, and particularly for the Calvinistic Puritans, to tear away those veils of compromise and bring man face to face with the awful abstraction he had created. The result was for a while a great hardening and strengthening of character, salutary indeed after what may be called the almost hypocritical compromise of Catholicism; but in the end human nature could not endure the rigidity of its own logic, and in revolting turned not to another compromise but to questioning the very hypothesis of its faith.

The inevitable reaction from the intolerable logic of the Protestants was Deism, in which God was stript altogether of his judicial and moral attributes and reduced to a kind of immanent, all-benevolent force in nature. "But now comes a modern Sage," says Warburton of Bolingbroke, ". . . who tells us 'that they made the Basis of Religion far too wide; that men have no further concern with GOD than TO BELIEVE THAT HE IS, which his *physical attributes* make fully manifest; but, that he is *a rewarder of them who diligently seek him,* Religion doth not require us to believe, since this depends on God's MORAL ATTRIBUTES, of which we have no conception.' " But the deistic position was manifestly untenable, for it left no place for the undeniable existence of evil in this world and life. From the unaccountable distribution of wrong and suffering the divine had argued the certainty of adjustment in a future state; the deist had flown in the face of facts by retaining the belief in a benevolent Providence while taking from it the power of supernatural retribution; the atheist was more logical, he denied the existence of Providence altogether and turned the universe over to chance or blind law. Such was the progress of thought from Baxter to Bolingbroke and from Bolingbroke to Hume.

The positive consequences of this evolution are written large in the literature of the eighteenth century. With the idea of an avenging deity and a supernatural test there disappeared also the sense of deep personal responsibility; the very notion of a radical and fundamental difference between good and evil was lost. The evil that is apparent in character comes to be regarded merely as the result of the restraining and thwarting institutions of society as these exist—why, no one can explain. Envy and jealousy and greed and the sheer lust of power, all those traits which were summed up in the single Greek word *pleonexia, the desire to have more,* are not inherent in the human heart, but are artificially introduced by property and a false civilization. Change these institutions or release the individual entirely from restrictions, and his nature will recoil spontaneously to its natural state of virtue. He needs only follow the impulse of his instinctive emotions to be sound and good. And as a man feels of himself, so he feels of others. There is no real distinction between the good and the evil, but all are naturally good and the superficial variations we see are caused by the greater or less freedom of development. Hence we should condemn no man even as we do not condemn ourselves. There is no place for sharp judgment, and the laws which impose penalties and restrictions and set up false discriminations between the innocent and the criminal are subject to suspicion and should be made as flexible as possible. In place of judgment we are to regard all mankind with sympathy; a sort of emotional solidarity becomes the one great virture, in which are included, or rather sunk, all the law and the prophets.

It was the great work of the eighteenth century, beginning in England and developing in France, to formulate this change and indoctrinate with it the mind of the unthinking masses. Here is not the place to follow the development in detail, and those who care to see its outcome may be referred to the keen and unjustly neglected chapters on the *philosophes* in La Harpe's *Lycée.* To those, indeed, who are acquainted with the philosophical writings that preceded and introduced the French Revolution, the epithet "new" as it is attached to our present-day morality may seem a bit presumptuous; for it would be difficult to find a single fundamental idea in current literature on this subject which could not be closely paralleled by a quotation from Rousseau, or Diderot, or Helvétius, or one of their compeers. Thus, in our exaltation of sympathy above judgment and of the unrestrained emotions generally as the final rule of character, we are but following Diderot's philosophy of the heart: "Les passions amorties dégradent les hommes extraordinaires",[5] and when we read in Ellen Key[6] and a host of other feminist liberators the apotheosis of love as higher than any divine or human obligations, we are but meeting again with Toussaint's religion a little disguised: "On aime de même Dieu et sa maîtresse."[7] Our revolt from constitutional law as a power imposed by the slower reflection of men upon their own immediate desires and opinions is essentially the same as the restlessness consecrated by the French *économistes* in the phrase, "le despotisme légal." And, to return whence we began, the economics of Hull House flow only too easily from Helvétius' definition of virtue as "le désir du bien public," and from his more specific statement: "The integrity which is related to an individual or to a small society is not the true integrity; integrity considered in relation to the public is the only kind that really deserves and generally obtains the name."

Miss Addams herself has been disturbed by these reminiscences. Thus she quotes from one of the older humanitarians a characteristic saying: "The love of those whom a man does not know is quite as elemental a sentiment as the love of those whom a man does know," and repudiates it as vague and unpractical beside the New Morality. She ought to know, and may be right, yet it is not easy to see wherein her own ethics are any less vague when she deplores the act of a boy who goes to work for his starving grandmother because in doing so he is unfitting himself for future service to society. And as for effectiveness, it might seem that the French Revolution was a practical result fairly equivalent in magnitude to what has been achieved by our college settlements. But Miss Addams is by no means peculiar in this assumption of originality. Nothing is more notable in the humanitarian literature of the day than the feeling that our own age is severed from the past and opens an entirely new epoch in history. *"The race has now crossed the great divide of human history!"* exclaims an hysterical doctor of divinity in a book just published. "The tendency of the long past has been toward *diversity,* that of the longer future will be toward *oneness.* The change in this stream of tendency is not a temporary deviation from its age-long course—a new bend in the river. It is an actual reversal of the current, which beyond a peradventure will prove permanent." To this ecstatic watcher the sudden reversal took place at no remote date, but yesterday; and by a thousand other watchers the same miracle is vociferously heralded. Beyond a peradventure! Not a little of this flattering assumption is due to the blind and passionate hope of the human heart clamouring against the voice of experience. So many prophets before now have cried out, looking at the ever-flowing current of time, and having faith in some Thessalian magic:

> Cessavere vices rerum.
> . . . Amnisque cucurrit
> Non qua pronus erat.[8]

So often the world has been disappointed; but at last we have seen—beyond a peradventure. If the vicissitudes of fate have not ceased, yet at least we have learned to look with complacency on the very law of mutation from which the eyes of men had hitherto turned away in bewildered horror, at last the stream has turned back upon its sources, and change itself is carrying us no longer towards diversity, but towards the consummation of a divine oneness.

But it would equally be an error to insist too dogmatically on the continuity of the present-day movement with that of the eighteenth century; for one generation is never quite as another. We must not forget that for a hundred years or thereabout there was a partial reaction against the doctrines of the *philosophes,* during which time the terrors of the Revolution lay like a warning nightmare in the imagination of the more thoughtful men. A hundred years is a long period for the memory to bridge, particularly in a time when the historical sense has been weakened. Superficially, too, the application of the

theory is in some respects different from what it was; the law
of social sympathy has been developed into different conceptions of socialism, and we have devised fresh schemes for giving efficacy to the immediate will of the people. Even deeper
is the change that has come over the attitude of religious or-
ganizations towards the movement. In the age of the Revolution the Church, both Catholic and Protestant, was still
strongly entrenched in the old beliefs and offered a violent
resistance to the substitutions of humanitarianism for responsibility to the priest and to God. Now this last barrier has been
almost swept away. Indeed, not the least remarkable feature
of this literature is the number of clergymen who are contributing to it, with their constant appeal to the New Morality
as the test of faith. Open one of these books before us—let us
take *The Christian Reconstruction of Modern Life*,[9] for the
promise of its title—and you will be pretty likely to come upon
such a passage as this: "Faith's fellowship with Jesus is one with
the realization of our fellowship in humanity"; or, on another
page: "If the fundamental of the true philosophy cannot be
found by common men, what advantage in any man's finding
it? If life's secret, direction, and power . . . is not attainable by
the lowliest, then a man of this age, living in the social passion
of our time, is forced to be indifferent to that which would be
the monopoly of a few gifted souls." If such a social passion
means anything, it means the reconstruction of life to the level
of the gutter. It is the modern sham righteousness which would
have called from Jesus the same utter scorn as that which he
poured upon the Pharisaical cant of his own day. Yet it is not
in religious books alone that you will meet with this sort of
irreligion. For one sermon you will hear on the obligation of
the individual soul to its maker and judge, and on the need of
personal regeneration and the beauty of holiness, you will hear
a score on the relation of a man to his fellows and on the virtue
of social sympathy. In effect, the first and great commandment, "Thou shalt love the Lord thy God with all thy heart and
with all thy soul and with all thy mind," has been almost forgotten for the second, "Thou shalt love thy neighbour as thyself."

Worship in the temple is no longer a call to contrition and repentance, but an organized flattery of our human nature, and the theological seminary is fast becoming a special school for investigating poverty and spreading agnosticism. In this sense, or degree, that humanitarianism is no longer opposed by organized religion, but has itself usurped the place of the Church, the New Morality may really justify its name.

What are the results of this glorification of humanity? What does the New Morality mean in life and conduct? Well, of such matters it is wise to speak cautiously. The actual morals of an age are an extremely complicated and elusive network of facts, and it is only too easy to generalize from incomplete observation. On the other hand we must guard against allowing ourselves to be deceived by the fallacy everywhere heard, that, because the preacher has always, even from the remotest record of Egypt, bewailed his own times as degenerate, therefore no age has fallen off in morality from its predecessor. Such an argument is a complete *non-sequitur;* there have been periods of degeneration, and there may yet be. As for our own age, only a fool would dogmatize; we can only balance and surmise. And in the first place a certain good must almost certainly be placed to the credit of humanitarianism. It has softened us and made us quicker to respond to the sufferings of others; the direct and frightful cruelty that runs through the annals of history like a crimson line has been largely eliminated from civilization, and with it a good deal of the brutality of human nature. We sometimes hear the present age compared with the later Roman Republic and the Empire, and in some respects speciously, but the callousness of the greater Romans to human misery and their hardness are almost unthinkable today. Consider a sentence or two from Appian: "The head and hand of Cicero were suspended for a long time from the rostra in the forum where formerly he had been accustomed to make public speeches, and more people came together to behold this spectacle than had previously come to listen to him. It is said that even at his meals Antony placed the head of Cicero before his table, until he became satiated with the horrid sight." Such an episode scarcely stands out from the hideous story of the Civil Wars; to the modern reader it brings a feeling almost of physical sickness. So much we seem to have gained, and the change in this respect even from our own seventeenth century shows that the credit is due in no small part to the general trend of humanitarianism.

But in other directions the progress is not so clear. Statistics are always treacherous witnesses, but so far as we can believe them and interpret them we can draw no comfort from the prevalence of crime and prostitution and divorce and insanity and suicide. At least, whatever may be the cause of this inner canker of society, our social passion seems to be powerless to cure it. Some might even argue that the preaching of any doctrine which minimizes personal responsibility is likely to increase the evil. Certainly a teacher who, like Miss Jane Addams, virtually attributes the lawless and criminal acts of our city hoodlums to a wholesome desire of adventure which the laws unrighteously repress, would appear to be encouraging the destructive and sensual proclivities which are too common in human nature, young and old. Nor are the way of honesty made clear by a well-known humanitarian judge of Denver, who refused to punish a boy for stealing a Sunday-School teacher's pocketbook, for the two good reasons, as his honour explained in a public address, "that the boy was not responsible, and, secondly, that there were bigger thieves in the pews upstairs." So, too, a respectable woman of New York who asks whether it may not be a greater wrong for a girl to submit to the slavery of low wages than to sell herself in the street, is manifestly not helping the tempted to resist. She is even doing what she can with her words to confuse the very bounds of moral and physical evil.

There is, in act, a terrible confusion hidden in the New Morality, an ulcerous evil that is ever working inward. Sympathy, creating the desire for even-handed justice, is in itself an excellent motive of conduct, and the stronger it grows, the better the world shall be. But sympathy, spoken with the word "social" prefixed, as it commonly is on the platforms of the day, begins to take on a dangerous connotation. And "social sympathy" erected into a theory which leaves out of account the responsibility of the individual and seeks to throw the blame of evil on the laws and on society, though it may effect desirable reforms here and there in institutions, is bound to leave the individual weakened in his powers of resistance against the temptations which can never be eliminated from human life. The whole effect of calling sympathy justice and putting it in the place of judgment is to relax the fibre of character and nourish the passions at the expense of reason and the will. And undoubtedly the conviction is every day gaining ground among cool observers of our life that the manners and morals of the people are beginning to suffer from this relaxation in many insidious ways apart from acts which come into the cognizance of the courts. The sensuality of the prevailing music and dancing, the plays that stir the country as organs of moral regeneration, the exaggeration of sex in the clothing seen in the street, are but symptoms more or less ominous to our mind as we do or do not connect them with the regnant theory of ethics. And in the end this form of social sympathy may itself quite conceivably bring back the brutality and cruelty from which it seems to have delivered us. The Roman who gloated over the head of his and the people's enemy lived two thousand years ago, and we think such bloodthirstiness is no longer possible in public life. Yet not much more than a century ago the preaching of social sympathy could send a Lebon and his kind over France with an insatiable lust for killing, complicated with Sadism, while in Paris the leader of the government of the most civilized country of Europe was justifying such a régime on the pious principle that, "when the sovereign people exercises its power, we can only bow before it; in all it does all is virtue and truth, and no excess, error, or crime is possible." The animal is not dead within us, but only asleep. If you think he has been really conquered, read what he has been doing in Congo and to the Putumayo Indians, or among the redeemers of the Balkan States. Or if you wish to get a glimpse of what he may yet do under the spur of social sympathy,

consider the callous indifference shown by the labour unions
to the revelation, if it deserves the name, of the system of
dynamiting and murder employed in the service of "class-
consciousness." These things are to be taken into account, not
as bugbears, for society at large is no doubt sound at heart and
will arouse itself at last against its false teachers, but as symptoms to warn and prepare.[10]

To some few the only way out of what seems a state of moral
blindness is through a return to an acknowledgment of the
responsibility of the individual soul to its maker and inflexible
judge. They may be right. Who can tell what reversal of belief
may lie before us or what religious revolution may be preparing in the heart of infidelity? But for the present, at least, that
supernatural control has lost its general efficacy and even from
the pulpit has only a slight and intermittent appeal. Nor does
such a loss appear without its compensations when we consider
the harshness of medieval theology or the obliquities of superstition that seem to be inherent in the purest of religions.
Meanwhile, the troubled individual, whatever his scepticism
may be, need not be withheld from confirming his moral faith
by turning from the perverted doctrine of the "Enlightenment" and from its recrudescence in modern humanitarianism to a larger and higher philosophy. For there is a faith which
existed long before the materialism of eighteenth century and
before the crude earlier anthropomorphism, and which per-
sisted unchanged, though often half-concealed, through those
ages and still persists as a kind of shamefast inheritance of
truth. It is not necessary to go to ancient books to recover that
faith. Let a man cease for a moment to look so strenuously
upon what is right for his neighbours. Let him shut out the
voices of the world and disregard the stream of informing
books which pour upon him from the modern press, as the
"floud of poyson" was spewed upon Spenser's Knight from
"Errours den":

Her fruitful cursed spawne of serpents small.

Let him retire into himself, and in the silence of such recollection examine his own motives and the sources of his self-approval and discontent. He will discover there in that dialogue with himself, if his abstraction is complete and sincere, that his nature is not simple and single, but dual, and the consequences to him in his judgment of life and in his conduct will be of incalculable importance. He will learn, with a conviction which no science or philosophy falsely so-called can shake, that beside the passions and wandering desires and blind impulses and the cravings for pleasure and the prod of sensations there is something within him and a part of him, rather in some way his truer self, which controls and checks and knows and pronounces judgment, unmoved amid all motion, unchanged amid continual change, of everlasting validity above the shifting valuations of the moment. He may not be able to express this insight in terms that will satisfy his own reason or will convince others, but if his insight is true he will not waver in loyalty to it, though he may sin against it times without number in spoken word and impulsive deed. Rather, his loyalty will be confirmed by experience. For he will discover that there is a happiness of the soul which is not the same as the pleasure of fulfilled desires, whether these be for good or for ill, a happiness which is not dependent upon the results of this or that choice among our desires, but upon the very act itself of choice and self-control, and which grows with the habit of staying the throng of besetting and conflicting impulses always until the judicial *fiat* has been pronounced. It is thus that happiness is the final test of morality, bringing with it a sense of responsibility to the supernatural command within the soul of the man himself, as binding as the laws of religion and based on no disputable revelation or outer authority. Such a morality is neither old nor new, and stands above the varying customs of society. It is not determined essentially by the relation of a man to his fellows or by their approval, but by the consciousness of rightness in the man's own breast,—in a word, by character. Its works are temperance, truth, honesty, trustworthiness, fortitude, magnanimity, elevation; and its crown is joy.

Then, under the guidance of this intuition, a man may turn his eyes upon the world with no fear of being swayed by the ephemeral winds of doctrine. Despite the clamour of the hour he will know that the obligation to society is not the primal law and is not the source of personal integrity, but is secondary to personal integrity. He will believe that social justice is in itself desirable, but he will hold that it is far more important to preach first the responsibility of each man to himself for his own character. He will admit that equality of opportunity is an ideal to be aimed at, but he will think this a small thing in comparison with the universality of duty. In his attitude towards mankind he will not deny the claims of sympathy, but he will listen first to the voice of judgment:

> Away with charity that soothes a lie,
> And thrusts the truth with scorn and anger by.

He will be sensitive to the vast injustices of life and its widespread sorrows, but he will not be seduced by that compassion into the hypocrisy of saying that "the love of those whom a man does not know is quite as elemental as sentiment as the love of those whom a man does know." Nor, in repudiating such a falsehood, will he, like the mistress of Hull Hall, lose his power of discrimination under the stress of "those vast and dominant suggestions of a new peace and holiness," that is "to issue forth from broken human nature itself, out of the pathetic striving of ordinary men." Rather, he will, at any cost, strive to clear away the clouds of cant, and so open his mind to the dictates of the everlasting morality.

---

[1]   This has been one of More's most published essays. After appearing in both the *Unpopular Review* (January, 1914) and the Ninth Series of *Shelburne Essays*, it was republished in F. W. Scott and J. Zeitlin, *Essays Formal and Informal* (1927), O. Cargill, *The Social Revolt* (1933), and L. Wann, *Century Readings in the English Essay* (1939).

[2]   By Florence Converse, published in 1900.

3   Published in 1909.

4   Harry Kendall Thaw (1871–?), tried for the murder of Stanford White on June 25, 1906, the trial ending on April 12, 1907, with a verdict of murder in the first degree. A second trial opened January 6, 1908, and ended January 29 of that year, with a verdict of not guilty by reason of insanity. On August 17, 1913, Thaw escaped from Matteawan state hospital, and a third trial freed him in June, 1915. Thaw's own account of his trials can be read in his *The Traitor; Being the Untampered With, Unrevised Account of the Trial and All that Led to It*, Philadelphia, 1926; or in F. A. Mackenzie's edition of Thaw's book, *The Trial of Harry Thaw*, London, 1928.

5   "Cool passions discredit extraordinary men."

6   Ellen Karoline Sofia Key (1849–1926), Swedish social writer.

7   "One loves God and his mistress in the same way."

8   "The vicissitude of things.
         . . . The stream ran
     Where it was not sloping."

9   Charles Henry Dickinson (1857–1938), *The Christian Reconstruction of Modern Life*, New York, 1913.

10 All this was written and printed, I need scarcely say before the outbreak of the European War. I should not to-day refer to the Congo and the Putumayo Indians for the savagery underlying civilization. [More's note]

Wealth and Culture[1]

If the influence of wealth on national culture is to be treated in a manner that will give it any distinct meaning, the word culture must be taken in its narrower sense as something included within the general social life, but not coextensive with it. Culture is a definite problem of the imagination and touches on the other faculties of a man only as the imagination reacts upon the formation of character. Yet culture is not the mere cultivation of beauty, for many of the great products of culture are not beautiful. It is more than this. It is the power of creating a realm in which we live apart from and alongside of our actual life. It is thus an enlargement, a doubling so to speak, of human existence; but it is not necessarily beautiful. A man who reads Zola doubles his existence by adding his experiences, but he scarcely renders his life more beautiful.

Now this superadded world of the imagination, the ability to dwell in which we call culture, must possess the power of illusion; it must for the time while we are under its spell impose itself upon us as a transcript of reality, and the recollection of its spell must even abide with us as an actual experience; otherwise it can have no serious interest in our life. But it must also, by some magical faculty of persuasion, lift us into a realm that is larger and freer than the reality in which we live, must seemingly unshackle us from the ever-tightening bounds and limitations that more and more as the years pass teach us how little our life may expand as we wished it to expand. Without this faculty of expansion the imagination is merely an instrument of sensuous indulgence that becomes an utter weariness in the end. The power of illusion and the faculty of expansion must thus exist side by side; but unfortunately they tend to counteract each other. The illusion of reality is in danger of being lost as the imagination transcends more daringly the limits of actual experience, and the converse holds equally true.

The question of first importance is then to determine what field of the imagination will enable this power of illusion and this faculty of expansion to exist together and mutually reinforce each other. And the answer is near at hand. The artist in his work must carry out the ideal of the people among whom he lives and for whom he works. In this way the pictures he creates in the realm of the imagination will possess the easy power of illusion in as much as they present what we are already disposed to accept as flowing directly from real life; and his labor in creating an ideal is lessened in as much as it is already in large part formed for him.

This is perhaps a truism, and yet a few illustrations may not fall amiss. To go back to the ancient literature of India, if I may judge from my own experience, the work which lingers in memory as the truest and most effective creation of the Hindu imagination, is the episode of Sâvitrî (it has been translated, but spoiled in the translation, by Sir Edwin Arnold) in the epic Mahâbhârata.[2] And the reason of this is plain. The story portrays with all the beauty of imaginative vision that wonderful forest-life, with its austerities of renunciation sweetened by human pathos and by sympathy with nature, which was the fairest ideal of the Hindu people—portrays it not as it actually existed, but as the faith of the people would have wished it to exist. And it need not be said that such an ideal picture reacted on reality, and did much to purify and render more beautiful the actual forest-life. So in Greece Pindar in his Hymns of Victory heightened and carried out the national ideal of perfect self-dependence and complete self-development, with its half concealed exultation of *Vae victis!*[3] and its everhaunting dread of a retributive Nemesis waiting to cast down those

whose pride soared too high. And we may see the young men
of Pindar standing before us carved in the marbles of Phidias.
The Middle Ages, in conformity with their inherent dualism,
possessed a double ideal; their imagination did, in fact, dwell
in a kind of perpetual oxymoron. Dante has fixed forever the
religious ideal of the soul that counts the world well lost for her
own salvation; Cervantes has caught the ideal of the soldier
knight just as it was passing away in the new life of the renaissance. And the renaissance itself had its portrayal of the ideal
man, its humanism, described in the Courtier of Castiglione.
Coming nearer to our own day, the ideals of the opening nineteenth century, the dreams of a pantheistic return to nature,
the hopes of individual liberty passing so lightly into license—
do we not read them in Wordsworth and Shelley and Byron?

These are but a few familiar illustrations chosen from many.
They are sufficient to show—if exposition be necessary—how
the imaginative life of a nation, its culture in the restricted
sense of the word, is only a carrying out, a realization in terms
of art, of the national ideal lying half revealed in the actual life
of the people.

And, if this be so, what national ideal has America today on
which its culture may be built up? Renunciation, self-development, religion, chivalry, humanism, pantheistic return to nature, liberty—all these have existed and have born their fair
fruits; what have we to offer in their place? The subject of this
symposium may stand as a sufficient answer, Wealth—wealth
and its complement which we call humanitarianism or socialism, and which is, in fact, nothing more than the extension and
dilution of this same ideal; wealth aiming at the control of vast
material forces, humanitarianism seeking, first of all and above
all, material comfort for the multitude while masquerading in
the guise of religion, and covering itself with the cloak of
brotherly love.

Now no one would be so blind as to assert that the love of
money and of material things is a new influence in the world;
the love of money has, of course, always existed, and has always
been a great force in human affairs. But its power today is

different in two important particulars. In the first place, the magnitude of the fortunes possessed by a few men is vastly greater than the world has seen in any previous age, with the possible exception of a short period in the history of Rome. The wealth of our richest men today is so enormous as to affect the imagination with a sort of hypnotic obsession; it dazzles and subdues our intelligence. And, secondly, this incalculable wealth is in the control of a new group of men, whether they be better or worse morally than the rich men of old. Formerly great wealth fell to successful soldiers and court favorites, or was inherited in noble families; it came indirectly to speak. The possessors of wealth may have been wicked and base, but this wealth in the public eye was merely an adjunct of their position. Today the development of mechanical forces is bringing wealth more and more into the hands of a different class of men. They owe their possessions to the direct control of the material sources of wealth, or to the manipulation of money itself. They stand for wealth and production of wealth and for nothing else. And they are the men who affect the imagination by their unknown powers. Whose are the names continually bruited now in the public ear? Not the sailor's who wins a great victory, is flattered with indiscriminate ovations today and forgotten tomorrow; not the statesman's who lives in retreat after a few years of service as President of the nation. No, the great men are those that manage the oil wells of the country, or the railroads, or the steel mills, and you may see their stronghold in the narrow lanes that wind about Wall Street.

I have traveled a good deal here and there, from city to city, but I always come back to this point of land which we call Wall Street as the most genuine expession of our national life. Walk through these sunless cañons and look up at the towering, threatening buildings. The architecture of these streets is impressive for its originality and its significance. It symbolizes perfectly the power that dwells and labors in this fastness and it is utterly distinct from anything the world has ever seen before. In comparison with these mountains of iron and stone the churches of the land (mere cockle shells for the most part), and the libraries, the colleges and the museums, dwindle in impressiveness to mere toys. Here is the palace and the fortress and the temple of wealth, and it signifies to America today what the Parthenon signified to Athens, or Notre Dame and the Louvre to Paris, or St. Peter's to Rome.

I remember a few years ago, when the tallest edifice of the city was erecting, the impression made by its skeleton rising high up into the air. The vast network of steel girders and columns seemed to my fancy to stand like the bars of a huge prison in which the human spirit was to be caged; and over this structure of steel was laid a thin veneering of ornamental stone not unlike the wanton and meaningless luxury of those who pass from accumulating wealth to spending it. The building stands now enormously high and oppressive by reason of its isolation; you cannot gaze up its endless rows of windows without a sinister sensation that the whole monstrous thing will topple over one day and crush you in its ruins. And beneath it, far beneath its upper stories, crouches a little homely church, old St. Paul's, with its tombstones crumbling in the shade!

The architecture of Wall Street, I think, presents the true culture, the true imaginative creation of the day, for the simple reason that it is the most genuine and adequate expression of the national ideal. But the influence of this material ideal does not stop here. Come with me to Harvard, our most cultured university, and see its effects. The academic department of that institution is yearly losing ground before new departments that teach the manipulation of those mechanical forces by which the fortunes of Wall Street are nourished. The very building in which the earlier ideals of culture are taught looks insignificant in comparison with the new engineering hall where the engines of commerce rumble and grind all day. And in the academic department itself the old humanistic studies dwindle and are hardly considered seriously, while the economic courses, which scarcely existed a score of years ago, attract more and more the real strength of the college. Even those studies of abstract science which flourish so nobly and of which we boast so complacently are but a higher development of the same all-absorbing desire, at any cost, to make ourselves masters of the material resources of the earth.

The influence of the new ideal on art is to convert art into the mere veneering and amusement of life, into a tasteless covering of luxury that hides the sordid rapacities of a Wall-Street life as those ornate and meaningless shells of stone conceal the true structure of a Wall-Street building. In place of an Italian palace, simple in its furniture and moderate in its adornment, you may find a mansion on Fifth Avenue into which the spoils of the ages are thrown together with a wanton and vulgar profusion such as the world has not dreamed of since the days of Imperial Rome. And in literature—the commonest aim is to sell a half million copies of a novel and grow rich. The novels speak for themselves; they are for the relaxation of the moment and bear no relation to the significant things of life. What is on the whole the most philosophic history of the United States, the incompleted work of John Fiske, makes the realization of this commercial ideal the end toward which the evolution of humanity has gravitated unerringly from the beginning, and magnifies this ideal as the highest conceivable. America leads the world in civilization because she has most frankly recognized this ideal.

But there is another side to this question as I have intimated. Some one will say that not wealth is the true ideal of the day, but humanitarianism, socialism, brotherly love, equal distribution of wealth. The retort is in one sense right, but in another and profounder sense changes nothing that has been said. Humanitarianism is in the end nothing else but the extension of the same ideal from the few to the many; a substitution at best of the ideal of comfort for the ideal of material power. I know that the socialist reformers look to the proper distribution of wealth as merely the first step which is to be followed by some greater spiritual reform. But as a matter of fact the spiritual ideal is at present a nebulous hypothesis; the creating of universal comfort is the actual aim and ideal held before the eyes. It is well in itself, but the present day exaggerated insistance on it arises from the absence of other ideals. It grows and absorbs our energies because it is without a serious rival. It is the flower of materialism, a mere dilution of the more concentrated ideal of wealth. The upholders of it look upon it as a propaganda against the ideal of wealth; they are in reality fostering what they seek to overthrow.

The effect of this sentimental form of the ideal on the national culture is great and will become greater; already the most serious work in American fiction today tends to deal with this humanitarian propaganda in one form or another. The only American novels I have read for some time which seemed to me to possess, along with artistic cunning, that vitality of art which comes from the inspiration of a popular ideal are Miss Wilkins's *Jerome* and *The Portion of Labor*.[4] The poems of Mr. Markham, although themselves intrinsically vulgar, show, I think, the only region in which really significant poetry may yet be written under the present empire of wealth.

Significant poetry, I say, but can hardly believe that any work of permanent greatness or loveliness can spring from such a source. On one side is the art of luxury—the vapid novels and meaningless pictures and houses that are made for money and for the pleasure of those who are absorbed in money; these show the cynical acceptance of the ideal of wealth and may not detain us further. On the other side is the art of humanitarianism, filled with the pathos of despair or the bitterness of revolt; it is at least a serious appeal to the heart, but it has no share in the joyous outcome of an art that grows out of a spiritual or broadly human ideal, and that will be held as a precious inheritance hereafter. The very bitterness and pathos of it all show that it speaks the revolt of a mind imprisoned within the same material ideal—of a mind that tortures itself to escape, but sees nothing and knows nothing beyond its prison walls. Both the cynical smile of prosperity and the bitter cry of humanitarianism in art are the natural projection of the popular ideal of life into the realm of the imagination. They represent respectively the feeling of those who have succeeded under the ideal of wealth and of those who have been crushed beneath it. Neither the one nor the other is lovely, but they both unite to form our national culture. The change, when it comes, will not come from a victory of the pathetic fallacy of socialism, as some fondly suppose, but from the rise of some new and fairer vision of life to supplant this present ideal of wealth which has been fostered into such predominance by the sudden and enormous increase in the mechanical facilities for producing wealth.

1   This early essay, published in the *Independent*, May 1, 1902, is important if for no other reason than it reveals More as something other than a defender of bourbon capitalism and as one of the wisest prophets of what sentimental humanitarianism, practiced by men like John D. Rockefeller, would eventually give rise to in the descendents of the American wealthy.

2   More's own translation of the episode appears in *The Demon of the Absolute*, pp. 165–83 ("Sâvitrî").

3   "Woe to the vanquished."

4   Mary E. Wilkins Freeman, *Jerome, A Poor Man* (1897) and *The Portion of Labor* (1901).

Progress[1]

In his latest work, *The Idea of Progress, An Inquiry into Its Origin and Growth*,[2] Professor J. B. Bury has narrated the development of what must still be regarded as the dominant idea of modern times, although several recent books in English and French and German show that scepticism is beginning to make terrible inroads into the complacency of our ante-bellum faith. He shows how and why the idea of Progress was foreign to the Greek and mediaeval mind; exhibits its feeble birth in the Renaissance, and describes its triumphant growth in the eighteenth century.

It does not fall within the scope of Mr. Bury's plan to decide whether the idea is false or true, mischievous or beneficent, although he does argue in conclusion that the conception of Progress, based as it is on the principle of change, is itself subject to change and must in time give way to some other dominating belief. In other words, Mr. Bury's purpose is historical and analytic rather than philosophical and synthetic. No one can quarrel with him for his self-imposed limits so far as these do not affect the object he has in view. But it may be fairly asked whether his exposition has not suffered in just this respect.

The belief or disbelief in Progress goes back to the intuitive answer of the heart to the question: Is man intrinsically good and is evil only accidental to him, or is evil an essential ingredient of his nature, deeply grounded in his being, and continually tending to drag him downwards? Mr. Bury does not fail to pose this question. He quotes Seneca's saying, *Erras si existimas vitia nobiscum esse; supervenerunt, ingesta sunt*,[3] and indicates some of its corrollaries; but he does not lay hold of it as a guiding clue. The various elements which compose the idea of Progress come up in his book in rather haphazard succession, and the impression left by his work as a whole is somewhat disjointed.

It is just the craving for flattery, the itch of an uneasy vanity, a longing to escape from the ancient indictment of the human heart as desperately wicked and deceitful above all things, that has been the driving force behind the whole movement of human thought from the Renaissance to the present day. Bacon felt this when he announced that the "happiness of mankind" was to be attained by discrediting the restrictive wisdom of the past, and by setting out on a course of physical discovery which should look to "the endowment of human life with new inventions and riches." Mankind had suffered, he thought, not from any innate overreaching after power, but from its mere lack of knowledge. Give men power over nature and the heart will take care of itself. The deists felt the same pull when they taught that "social evils were due neither to innate and incorrigible disabilities of the human being nor to the nature of things, but simply to ignorance and prejudice." Let men once be told that the universe is totally reasonable in design and of course they will be reasonable in their conduct. Saint-Pierre[4] was victim of the same illusion when he propounded his innumerable projects of government reform: only remove the oppression of bad laws and society will blossom with instinctive virtues. Rousseau made it the principle of education when he showed how a child, if left to develop its own nature without restraint or discipline, would grow up into a perfect man. And at last the philosophers of evolution gave it the sanction of science when they declared that, as one species is transmuted into a higher species by the operation of a mechanical law of fitness, so the generations of mankind grow from better to better by the mere gravity of an innate propensity, without taking thought and without painful self-direction. The idea of

Progress as it was finally formulated in the nineteenth century might be described as organized vanity decking itself out in the flummery of science: *l' amour-propre est le plus grand de tous les flatteurs.*[5]

The consequences of this formulated flattery are clear enough. On the credit side must be placed a spirit of hopefulness, a courage not easily dismayed, a consolatory trust that the future will make good the sad mishaps of the past. But against this must be set a terrible debit—the contemptuous attitude towards the past, the abandonment of the school of experience for the pleasanter Kindergarten of impulse, the restiveness under any form of discipline or restraint, the feeling that one man is as good as another—"and a deal better too!"—the introduction of a sort of down-at-the-heels *laisser-faire* into morals; all of which may be coupled with a fine intolerance of any benighted souls who profess to follow other lights than those shining at the moment and are indisposed to face with the current of the tide.

These consequences, good and bad, are seen in a way by Mr. Bury, and are indicated here and there in his comments. But he does not bring them to a psychological focus; nor does he mention what is perhaps the most striking result of all, the almost universal resurgence of youth against age, the common belief that the world is for the young and that the old are merely clogs on the chariot wheels of triumphant Progress. Naturally, if in the nature of things the present is an advance on the past, the coming generation by virtue of its date is wiser and better than the passing. Why should a scholar pay heed to a teacher droning out of the backward and abysm of time? Why should a child listen to the admonitions of a parent grumbling from the shelf where he properly belongs? And the odd thing is, not that scholar and child should think thus, but that teacher and parent should submit so patiently to this rule of moral parricide. If there is any truth in the saying that civilization is only the imperfectly exercised control of youth by age, then the idea of Progress is the voice of barbarism.

1   This article is taken from the *Villager* for April 9, 1921. It reveals how unorigi-
     nal the protestations of youth really are here in the nineteen-seventies.
• 2   Published first in 1920.
3   "You are mistaken if you think there are imperfections in us; they have been
     erased, they have been cast out."
4   Jacques Henri Bernardin de Saint-Pierre (1737–1814), disciple of Rousseau and
     author of *Paul et Virginia* (1787).
5   "Vanity is the greatest of all flatterers."